VALENTINE

No matter how hard she tries, Valentine just can't leave the killing game behind. Her life as an assassin has made her a liability to everyone she's ever known -- and the lingering mental effects of the CIA's MkUltra program have clouded her memory, making her past a puzzle waiting to be pieced together.

Could a trip to Valentine's hometown be the key to unlocking her memories? With a broken spirit and a bruised body, Valentine limps home to uncover a past that may be her only hope for a future. In a world where it's kill or be killed, it's Valentine's life that's become a death sentence.

VALENTINE

THE KILLING MOON

story and art by Daniel Cooney

lettered and designed by Daniel Cooney

edited by Carolina Stewart & Daniel Cooney

Red Eye Press
www.redeyepress.net

First Edition: July 2008
ISBN -10: 0-9724673-8-6
ISBN -13: 978-0-9724673-8-4

Printed in Canada

For Carolina, who inspires and amazes me every day.
– with love, Dan

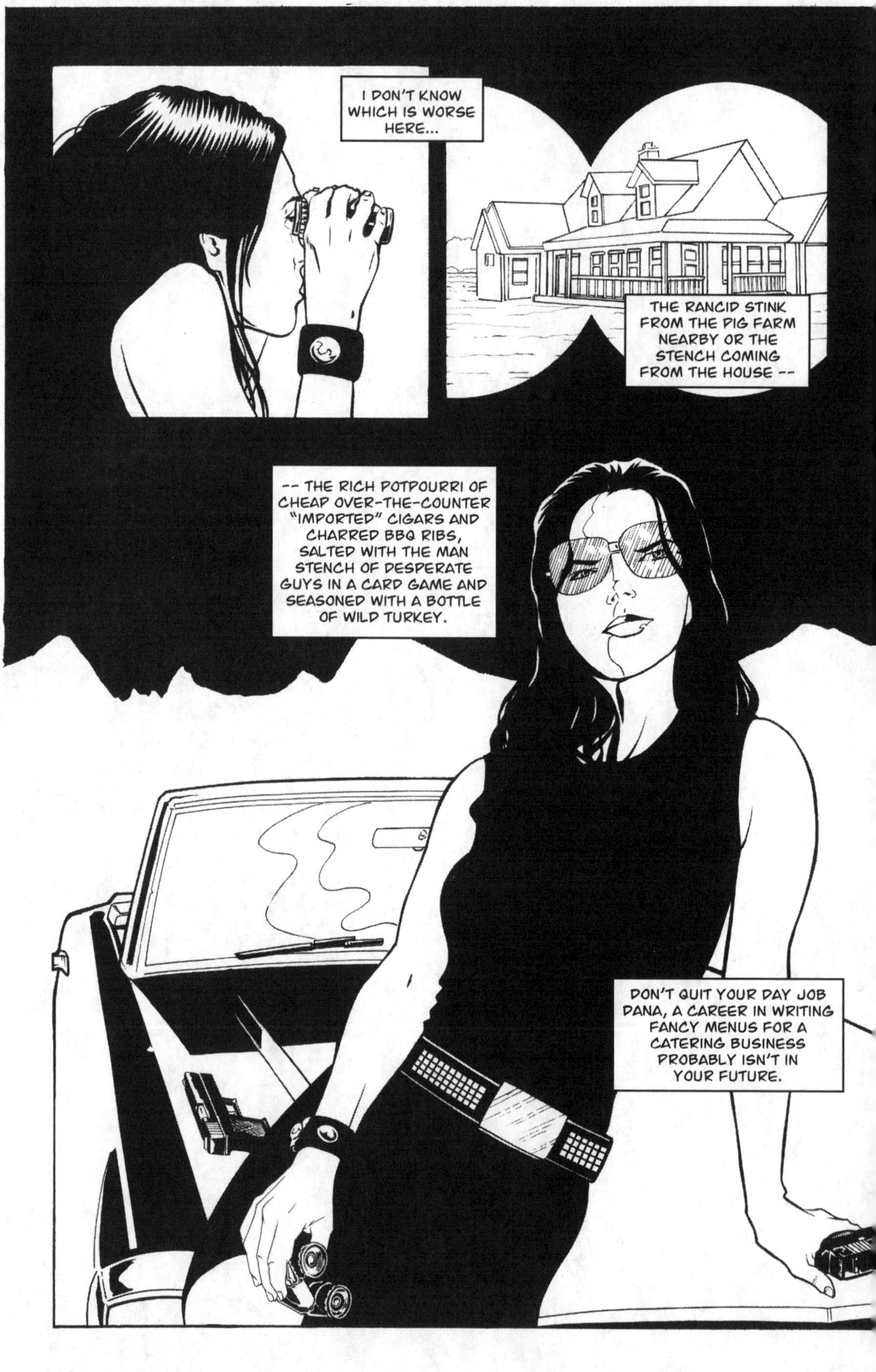
I DON'T KNOW WHICH IS WORSE HERE...
THE RANCID STINK FROM THE PIG FARM NEARBY OR THE STENCH COMING FROM THE HOUSE --
-- THE RICH POTPOURRI OF CHEAP OVER-THE-COUNTER "IMPORTED" CIGARS AND CHARRED BBQ RIBS, SALTED WITH THE MAN STENCH OF DESPERATE GUYS IN A CARD GAME AND SEASONED WITH A BOTTLE OF WILD TURKEY.
DON'T QUIT YOUR DAY JOB DANA, A CAREER IN WRITING FANCY MENUS FOR A CATERING BUSINESS PROBABLY ISN'T IN YOUR FUTURE.

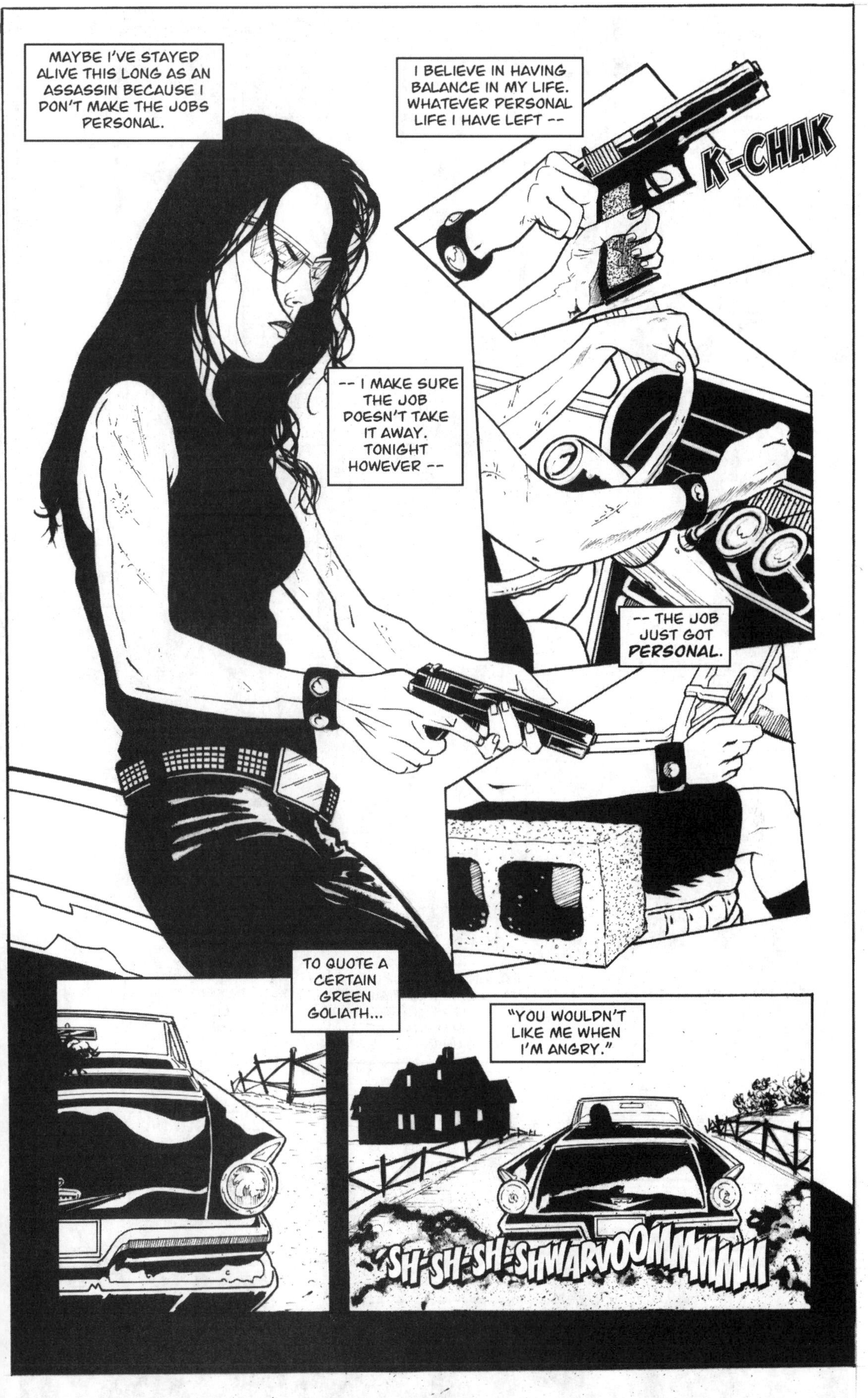
MAYBE I'VE STAYED ALIVE THIS LONG AS AN ASSASSIN BECAUSE I DON'T MAKE THE JOBS PERSONAL.
I BELIEVE IN HAVING BALANCE IN MY LIFE. WHATEVER PERSONAL LIFE I HAVE LEFT --
K-CHAK
-- I MAKE SURE THE JOB DOESN'T TAKE IT AWAY. TONIGHT HOWEVER --
-- THE JOB JUST GOT PERSONAL.
TO QUOTE A CERTAIN GREEN GOLIATH...
"YOU WOULDN'T LIKE ME WHEN I'M ANGRY."
SH-SH-SH-SHWARVOOMMMMM

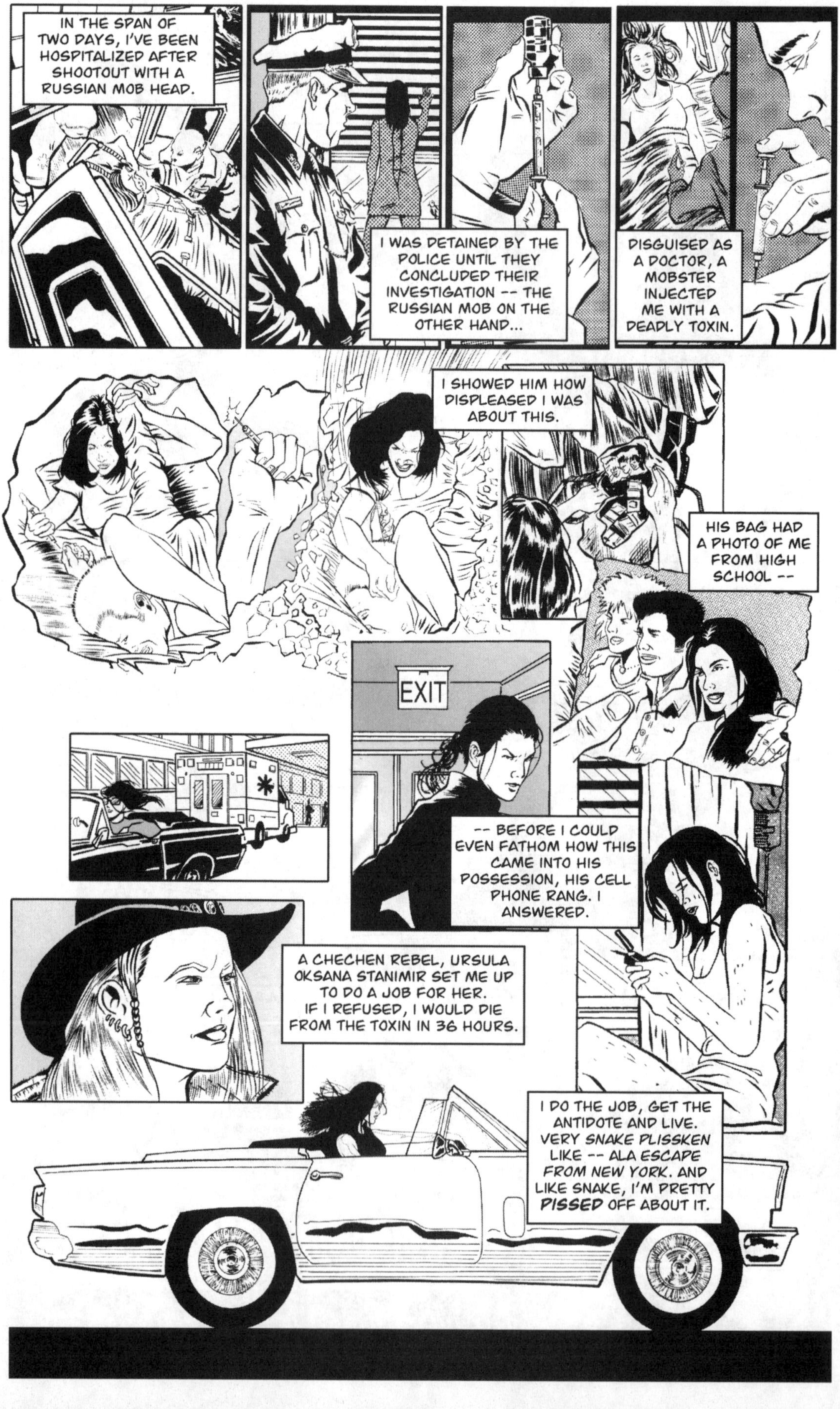
IN THE SPAN OF TWO DAYS, I'VE BEEN HOSPITALIZED AFTER SHOOTOUT WITH A RUSSIAN MOB HEAD.
I WAS DETAINED BY THE POLICE UNTIL THEY CONCLUDED THEIR INVESTIGATION -- THE RUSSIAN MOB ON THE OTHER HAND...
DISGUISED AS A DOCTOR, A MOBSTER INJECTED ME WITH A DEADLY TOXIN.
I SHOWED HIM HOW DISPLEASED I WAS ABOUT THIS.
HIS BAG HAD A PHOTO OF ME FROM HIGH SCHOOL --
EXIT
-- BEFORE I COULD EVEN FATHOM HOW THIS CAME INTO HIS POSSESSION, HIS CELL PHONE RANG. I ANSWERED.
A CHECHEN REBEL, URSULA OKSANA STANIMIR SET ME UP TO DO A JOB FOR HER. IF I REFUSED, I WOULD DIE FROM THE TOXIN IN 36 HOURS.
I DO THE JOB, GET THE ANTIDOTE AND LIVE. VERY SNAKE PLISSKEN LIKE -- ALA ESCAPE FROM NEW YORK. AND LIKE SNAKE, I'M PRETTY PISSED OFF ABOUT IT.

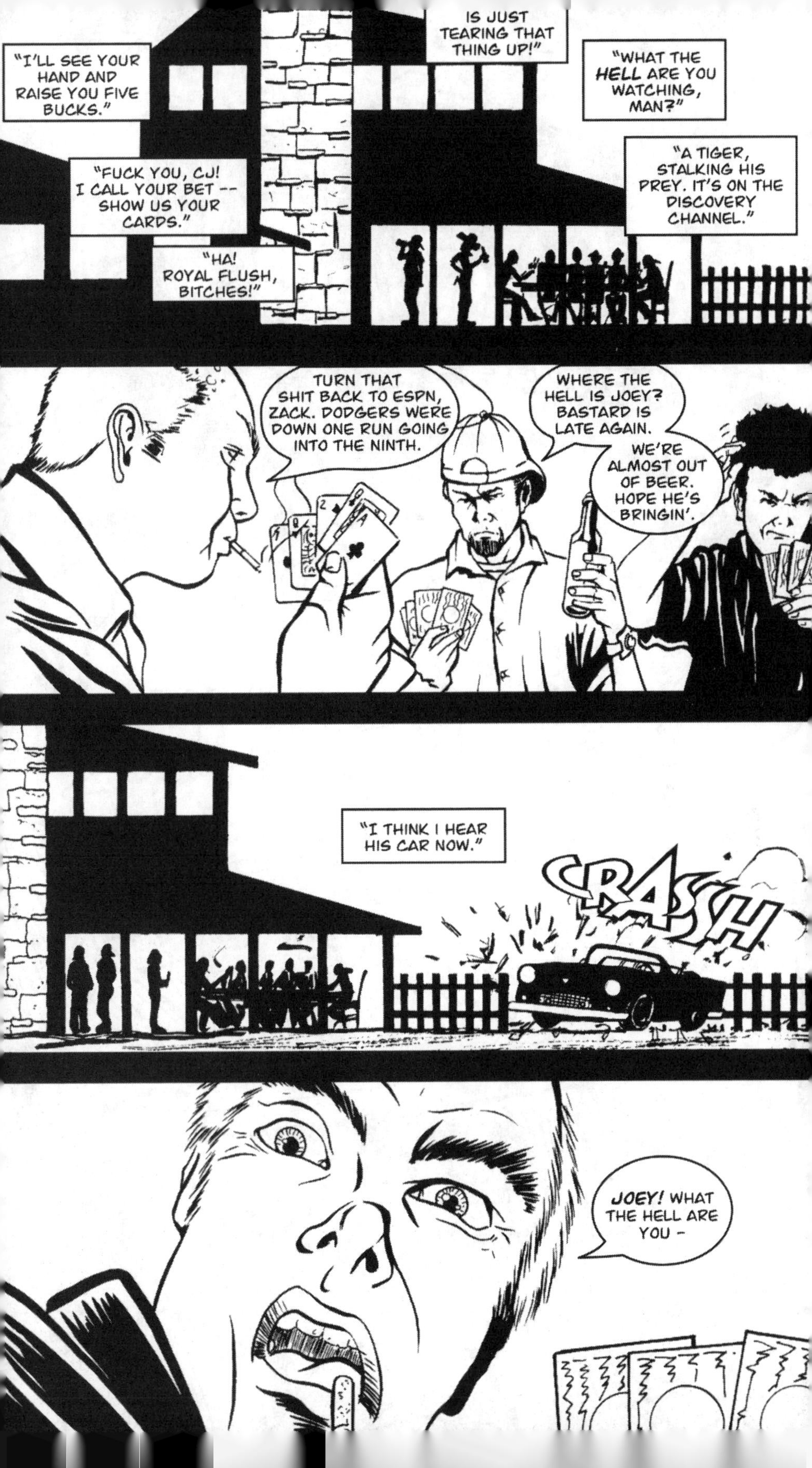
IS JUST TEARING THAT THING UP!"
"I'LL SEE YOUR HAND AND RAISE YOU FIVE BUCKS."
"WHAT THE HELL ARE YOU WATCHING, MAN?"
"A TIGER, STALKING HIS PREY. IT'S ON THE DISCOVERY CHANNEL."
"FUCK YOU, CJ! I CALL YOUR BET -- SHOW US YOUR CARDS."
"HA! ROYAL FLUSH, BITCHES!"
TURN THAT SHIT BACK TO ESPN, ZACK. DODGERS WERE DOWN ONE RUN GOING INTO THE NINTH.
WHERE THE HELL IS JOEY? BASTARD IS LATE AGAIN.
WE'RE ALMOST OUT OF BEER. HOPE HE'S BRINGIN'.
"I THINK I HEAR HIS CAR NOW."
CRASH
JOEY! WHAT THE HELL ARE YOU -

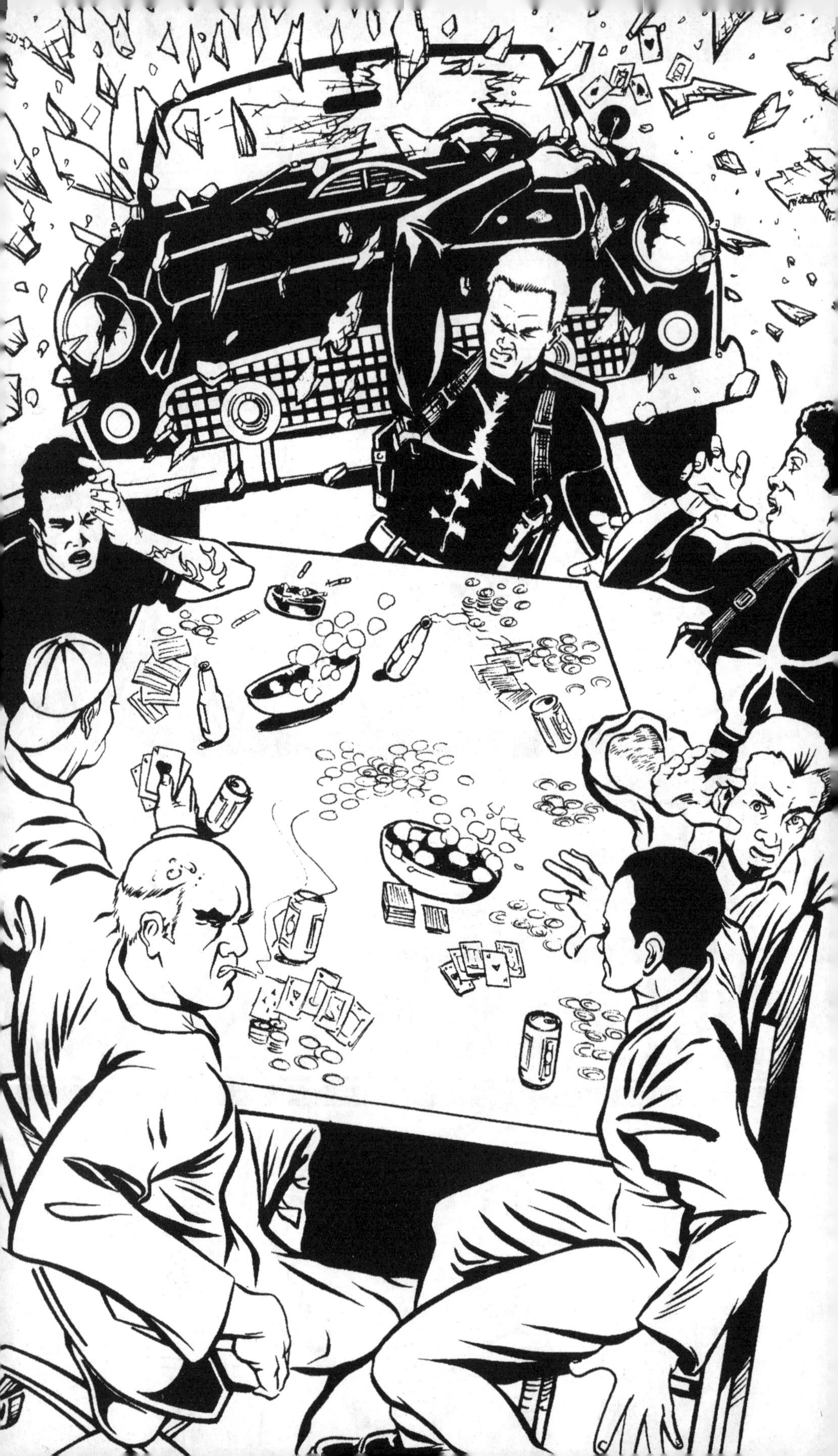

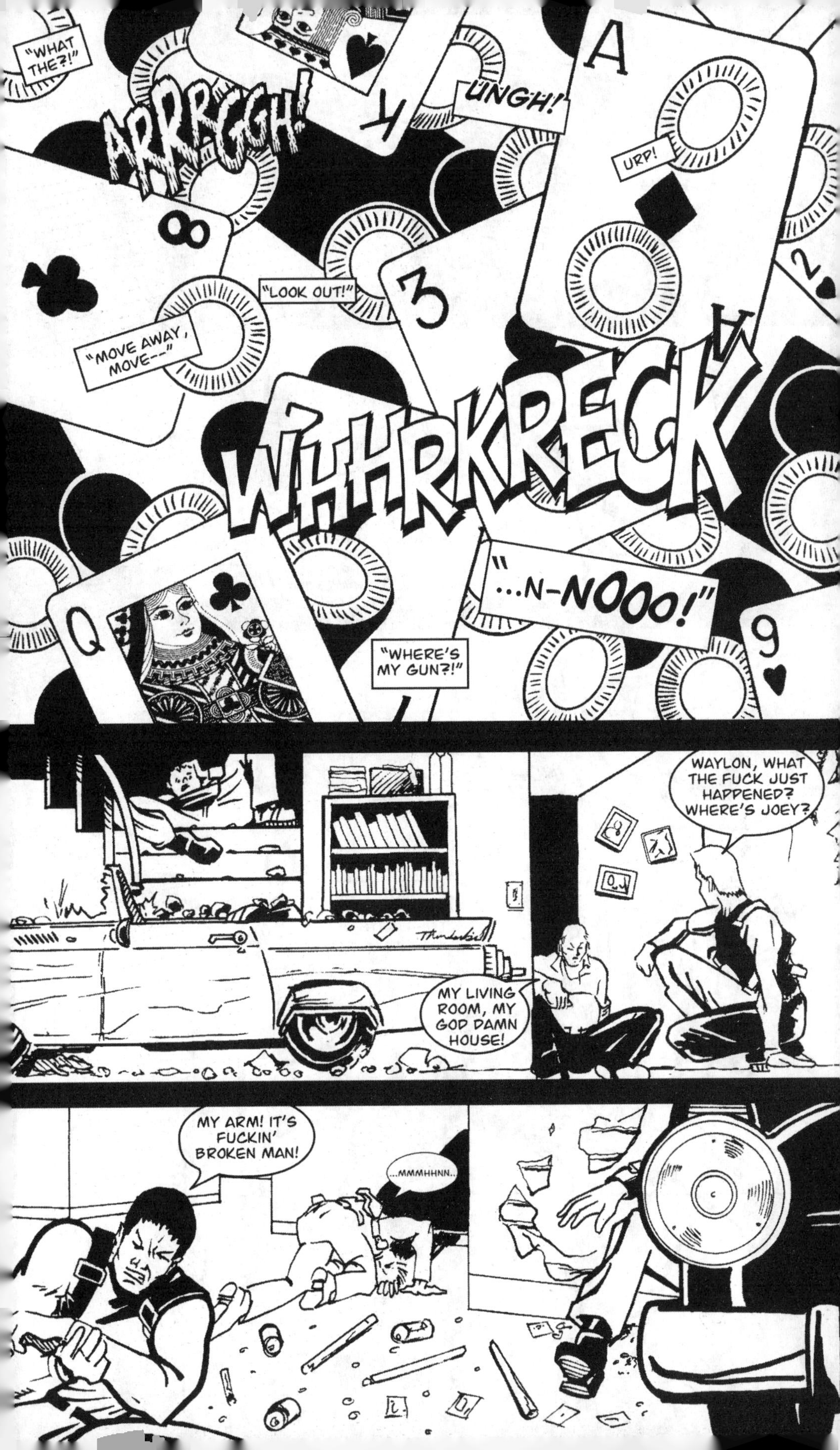
"WHAT THE?!"
ARRRGGH!
ÜNGH!
URP!
"LOOK OUT!"
"MOVE AWAY, MOVE--"
WHHRKRECK
"...N-NOOO!"
"WHERE'S MY GUN?!"
WAYLON, WHAT THE FUCK JUST HAPPENED? WHERE'S JOEY?
MY LIVING ROOM, MY GOD DAMN HOUSE!
MY ARM! IT'S FUCKIN' BROKEN MAN!
...MMMHHNN...

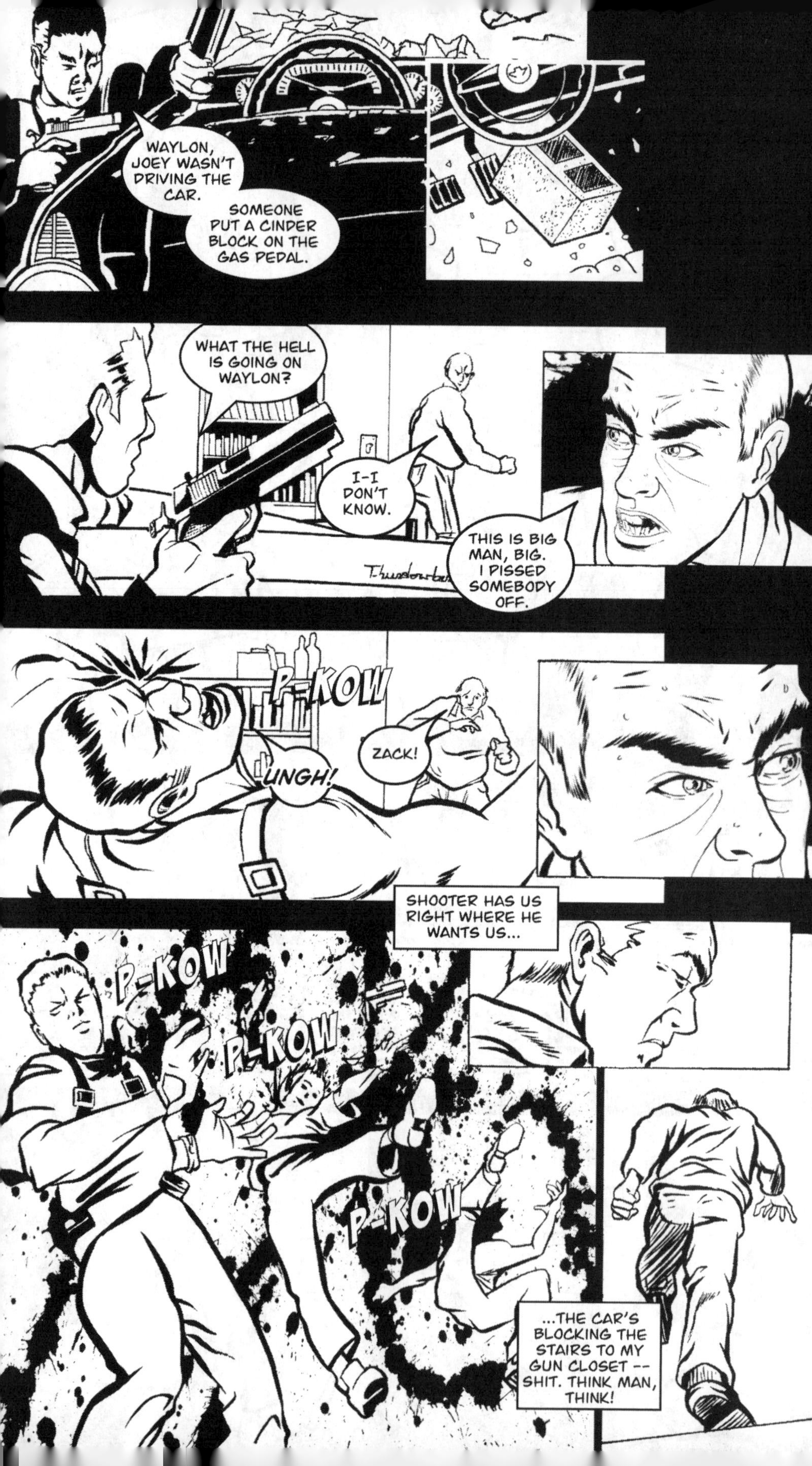
WAYLON, JOEY WASN'T DRIVING THE CAR.
SOMEONE PUT A CINDER BLOCK ON THE GAS PEDAL.
WHAT THE HELL IS GOING ON WAYLON?
I-I DON'T KNOW.
THIS IS BIG MAN, BIG. I PISSED SOMEBODY OFF.
P-KOW
UNGH!
ZACK!
SHOOTER HAS US RIGHT WHERE HE WANTS US...
P-KOW
P-KOW
P-KOW
...THE CAR'S BLOCKING THE STAIRS TO MY GUN CLOSET -- SHIT. THINK MAN, THINK!

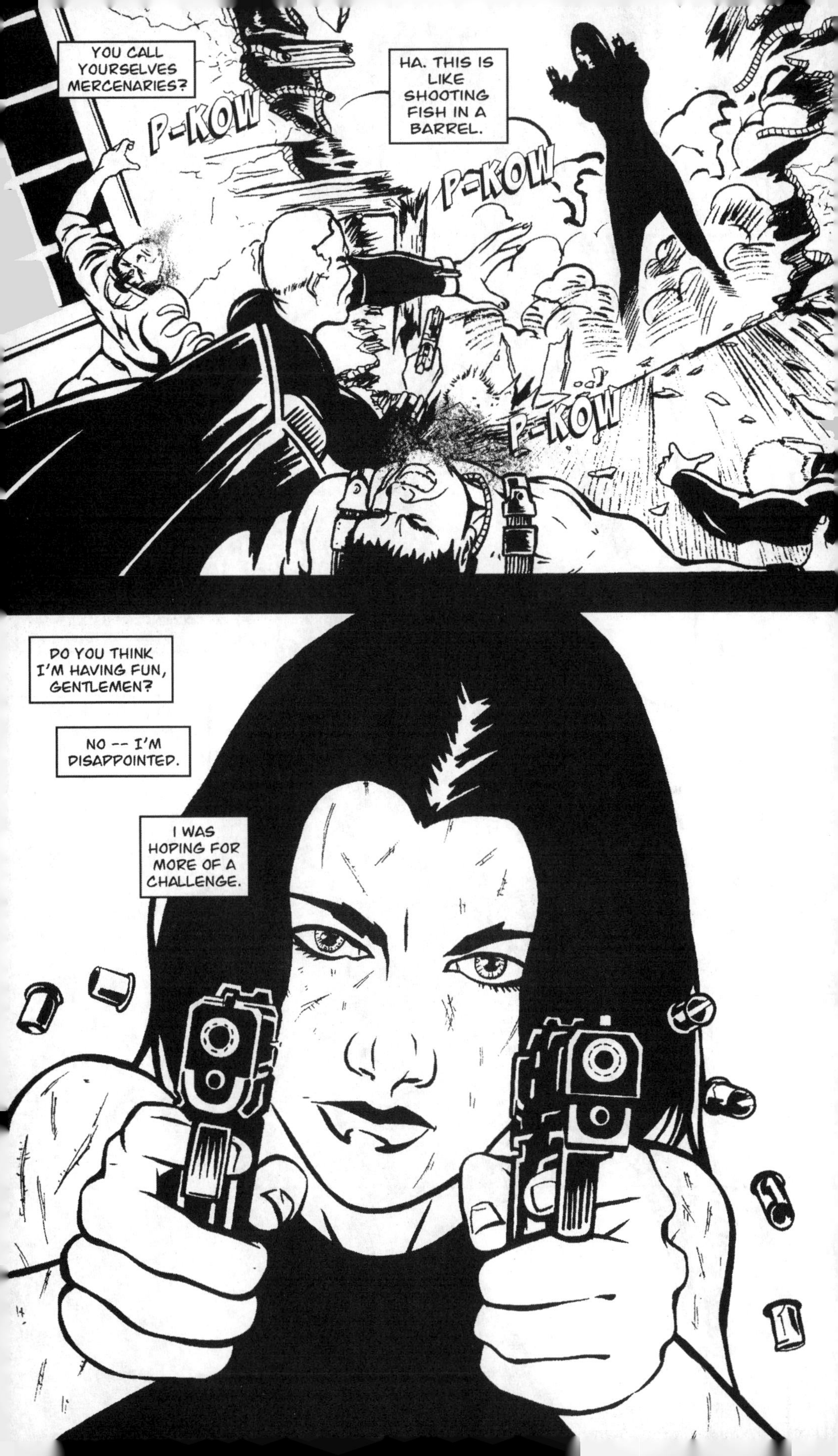
YOU CALL YOURSELVES MERCENARIES?
P-KOW
HA. THIS IS LIKE SHOOTING FISH IN A BARREL.
P-KOW
P-KOW
DO YOU THINK I'M HAVING FUN, GENTLEMEN?
NO -- I'M DISAPPOINTED.
I WAS HOPING FOR MORE OF A CHALLENGE.

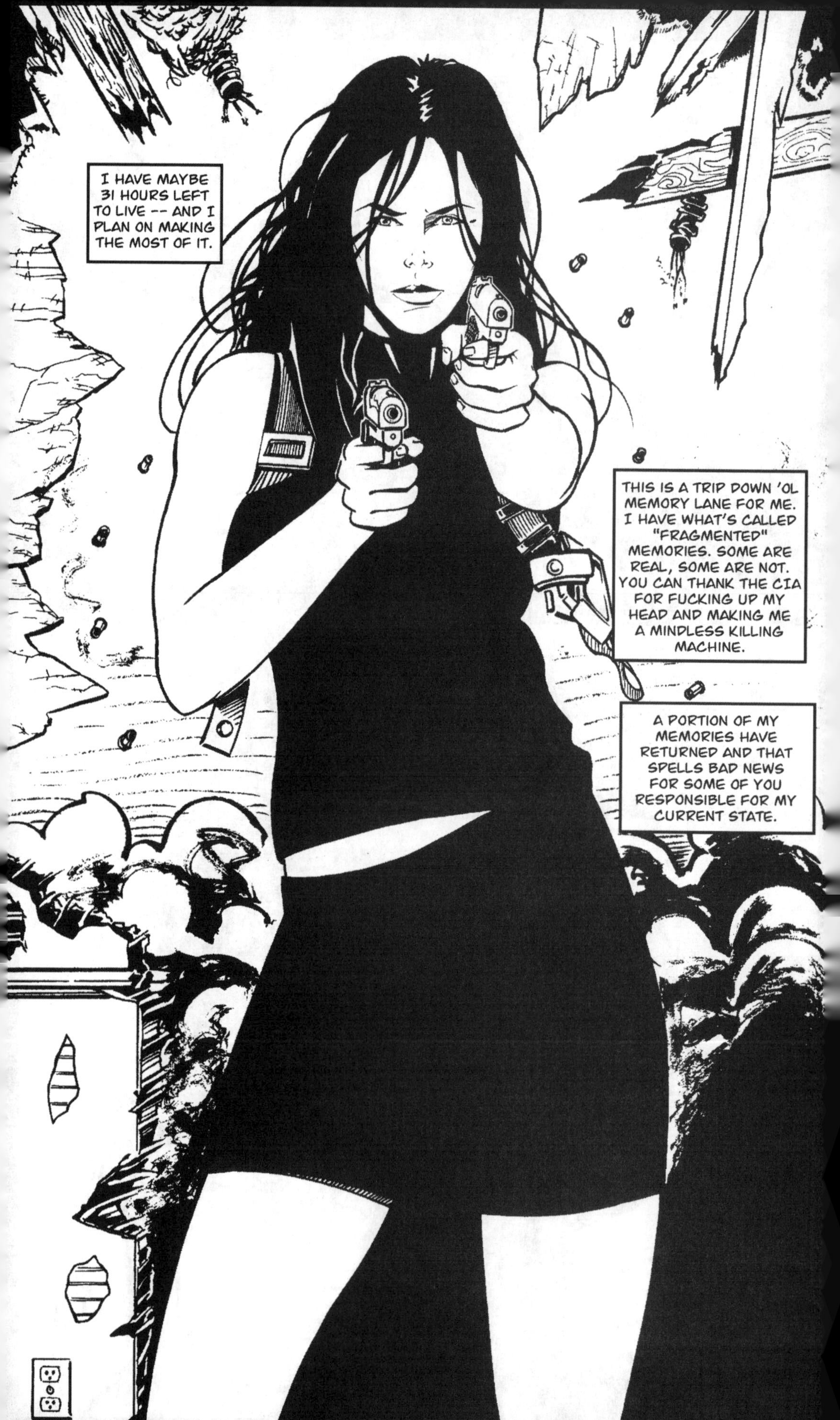
I HAVE MAYBE 31 HOURS LEFT TO LIVE -- AND I PLAN ON MAKING THE MOST OF IT.
THIS IS A TRIP DOWN 'OL MEMORY LANE FOR ME. I HAVE WHAT'S CALLED "FRAGMENTED" MEMORIES. SOME ARE REAL, SOME ARE NOT. YOU CAN THANK THE CIA FOR FUCKING UP MY HEAD AND MAKING ME A MINDLESS KILLING MACHINE.
A PORTION OF MY MEMORIES HAVE RETURNED AND THAT SPELLS BAD NEWS FOR SOME OF YOU RESPONSIBLE FOR MY CURRENT STATE.

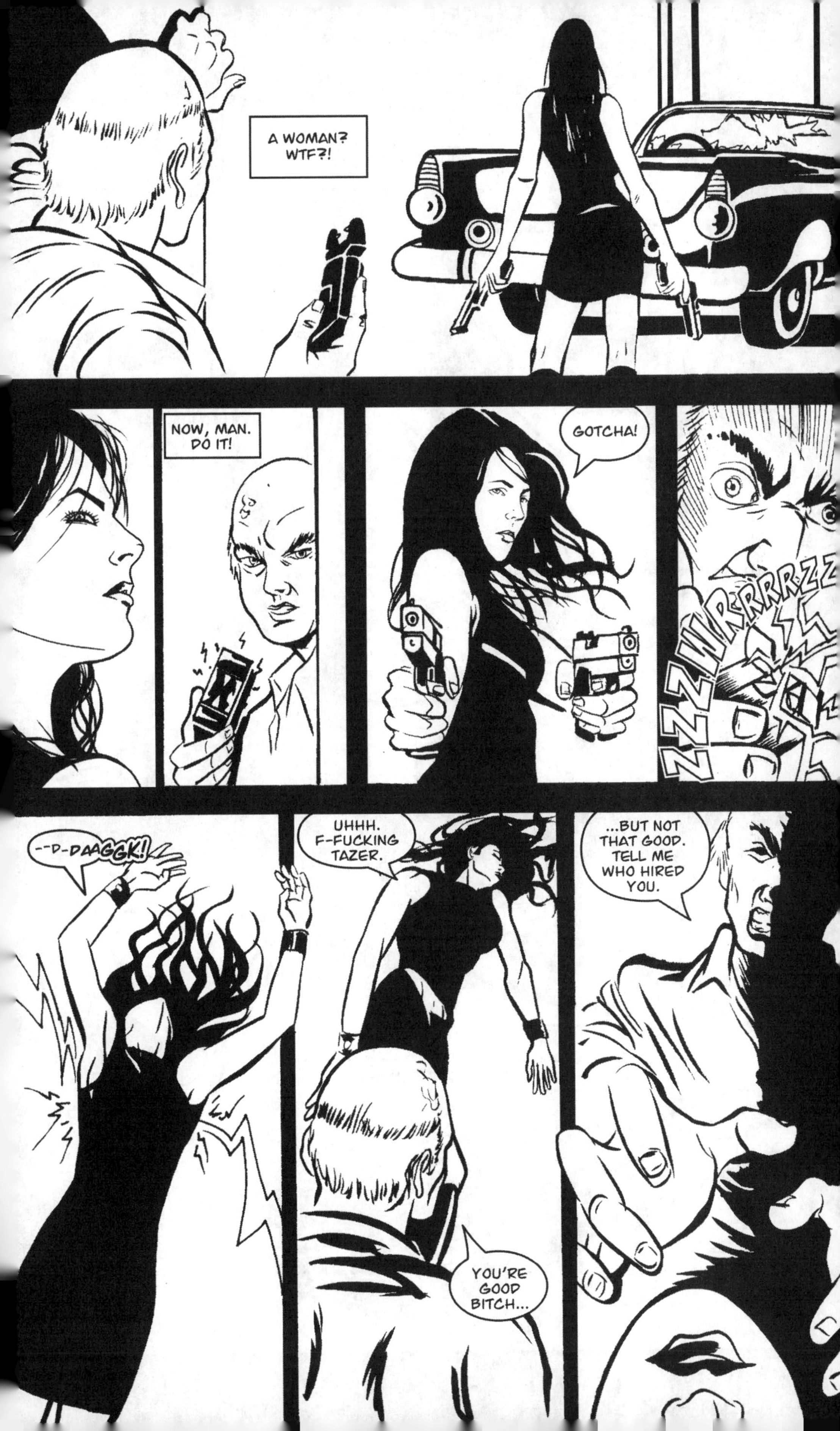
A WOMAN? WTF?!
NOW, MAN. DO IT!
GOTCHA!
ZZZWRRRRZZ
--D-DAAGGK!
UHHH. F-FUCKING TAZER.
YOU'RE GOOD BITCH...
...BUT NOT THAT GOOD. TELL ME WHO HIRED YOU.

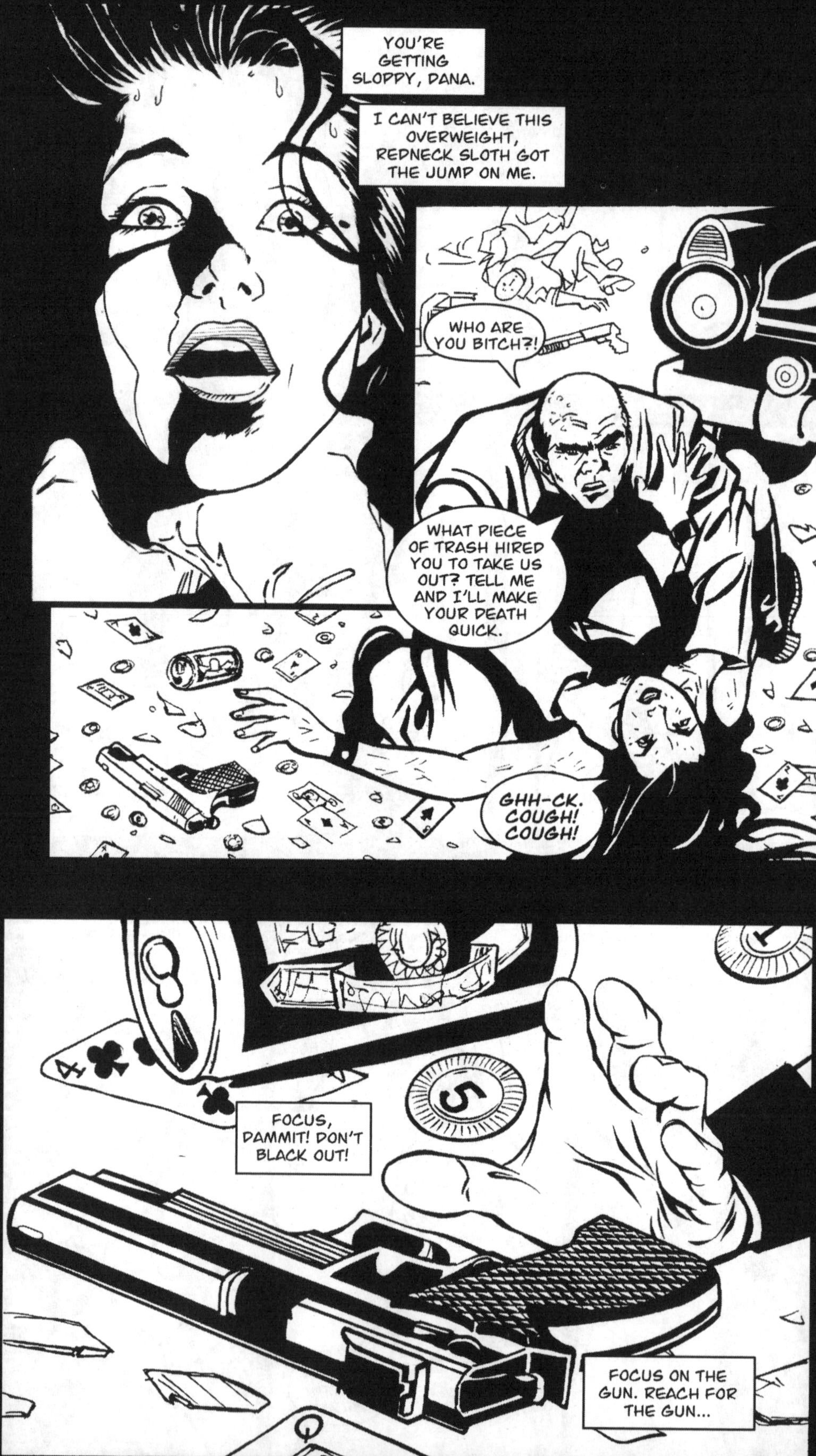
YOU'RE GETTING SLOPPY, DANA.
I CAN'T BELIEVE THIS OVERWEIGHT, REDNECK SLOTH GOT THE JUMP ON ME.
WHO ARE YOU BITCH?!
WHAT PIECE OF TRASH HIRED YOU TO TAKE US OUT? TELL ME AND I'LL MAKE YOUR DEATH QUICK.
GHH-CK. COUGH! COUGH!
FOCUS, DAMMIT! DON'T BLACK OUT!
FOCUS ON THE GUN. REACH FOR THE GUN...

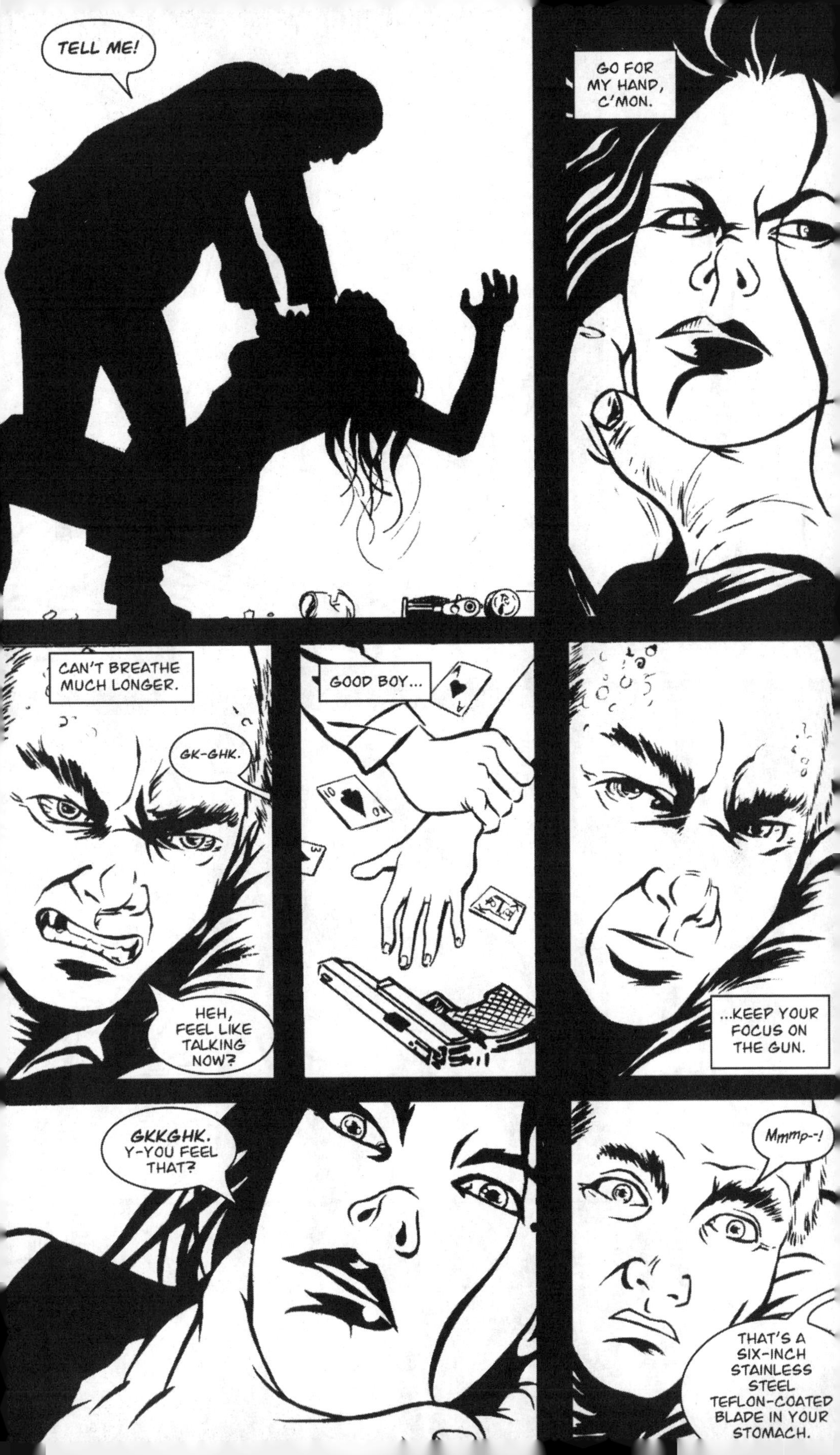
TELL ME!
GO FOR MY HAND, C'MON.
CAN'T BREATHE MUCH LONGER.
GK-GHK.
HEH, FEEL LIKE TALKING NOW?
GOOD BOY...
...KEEP YOUR FOCUS ON THE GUN.
GKKGHK. Y-YOU FEEL THAT?
Mmmp--!
THAT'S A SIX-INCH STAINLESS STEEL TEFLON-COATED BLADE IN YOUR STOMACH.

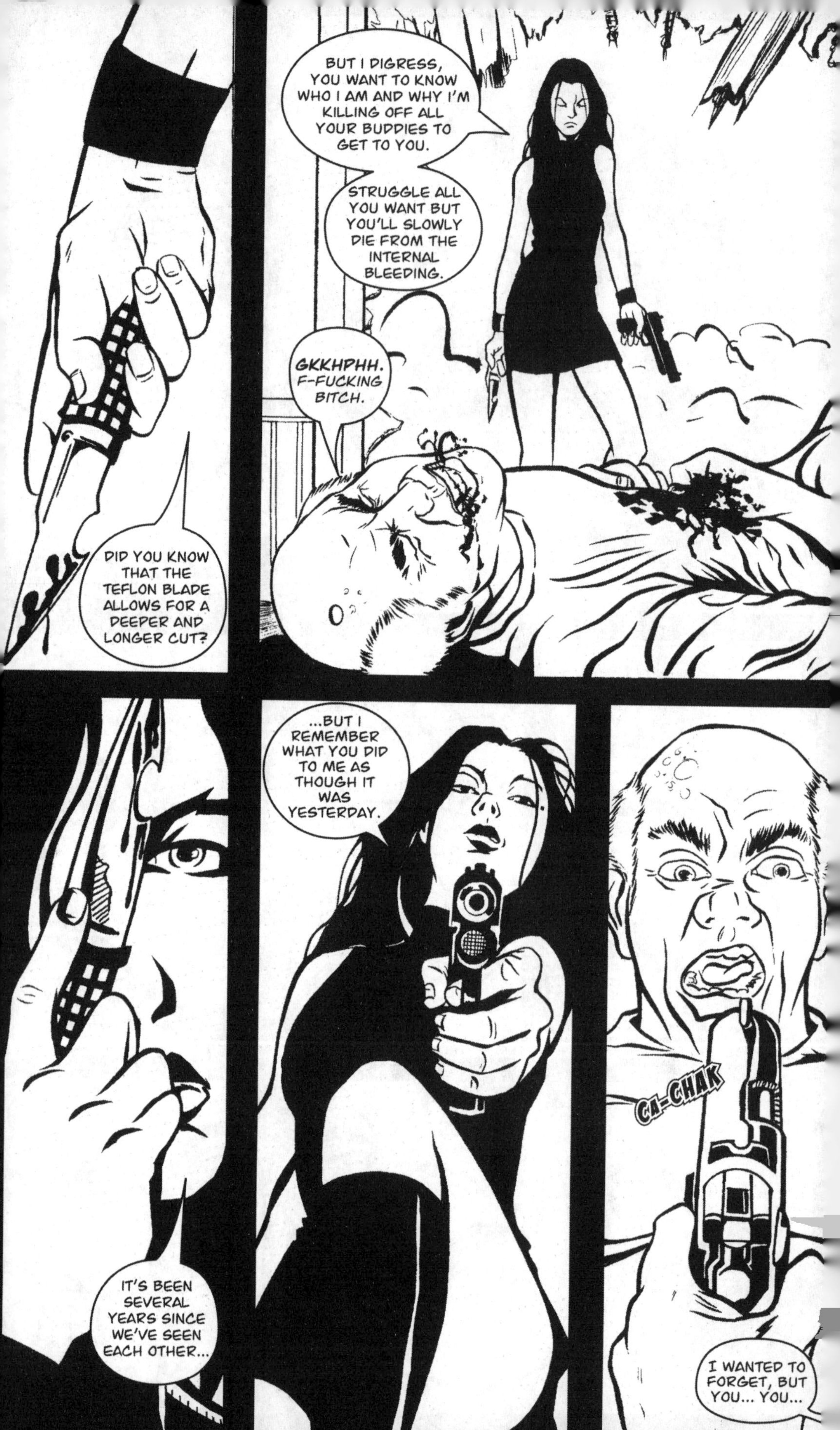
DID YOU KNOW THAT THE TEFLON BLADE ALLOWS FOR A DEEPER AND LONGER CUT?
BUT I DIGRESS, YOU WANT TO KNOW WHO I AM AND WHY I'M KILLING OFF ALL YOUR BUDDIES TO GET TO YOU.
STRUGGLE ALL YOU WANT BUT YOU'LL SLOWLY DIE FROM THE INTERNAL BLEEDING.
GKKHPHH. F-FUCKING BITCH.
IT'S BEEN SEVERAL YEARS SINCE WE'VE SEEN EACH OTHER...
...BUT I REMEMBER WHAT YOU DID TO ME AS THOUGH IT WAS YESTERDAY.
CA-CHAK
I WANTED TO FORGET, BUT YOU... YOU...

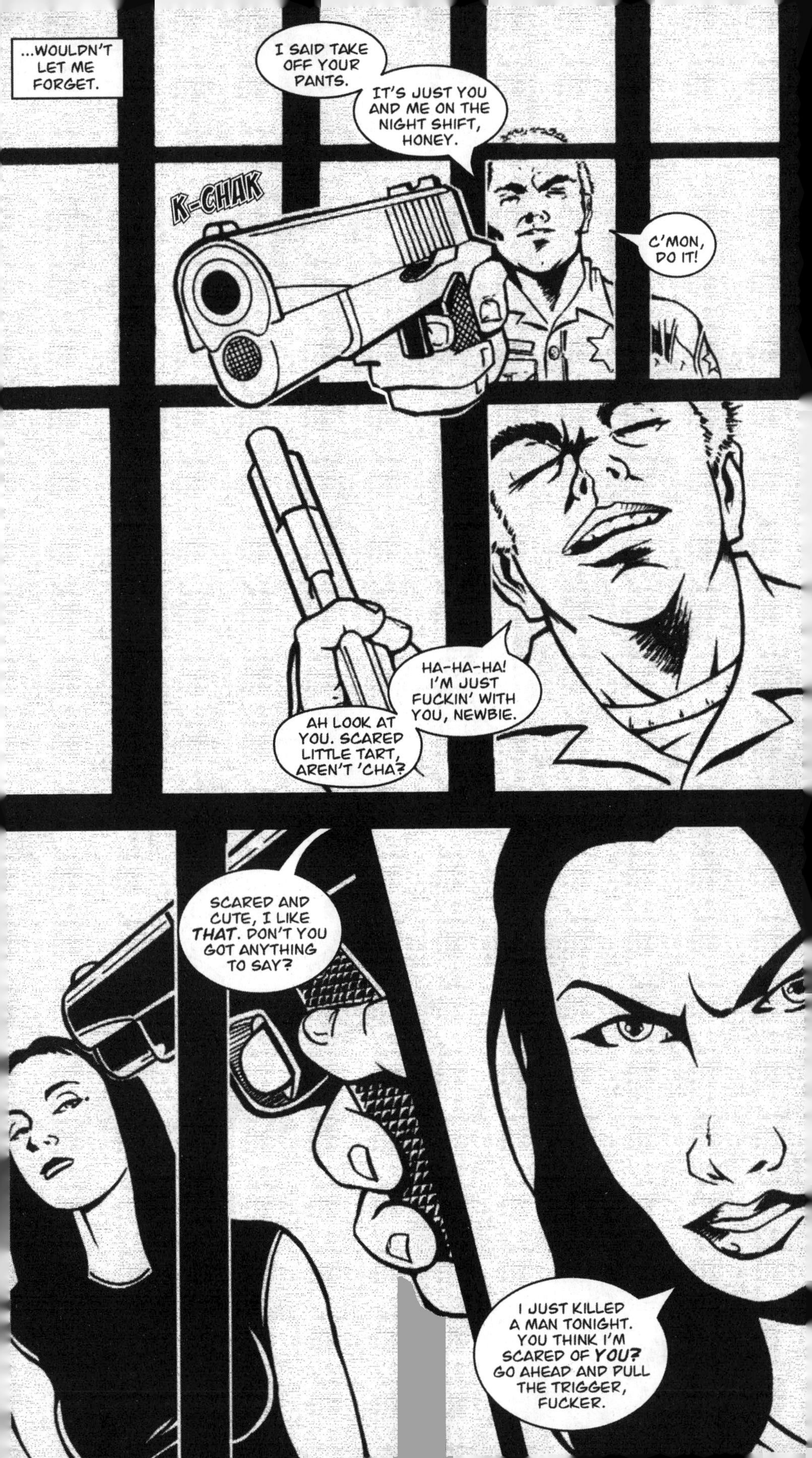
...WOULDN'T LET ME FORGET.
I SAID TAKE OFF YOUR PANTS.
IT'S JUST YOU AND ME ON THE NIGHT SHIFT, HONEY.
K-CHAK
C'MON, DO IT!
HA-HA-HA! I'M JUST FUCKIN' WITH YOU, NEWBIE.
AH LOOK AT YOU. SCARED LITTLE TART, AREN'T 'CHA?
SCARED AND CUTE, I LIKE THAT. DON'T YOU GOT ANYTHING TO SAY?
I JUST KILLED A MAN TONIGHT. YOU THINK I'M SCARED OF YOU? GO AHEAD AND PULL THE TRIGGER, FUCKER.

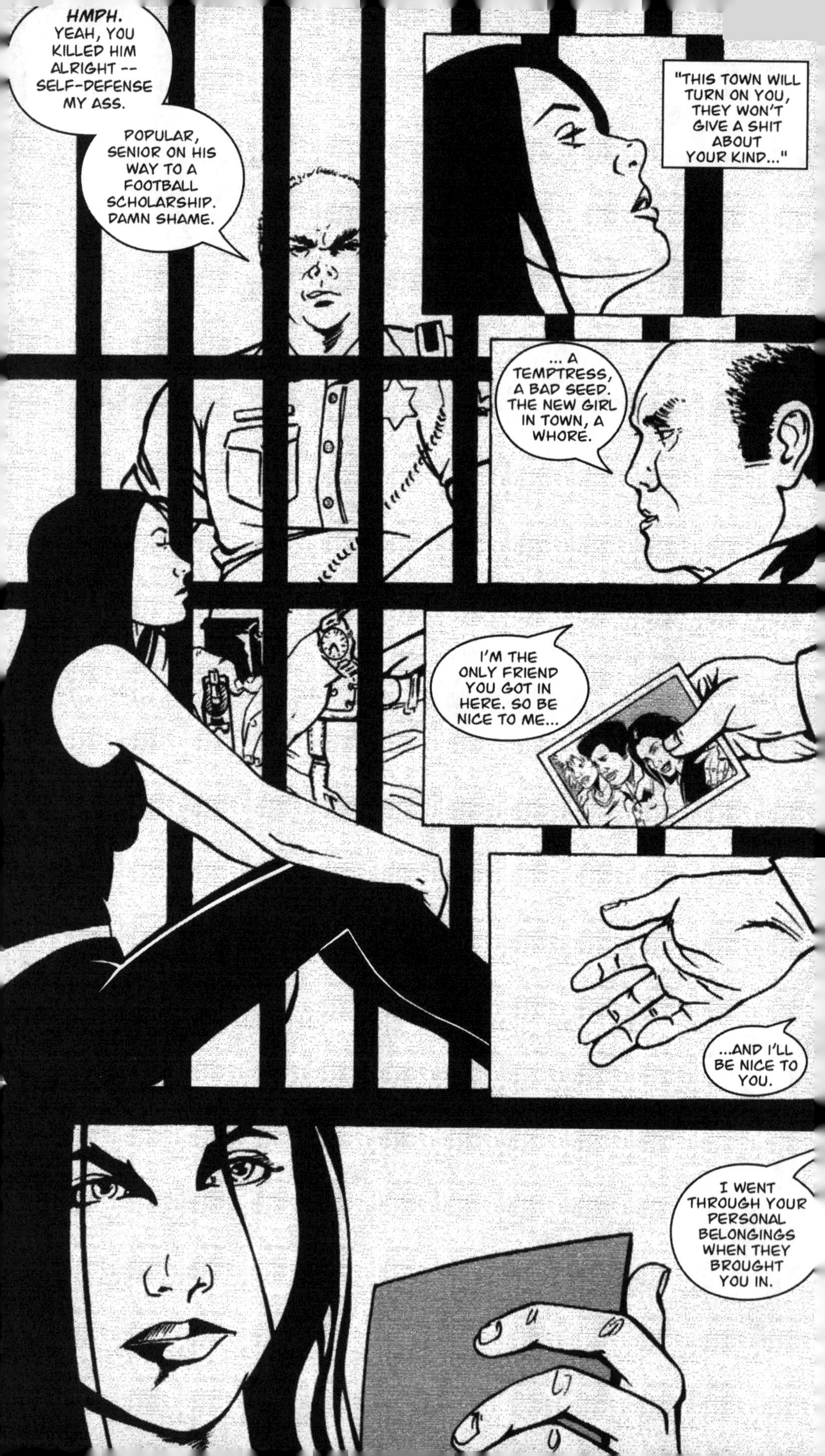
HMPH. YEAH, YOU KILLED HIM ALRIGHT -- SELF-DEFENSE MY ASS.
POPULAR, SENIOR ON HIS WAY TO A FOOTBALL SCHOLARSHIP. DAMN SHAME.
"THIS TOWN WILL TURN ON YOU, THEY WON'T GIVE A SHIT ABOUT YOUR KIND..."
... A TEMPTRESS, A BAD SEED. THE NEW GIRL IN TOWN, A WHORE.
I'M THE ONLY FRIEND YOU GOT IN HERE. SO BE NICE TO ME...
...AND I'LL BE NICE TO YOU.
I WENT THROUGH YOUR PERSONAL BELONGINGS WHEN THEY BROUGHT YOU IN.

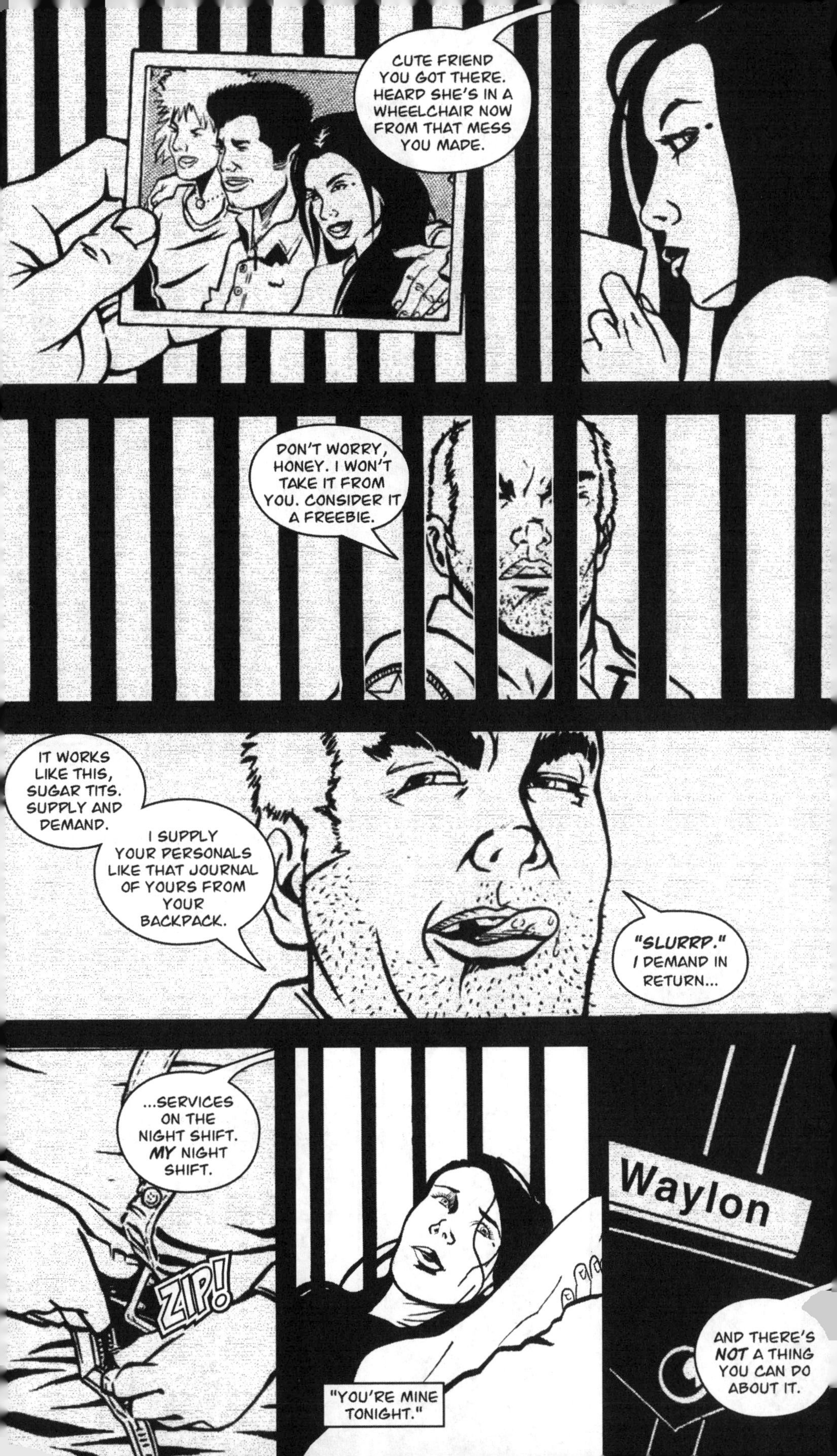

CUTE FRIEND YOU GOT THERE. HEARD SHE'S IN A WHEELCHAIR NOW FROM THAT MESS YOU MADE.
DON'T WORRY, HONEY. I WON'T TAKE IT FROM YOU. CONSIDER IT A FREEBIE.
IT WORKS LIKE THIS, SUGAR TITS. SUPPLY AND DEMAND.
I SUPPLY YOUR PERSONALS LIKE THAT JOURNAL OF YOURS FROM YOUR BACKPACK.
"SLURRP." I DEMAND IN RETURN...
...SERVICES ON THE NIGHT SHIFT. MY NIGHT SHIFT.
ZIP!
"YOU'RE MINE TONIGHT."
Waylon
AND THERE'S NOT A THING YOU CAN DO ABOUT IT.

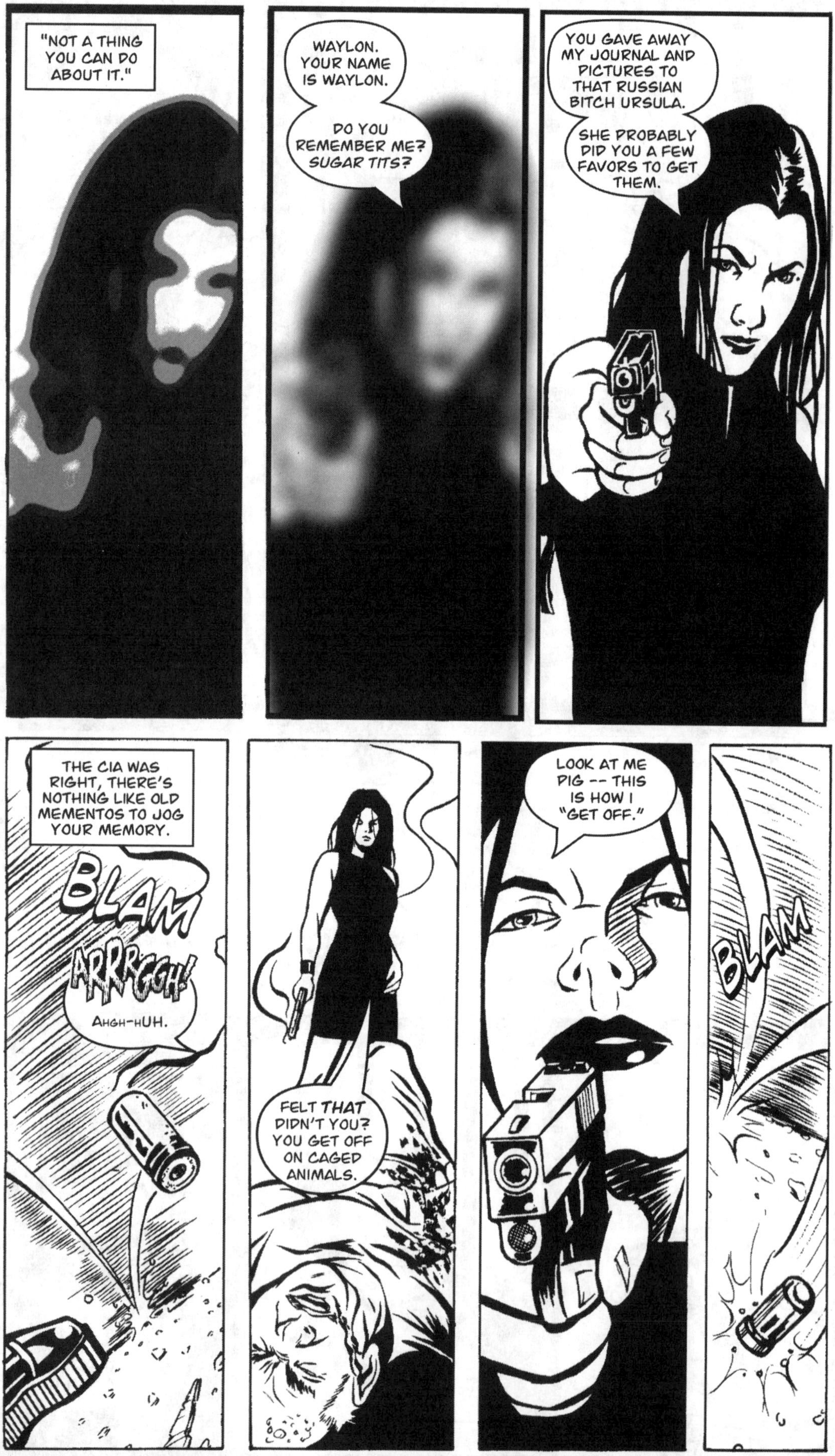
"NOT A THING YOU CAN DO ABOUT IT."
WAYLON. YOUR NAME IS WAYLON.
DO YOU REMEMBER ME? SUGAR TITS?
YOU GAVE AWAY MY JOURNAL AND PICTURES TO THAT RUSSIAN BITCH URSULA.
SHE PROBABLY DID YOU A FEW FAVORS TO GET THEM.
THE CIA WAS RIGHT, THERE'S NOTHING LIKE OLD MEMENTOS TO JOG YOUR MEMORY.
BLAM
ARRRGGH!
AHGH-HUH.
FELT THAT DIDN'T YOU? YOU GET OFF ON CAGED ANIMALS.
LOOK AT ME PIG -- THIS IS HOW I "GET OFF."
BLAM

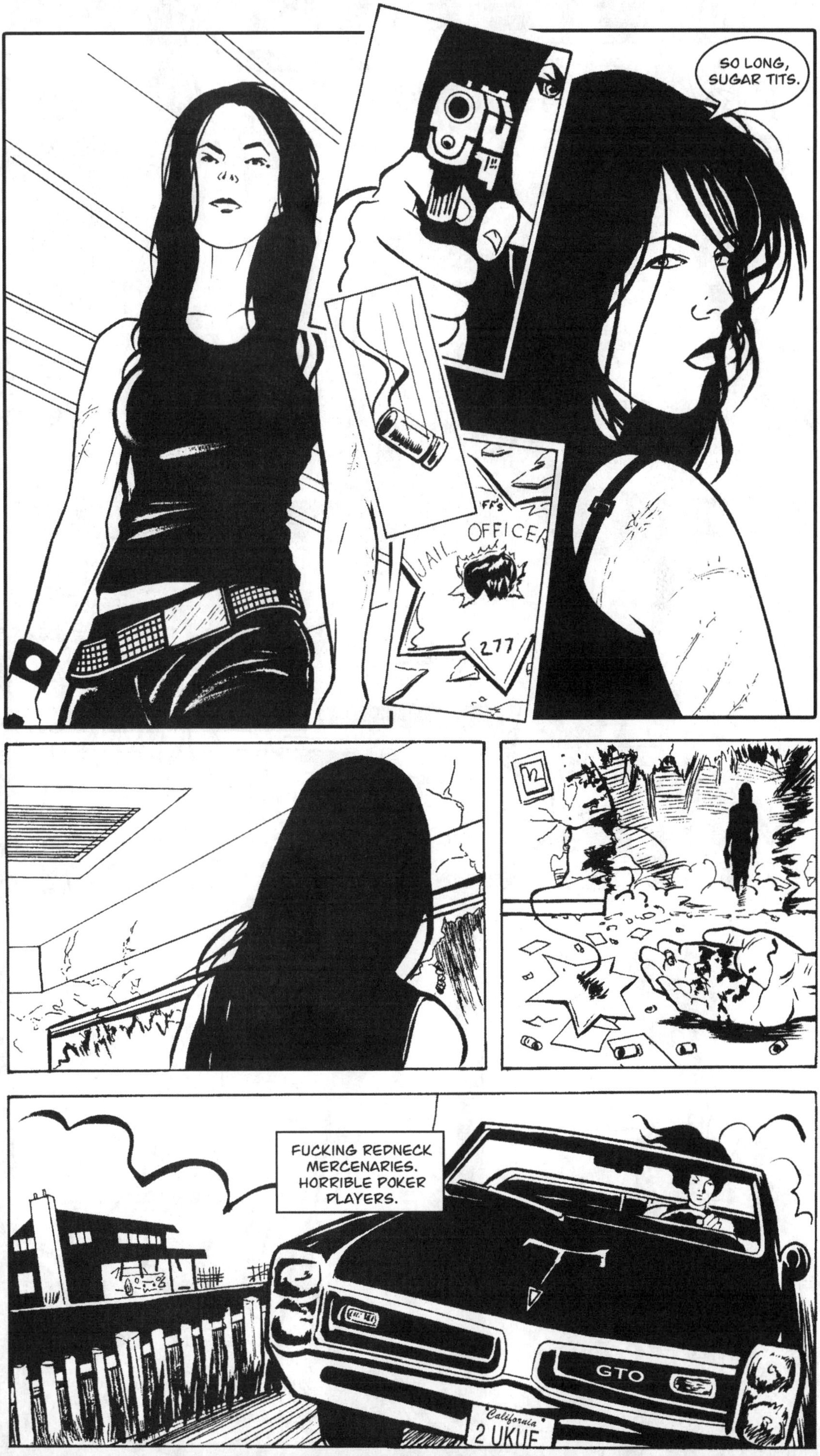
SO LONG, SUGAR TITS.
OFFICER
JAIL
277
FUCKING REDNECK MERCENARIES. HORRIBLE POKER PLAYERS.
GTO
California
2 UKUF

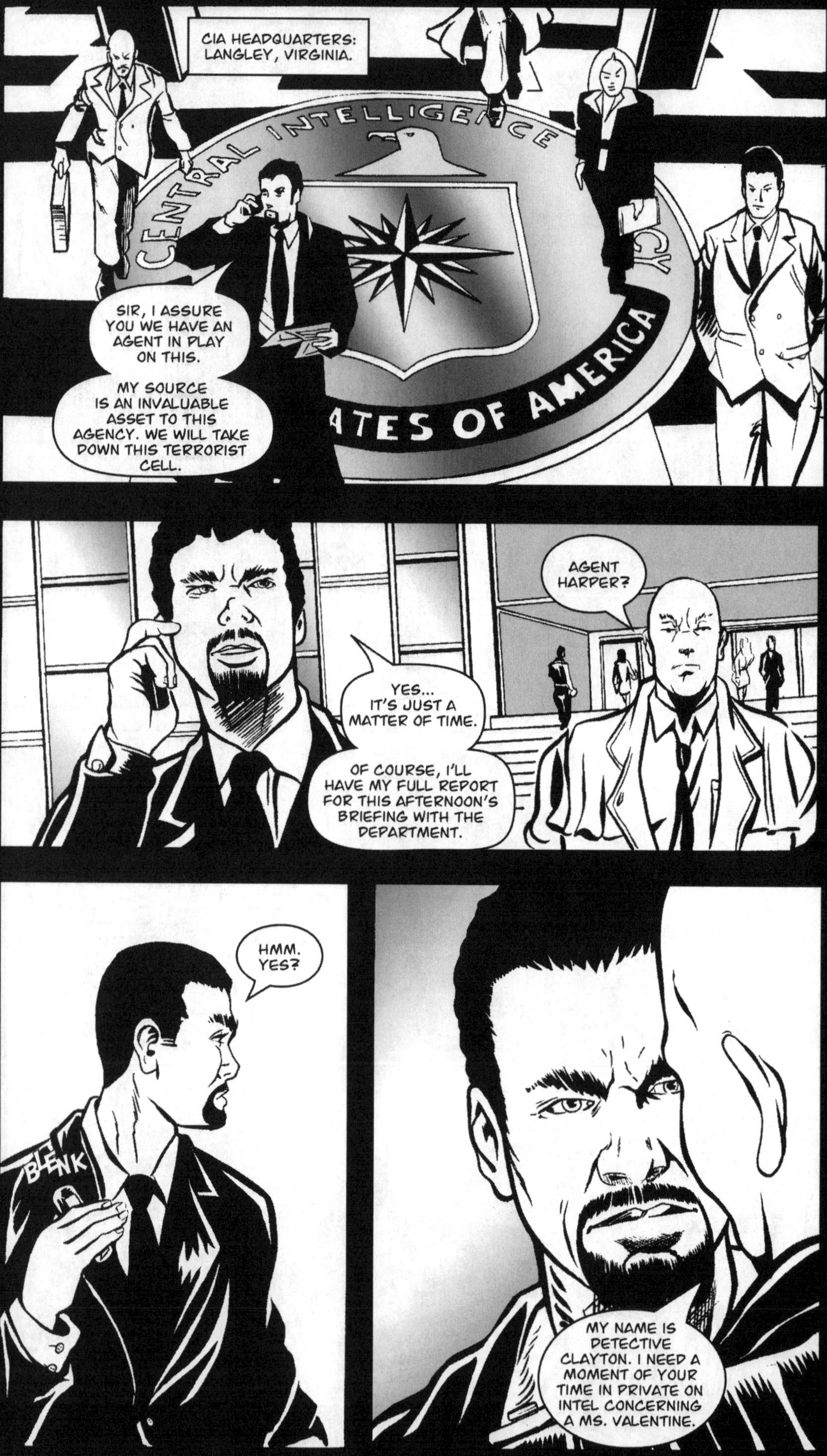
CIA HEADQUARTERS: LANGLEY, VIRGINIA.
CENTRAL INTELLIGENCE AGENCY
UNITED STATES OF AMERICA
SIR, I ASSURE YOU WE HAVE AN AGENT IN PLAY ON THIS.
MY SOURCE IS AN INVALUABLE ASSET TO THIS AGENCY. WE WILL TAKE DOWN THIS TERRORIST CELL.
AGENT HARPER?
YES... IT'S JUST A MATTER OF TIME.
OF COURSE, I'LL HAVE MY FULL REPORT FOR THIS AFTERNOON'S BRIEFING WITH THE DEPARTMENT.
HMM. YES?
BLENK
MY NAME IS DETECTIVE CLAYTON. I NEED A MOMENT OF YOUR TIME IN PRIVATE ON INTEL CONCERNING A MS. VALENTINE.

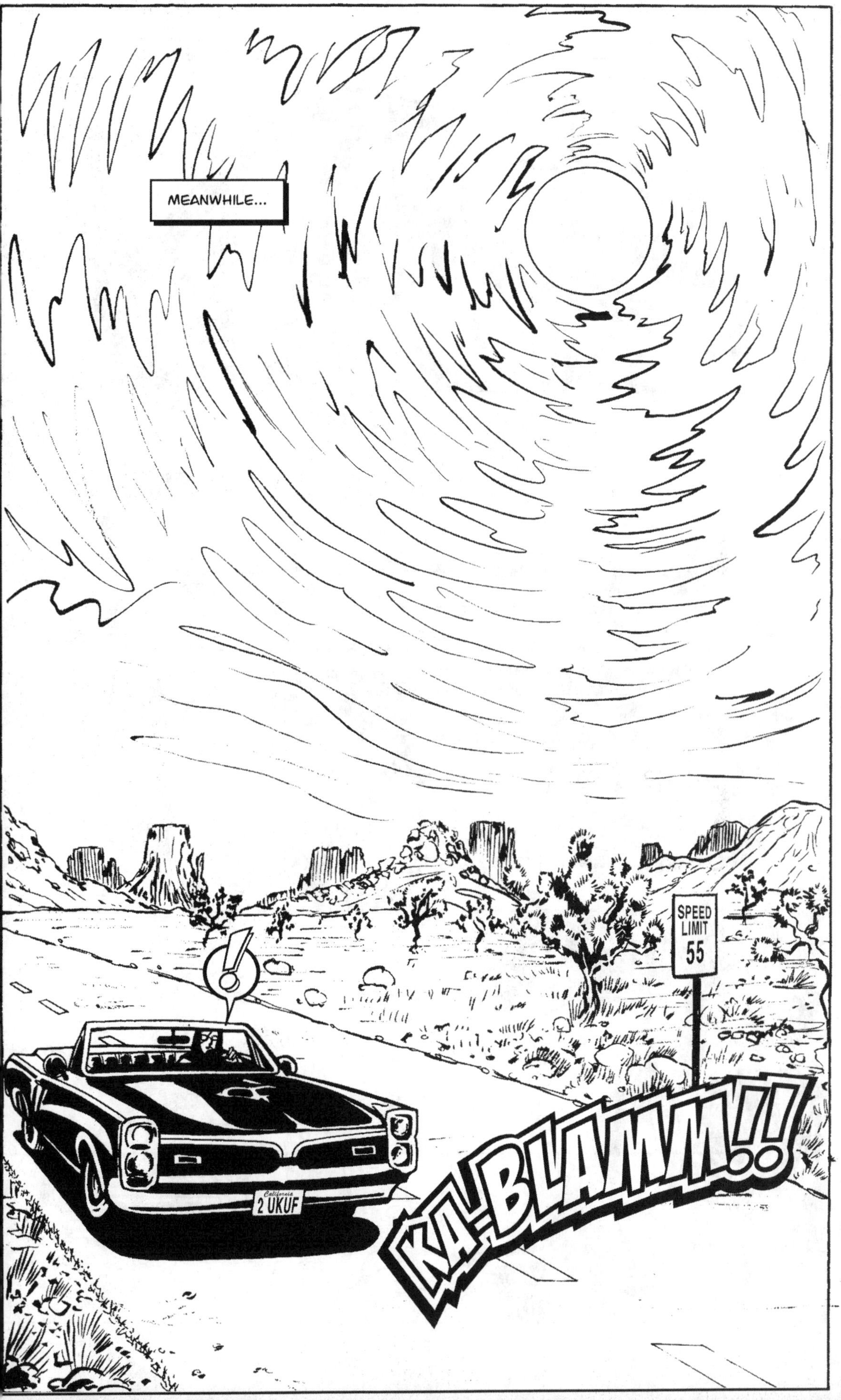
MEANWHILE...
!
SPEED LIMIT 55
California
2 UKUF
KA-BLAMM!!

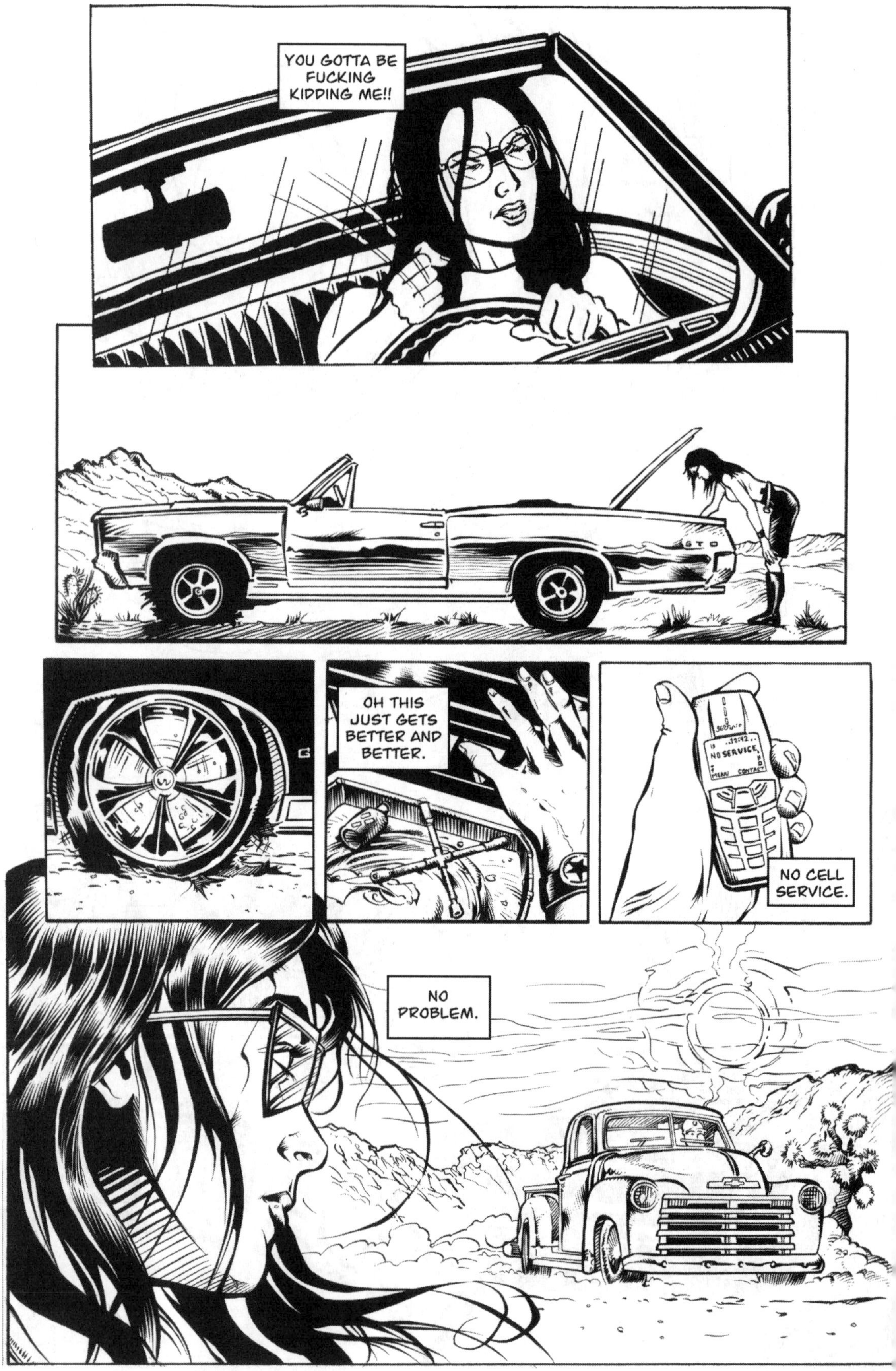
YOU GOTTA BE FUCKING KIDDING ME!!
OH THIS JUST GETS BETTER AND BETTER.
NO SERVICE
NO CELL SERVICE.
NO PROBLEM.

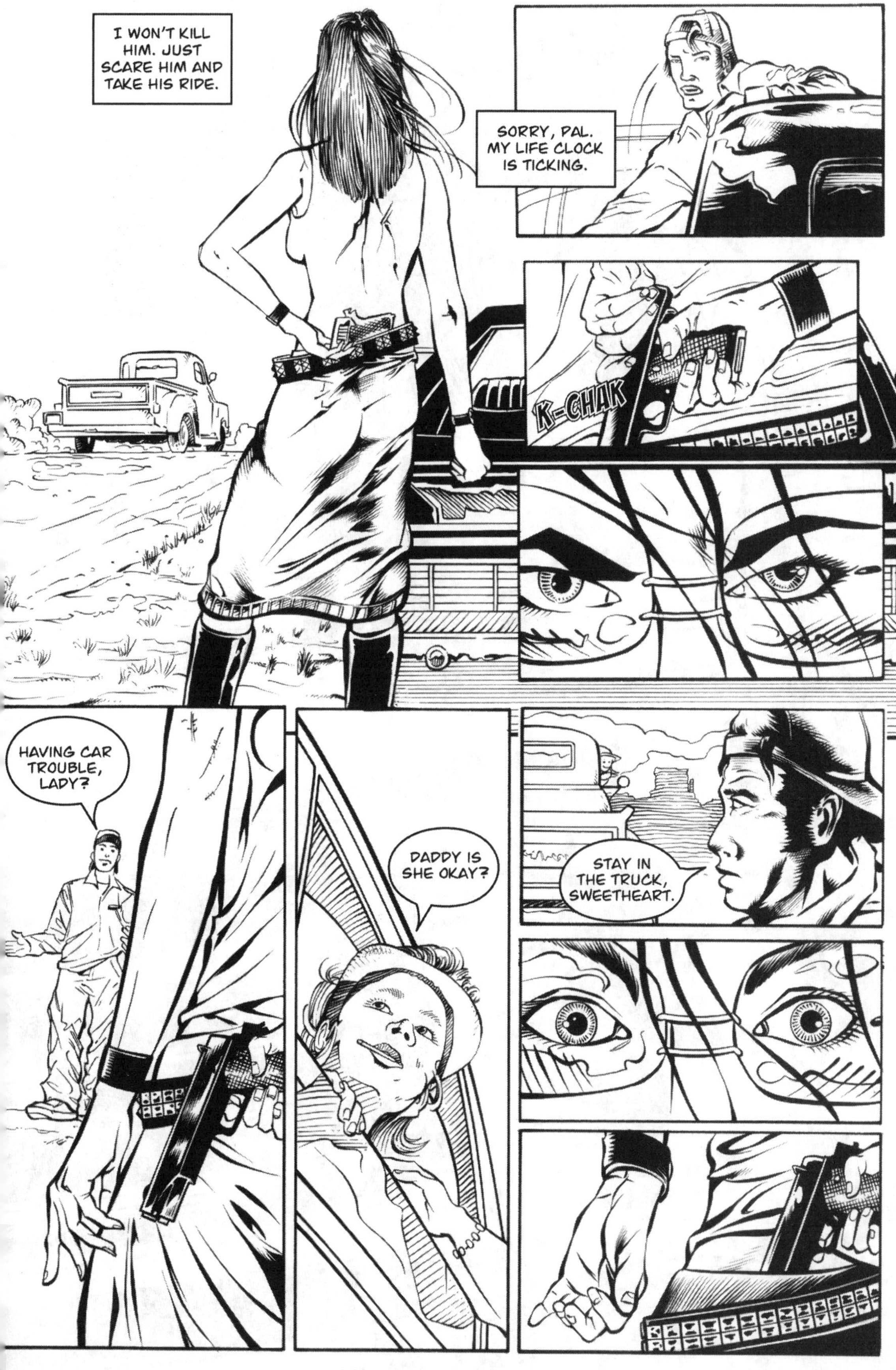
I WON'T KILL HIM. JUST SCARE HIM AND TAKE HIS RIDE.
SORRY, PAL. MY LIFE CLOCK IS TICKING.
K-CHAK
HAVING CAR TROUBLE, LADY?
DADDY IS SHE OKAY?
STAY IN THE TRUCK, SWEETHEART.

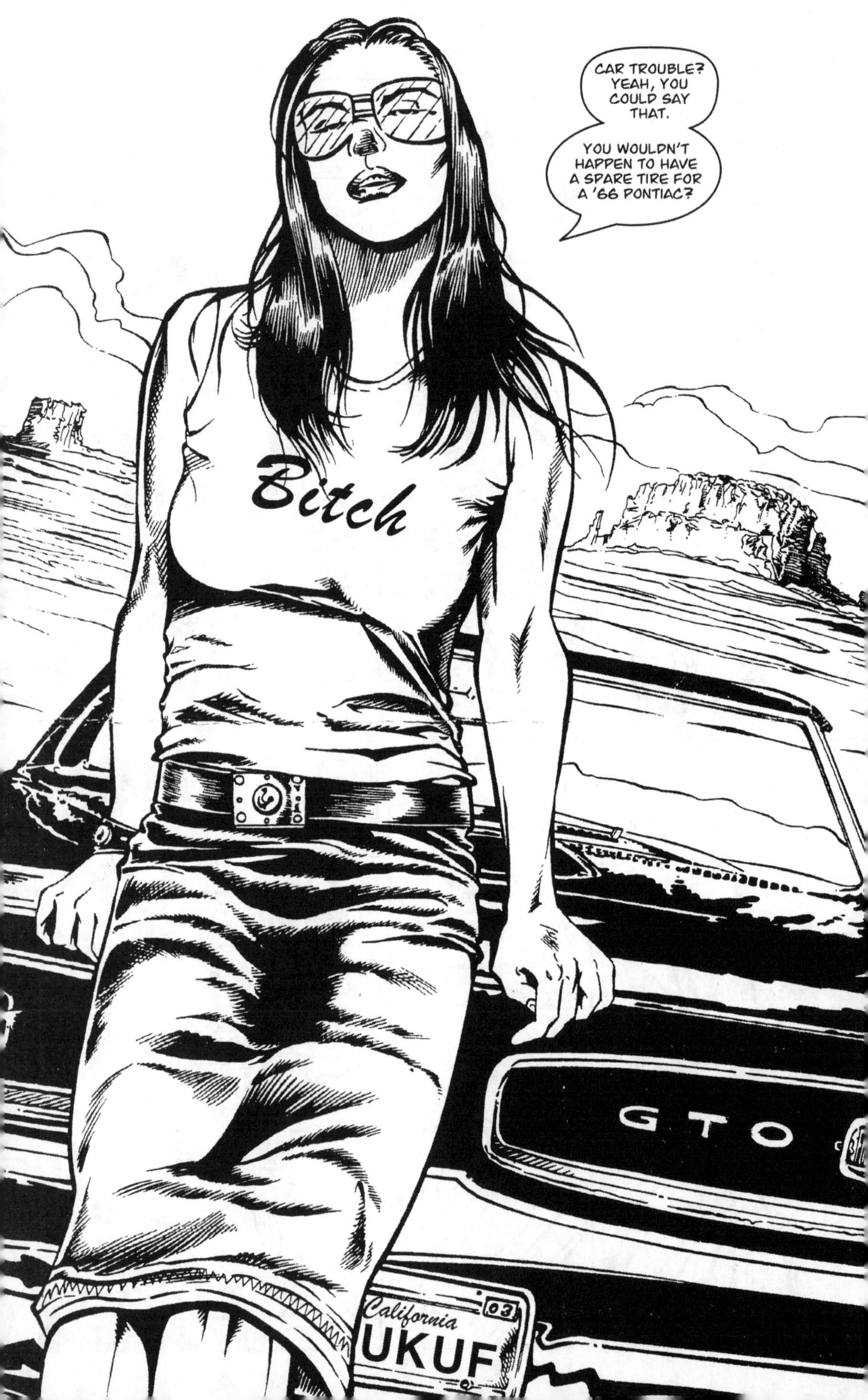
CAR TROUBLE? YEAH, YOU COULD SAY THAT.
YOU WOULDN'T HAPPEN TO HAVE A SPARE TIRE FOR A '66 PONTIAC?
Bitch
GTO
California 03
UKUF

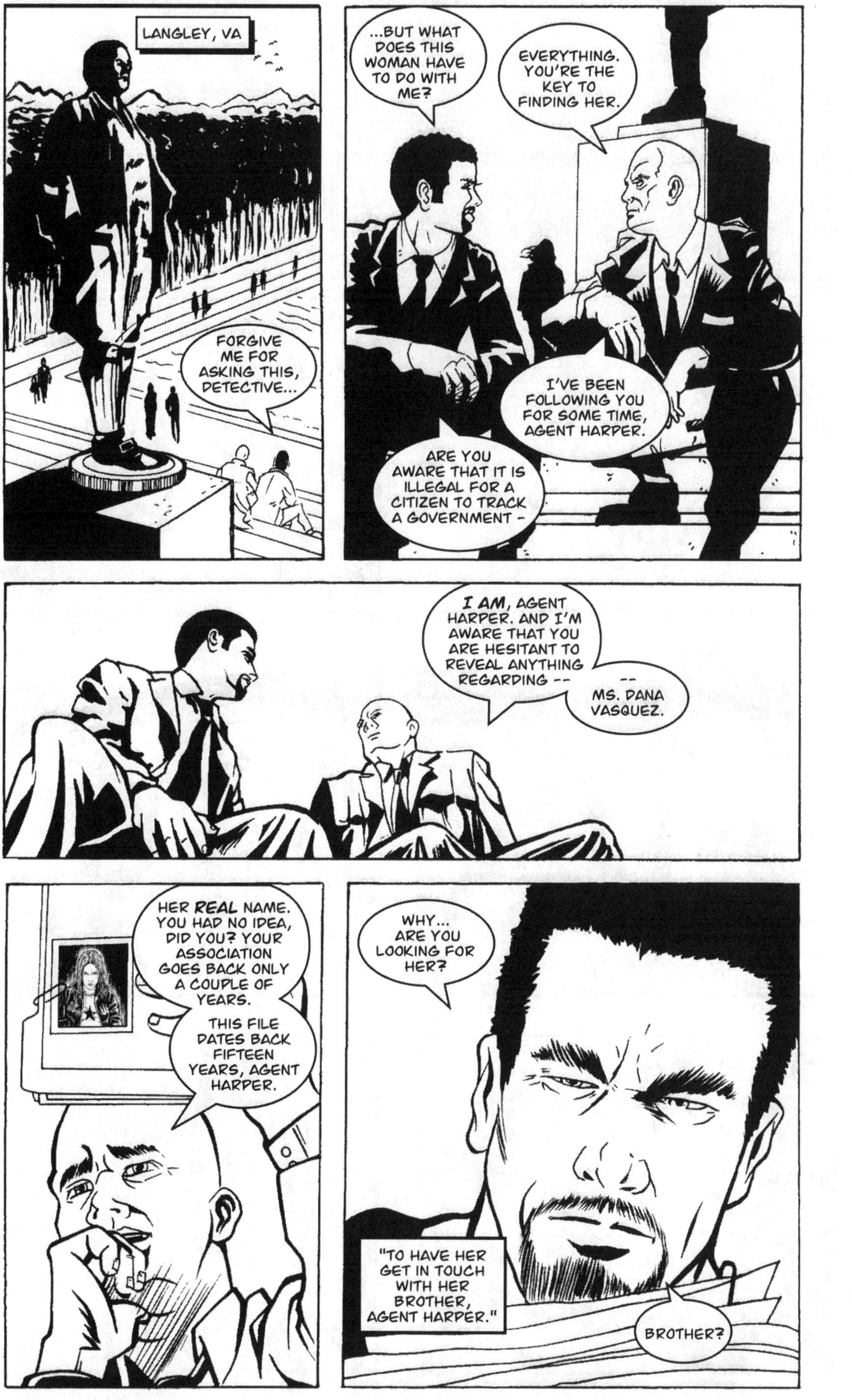
LANGLEY, VA
FORGIVE ME FOR ASKING THIS, DETECTIVE...
...BUT WHAT DOES THIS WOMAN HAVE TO DO WITH ME?
EVERYTHING. YOU'RE THE KEY TO FINDING HER.
I'VE BEEN FOLLOWING YOU FOR SOME TIME, AGENT HARPER.
ARE YOU AWARE THAT IT IS ILLEGAL FOR A CITIZEN TO TRACK A GOVERNMENT -
I AM, AGENT HARPER. AND I'M AWARE THAT YOU ARE HESITANT TO REVEAL ANYTHING REGARDING --
-- MS. DANA VASQUEZ.
HER REAL NAME. YOU HAD NO IDEA, DID YOU? YOUR ASSOCIATION GOES BACK ONLY A COUPLE OF YEARS.
THIS FILE DATES BACK FIFTEEN YEARS, AGENT HARPER.
WHY... ARE YOU LOOKING FOR HER?
"TO HAVE HER GET IN TOUCH WITH HER BROTHER, AGENT HARPER."
BROTHER?

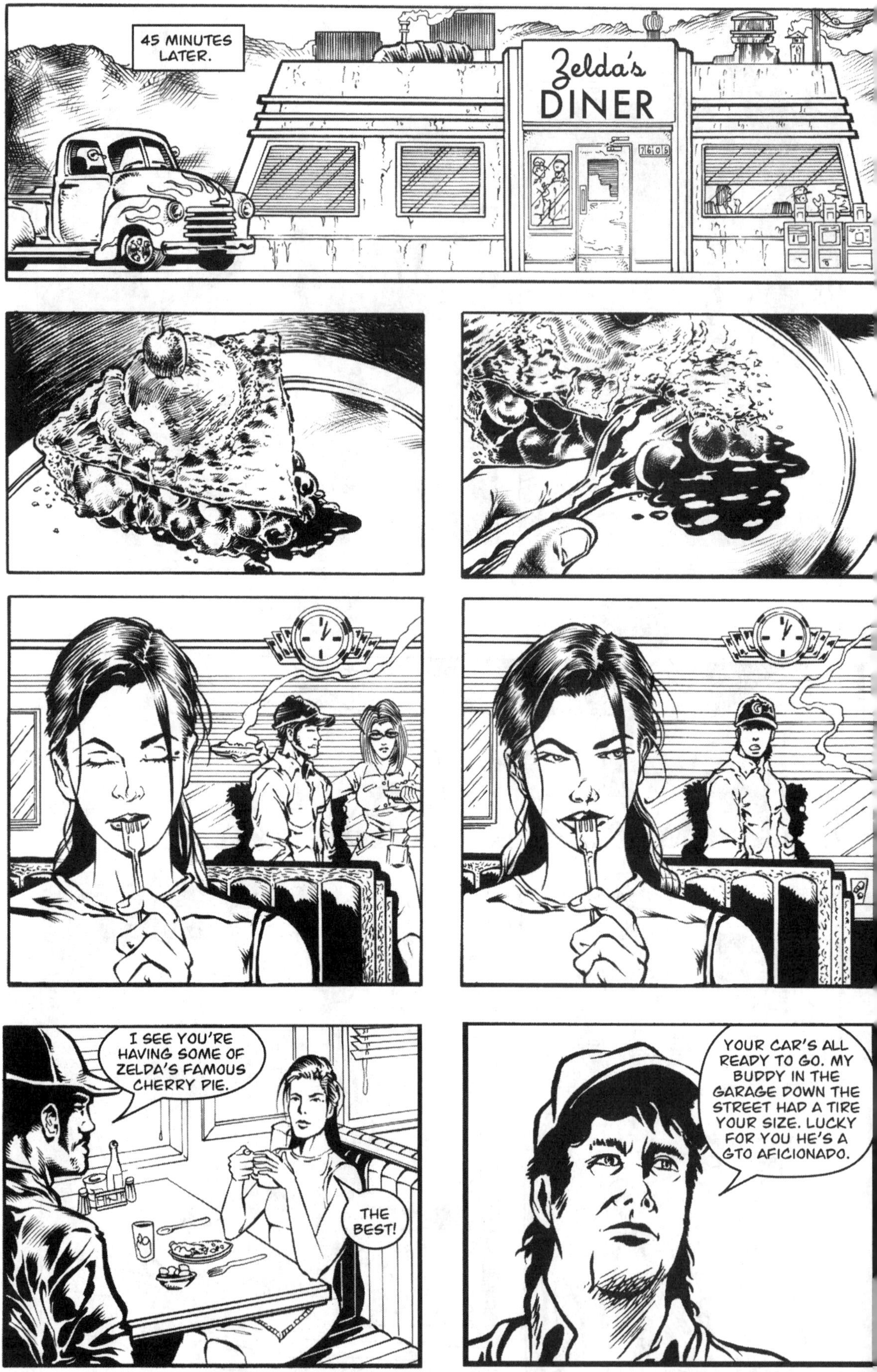
45 MINUTES LATER.
Zelda's DINER
I SEE YOU'RE HAVING SOME OF ZELDA'S FAMOUS CHERRY PIE.
THE BEST!
YOUR CAR'S ALL READY TO GO. MY BUDDY IN THE GARAGE DOWN THE STREET HAD A TIRE YOUR SIZE. LUCKY FOR YOU HE'S A GTO AFICIONADO.

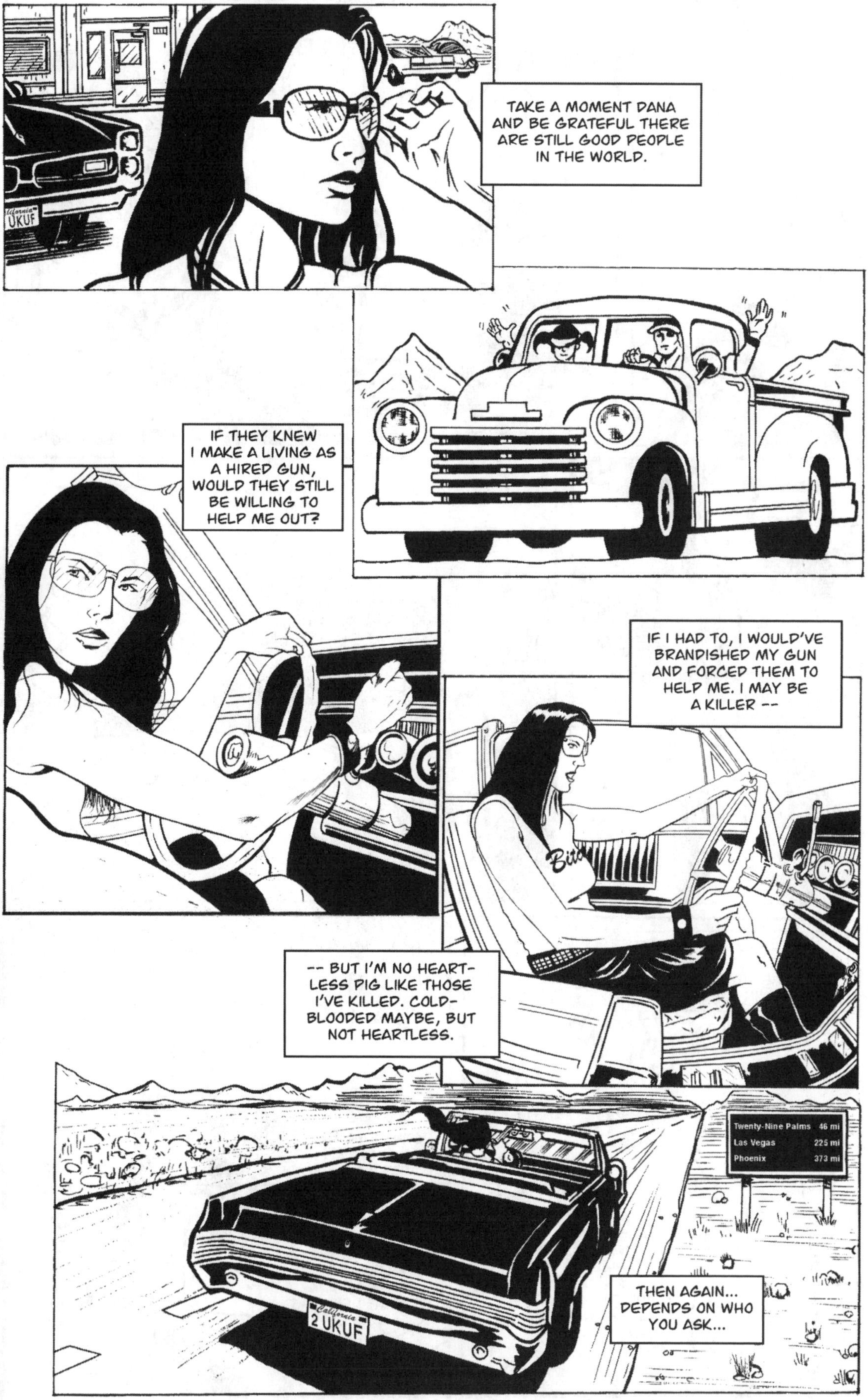
TAKE A MOMENT DANA AND BE GRATEFUL THERE ARE STILL GOOD PEOPLE IN THE WORLD.
UKUF
IF THEY KNEW I MAKE A LIVING AS A HIRED GUN, WOULD THEY STILL BE WILLING TO HELP ME OUT?
IF I HAD TO, I WOULD'VE BRANDISHED MY GUN AND FORCED THEM TO HELP ME. I MAY BE A KILLER --
-- BUT I'M NO HEART-LESS PIG LIKE THOSE I'VE KILLED. COLD-BLOODED MAYBE, BUT NOT HEARTLESS.
Twenty-Nine Palms 46 mi
Las Vegas 225 mi
Phoenix 373 mi
California
2 UKUF
THEN AGAIN... DEPENDS ON WHO YOU ASK...

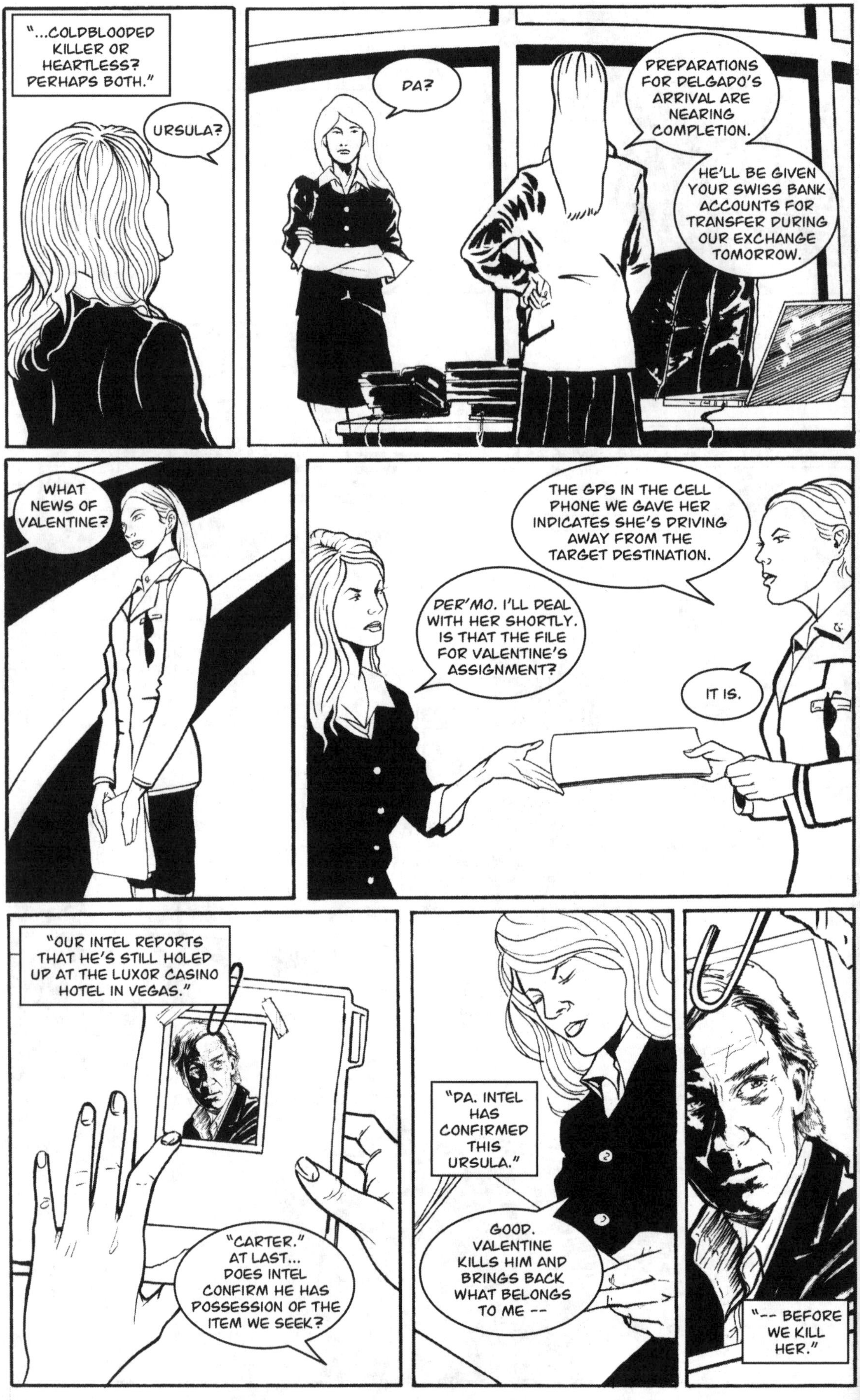
"...COLDBLOODED KILLER OR HEARTLESS? PERHAPS BOTH."
URSULA?
DA?
PREPARATIONS FOR DELGADO'S ARRIVAL ARE NEARING COMPLETION.
HE'LL BE GIVEN YOUR SWISS BANK ACCOUNTS FOR TRANSFER DURING OUR EXCHANGE TOMORROW.
WHAT NEWS OF VALENTINE?
THE GPS IN THE CELL PHONE WE GAVE HER INDICATES SHE'S DRIVING AWAY FROM THE TARGET DESTINATION.
DER'MO. I'LL DEAL WITH HER SHORTLY. IS THAT THE FILE FOR VALENTINE'S ASSIGNMENT?
IT IS.
"OUR INTEL REPORTS THAT HE'S STILL HOLED UP AT THE LUXOR CASINO HOTEL IN VEGAS."
"CARTER." AT LAST... DOES INTEL CONFIRM HE HAS POSSESSION OF THE ITEM WE SEEK?
"DA. INTEL HAS CONFIRMED THIS URSULA."
GOOD. VALENTINE KILLS HIM AND BRINGS BACK WHAT BELONGS TO ME --
"-- BEFORE WE KILL HER."

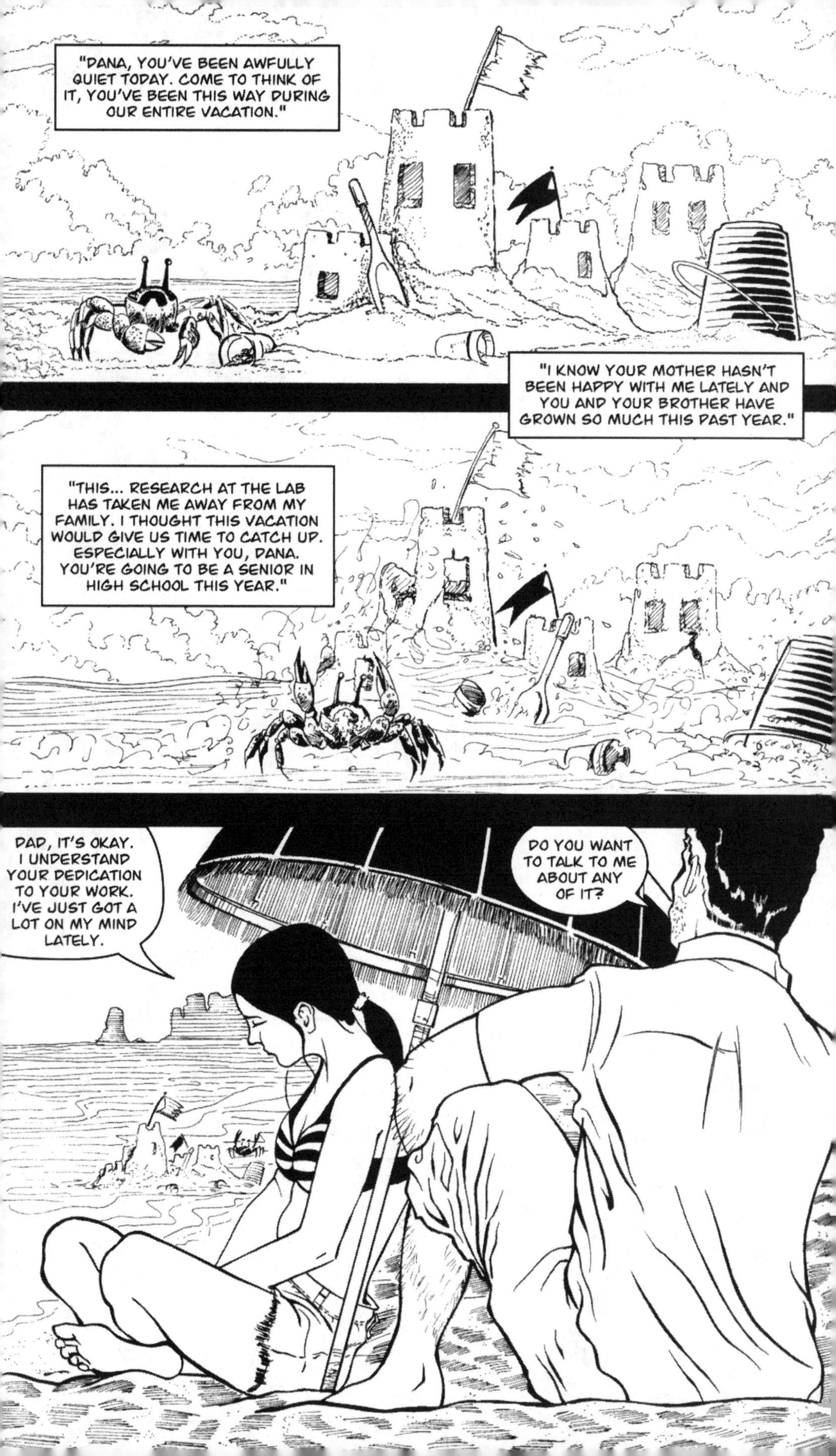
"DANA, YOU'VE BEEN AWFULLY QUIET TODAY. COME TO THINK OF IT, YOU'VE BEEN THIS WAY DURING OUR ENTIRE VACATION."
"I KNOW YOUR MOTHER HASN'T BEEN HAPPY WITH ME LATELY AND YOU AND YOUR BROTHER HAVE GROWN SO MUCH THIS PAST YEAR."
"THIS... RESEARCH AT THE LAB HAS TAKEN ME AWAY FROM MY FAMILY. I THOUGHT THIS VACATION WOULD GIVE US TIME TO CATCH UP. ESPECIALLY WITH YOU, DANA. YOU'RE GOING TO BE A SENIOR IN HIGH SCHOOL THIS YEAR."
DAD, IT'S OKAY. I UNDERSTAND YOUR DEDICATION TO YOUR WORK. I'VE JUST GOT A LOT ON MY MIND LATELY.
DO YOU WANT TO TALK TO ME ABOUT ANY OF IT?

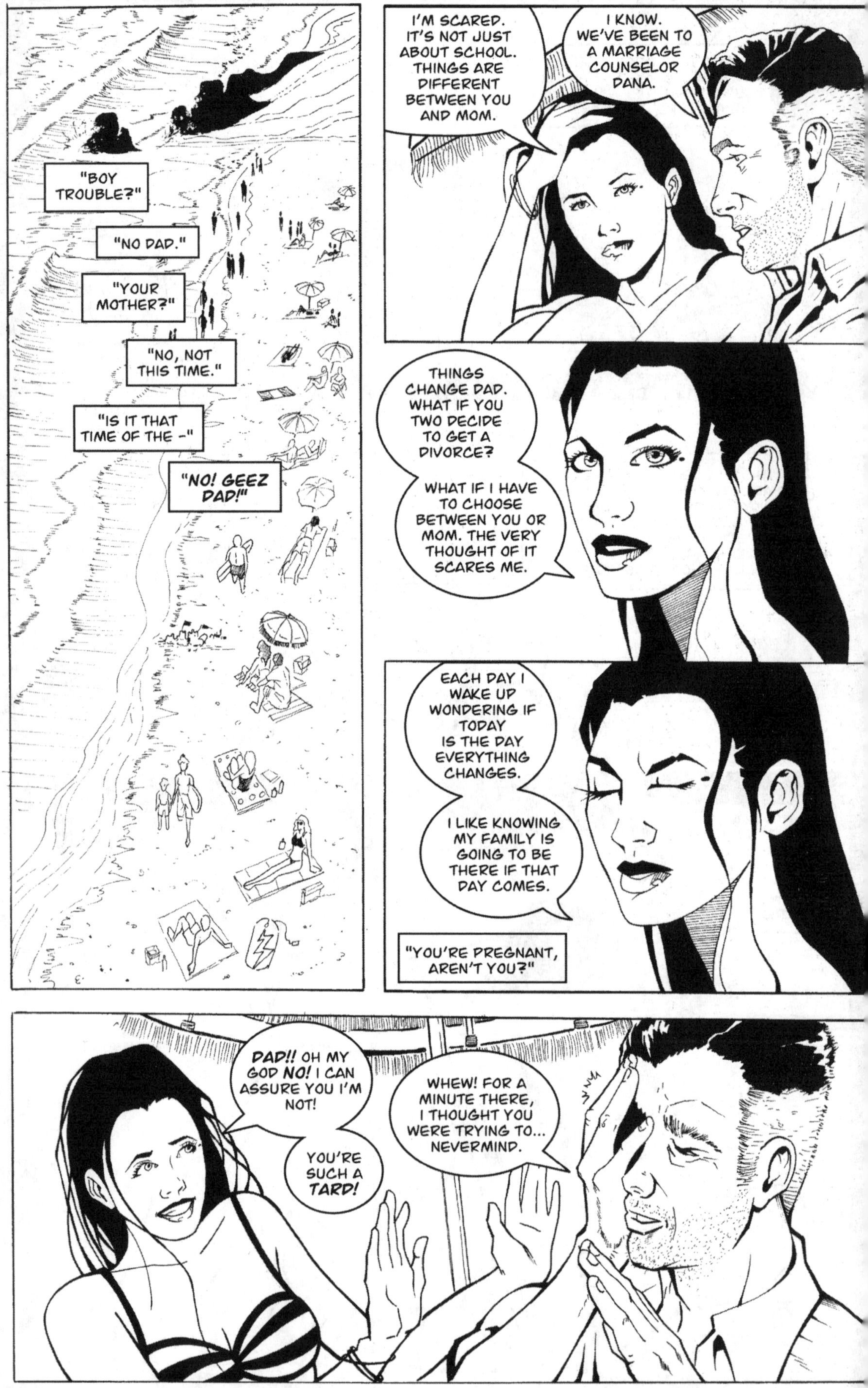
"BOY TROUBLE?"
"NO DAD."
"YOUR MOTHER?"
"NO, NOT THIS TIME."
"IS IT THAT TIME OF THE -"
"NO! GEEZ DAD!"
I'M SCARED. IT'S NOT JUST ABOUT SCHOOL. THINGS ARE DIFFERENT BETWEEN YOU AND MOM.
I KNOW. WE'VE BEEN TO A MARRIAGE COUNSELOR DANA.
THINGS CHANGE DAD. WHAT IF YOU TWO DECIDE TO GET A DIVORCE?
WHAT IF I HAVE TO CHOOSE BETWEEN YOU OR MOM. THE VERY THOUGHT OF IT SCARES ME.
EACH DAY I WAKE UP WONDERING IF TODAY IS THE DAY EVERYTHING CHANGES.
I LIKE KNOWING MY FAMILY IS GOING TO BE THERE IF THAT DAY COMES.
"YOU'RE PREGNANT, AREN'T YOU?"
DAD!! OH MY GOD NO! I CAN ASSURE YOU I'M NOT!
YOU'RE SUCH A TARD!
WHEW! FOR A MINUTE THERE, I THOUGHT YOU WERE TRYING TO... NEVERMIND.

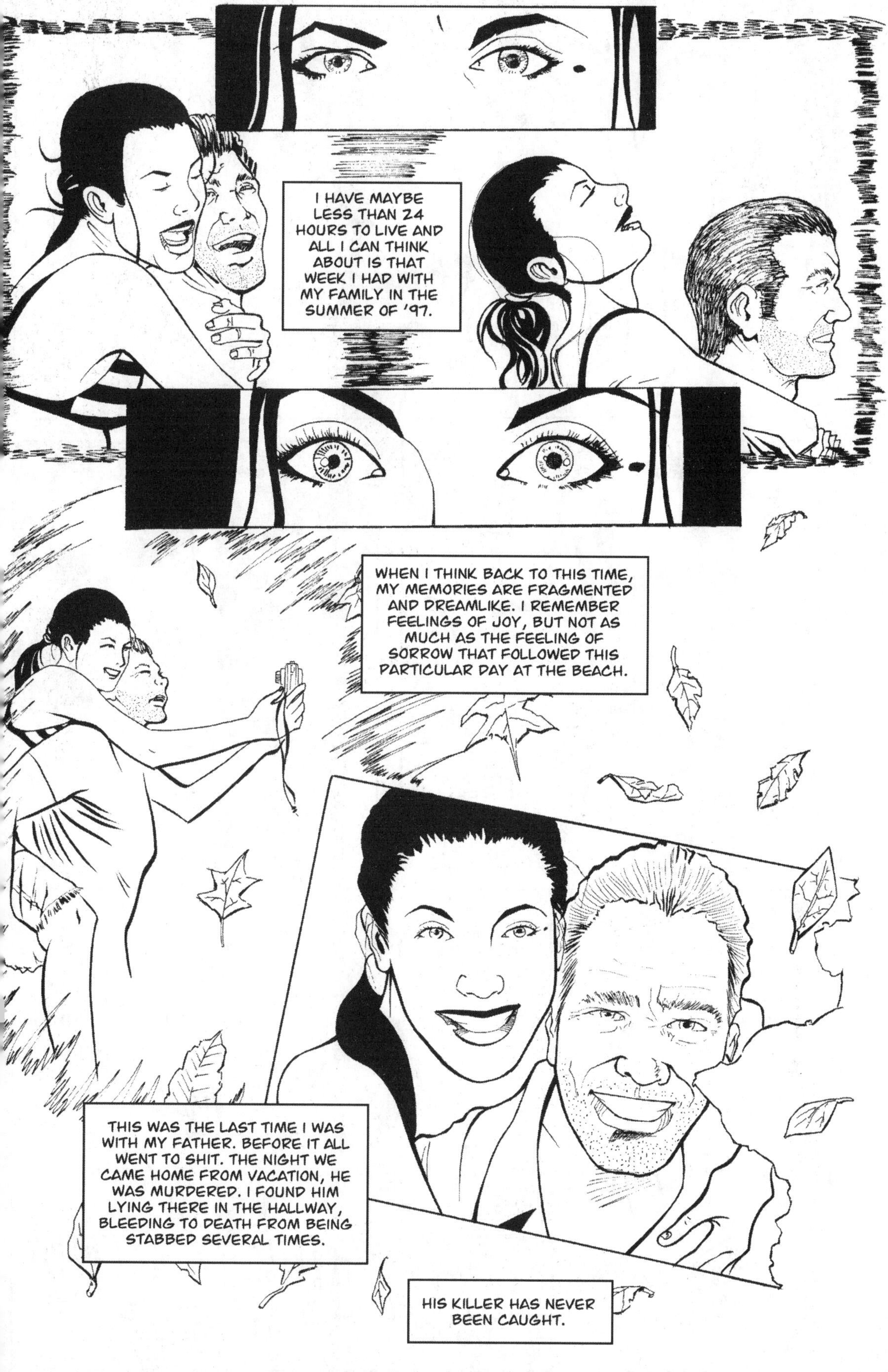
I HAVE MAYBE LESS THAN 24 HOURS TO LIVE AND ALL I CAN THINK ABOUT IS THAT WEEK I HAD WITH MY FAMILY IN THE SUMMER OF '97.
WHEN I THINK BACK TO THIS TIME, MY MEMORIES ARE FRAGMENTED AND DREAMLIKE. I REMEMBER FEELINGS OF JOY, BUT NOT AS MUCH AS THE FEELING OF SORROW THAT FOLLOWED THIS PARTICULAR DAY AT THE BEACH.
THIS WAS THE LAST TIME I WAS WITH MY FATHER. BEFORE IT ALL WENT TO SHIT. THE NIGHT WE CAME HOME FROM VACATION, HE WAS MURDERED. I FOUND HIM LYING THERE IN THE HALLWAY, BLEEDING TO DEATH FROM BEING STABBED SEVERAL TIMES.
HIS KILLER HAS NEVER BEEN CAUGHT.

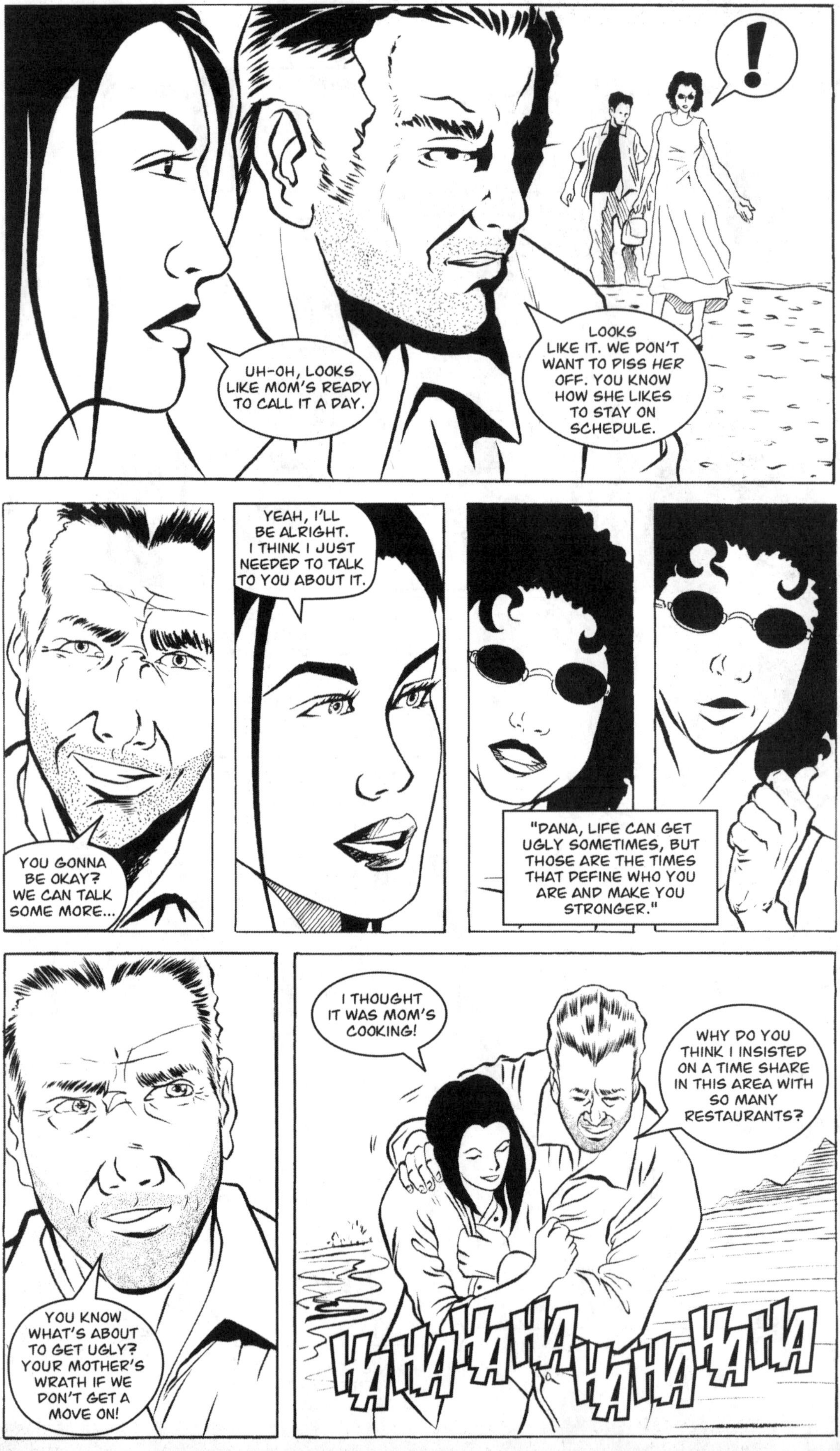
!
UH-OH, LOOKS LIKE MOM'S READY TO CALL IT A DAY.
LOOKS LIKE IT. WE DON'T WANT TO PISS HER OFF. YOU KNOW HOW SHE LIKES TO STAY ON SCHEDULE.
YOU GONNA BE OKAY? WE CAN TALK SOME MORE...
YEAH, I'LL BE ALRIGHT. I THINK I JUST NEEDED TO TALK TO YOU ABOUT IT.
"DANA, LIFE CAN GET UGLY SOMETIMES, BUT THOSE ARE THE TIMES THAT DEFINE WHO YOU ARE AND MAKE YOU STRONGER."
YOU KNOW WHAT'S ABOUT TO GET UGLY? YOUR MOTHER'S WRATH IF WE DON'T GET A MOVE ON!
I THOUGHT IT WAS MOM'S COOKING!
WHY DO YOU THINK I INSISTED ON A TIME SHARE IN THIS AREA WITH SO MANY RESTAURANTS?
HA HA HA HA HA HA HA HA HA HA

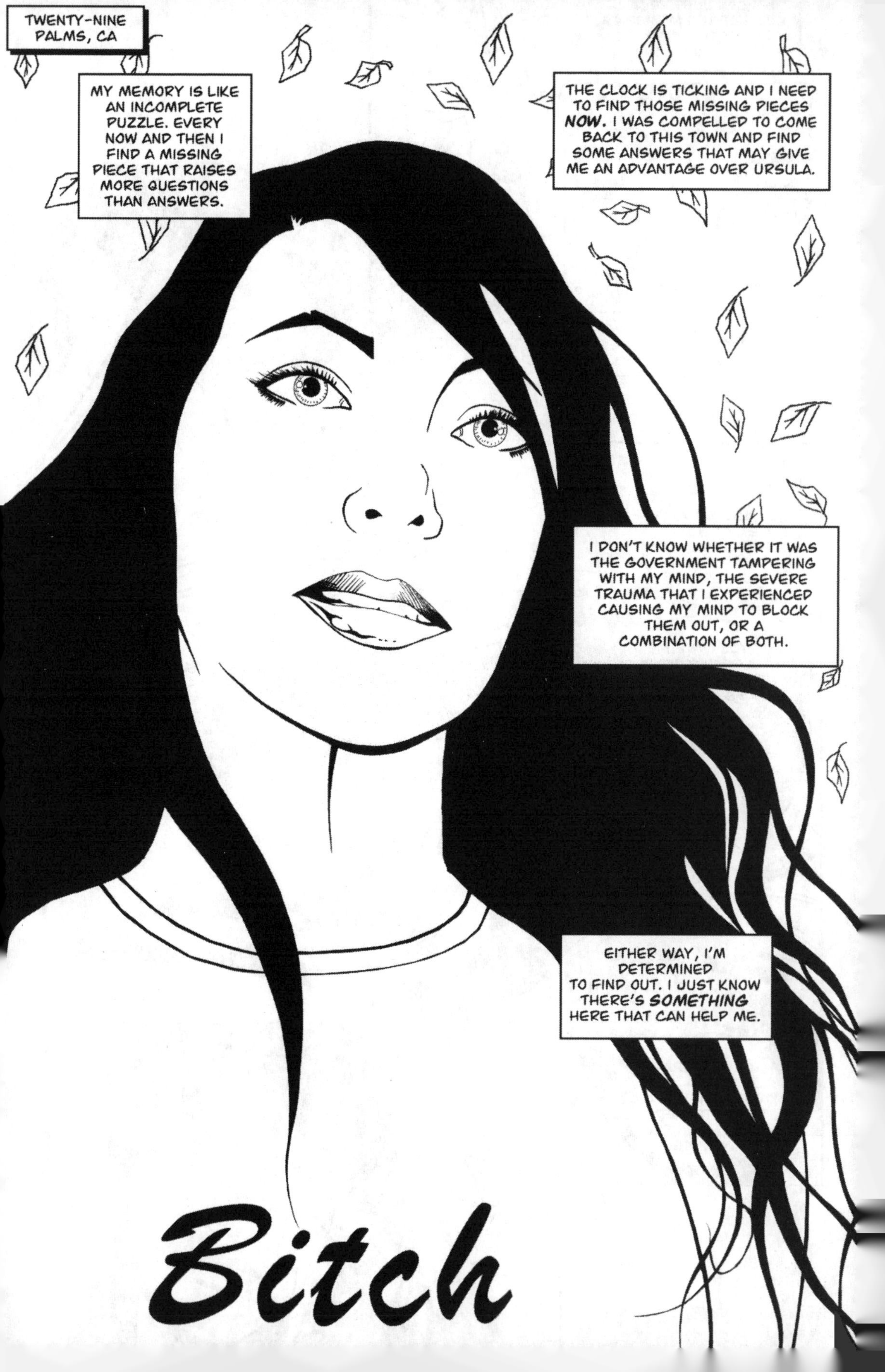
TWENTY-NINE PALMS, CA
MY MEMORY IS LIKE AN INCOMPLETE PUZZLE. EVERY NOW AND THEN I FIND A MISSING PIECE THAT RAISES MORE QUESTIONS THAN ANSWERS.
THE CLOCK IS TICKING AND I NEED TO FIND THOSE MISSING PIECES NOW. I WAS COMPELLED TO COME BACK TO THIS TOWN AND FIND SOME ANSWERS THAT MAY GIVE ME AN ADVANTAGE OVER URSULA.
I DON'T KNOW WHETHER IT WAS THE GOVERNMENT TAMPERING WITH MY MIND, THE SEVERE TRAUMA THAT I EXPERIENCED CAUSING MY MIND TO BLOCK THEM OUT, OR A COMBINATION OF BOTH.
EITHER WAY, I'M DETERMINED TO FIND OUT. I JUST KNOW THERE'S SOMETHING HERE THAT CAN HELP ME.
Bitch

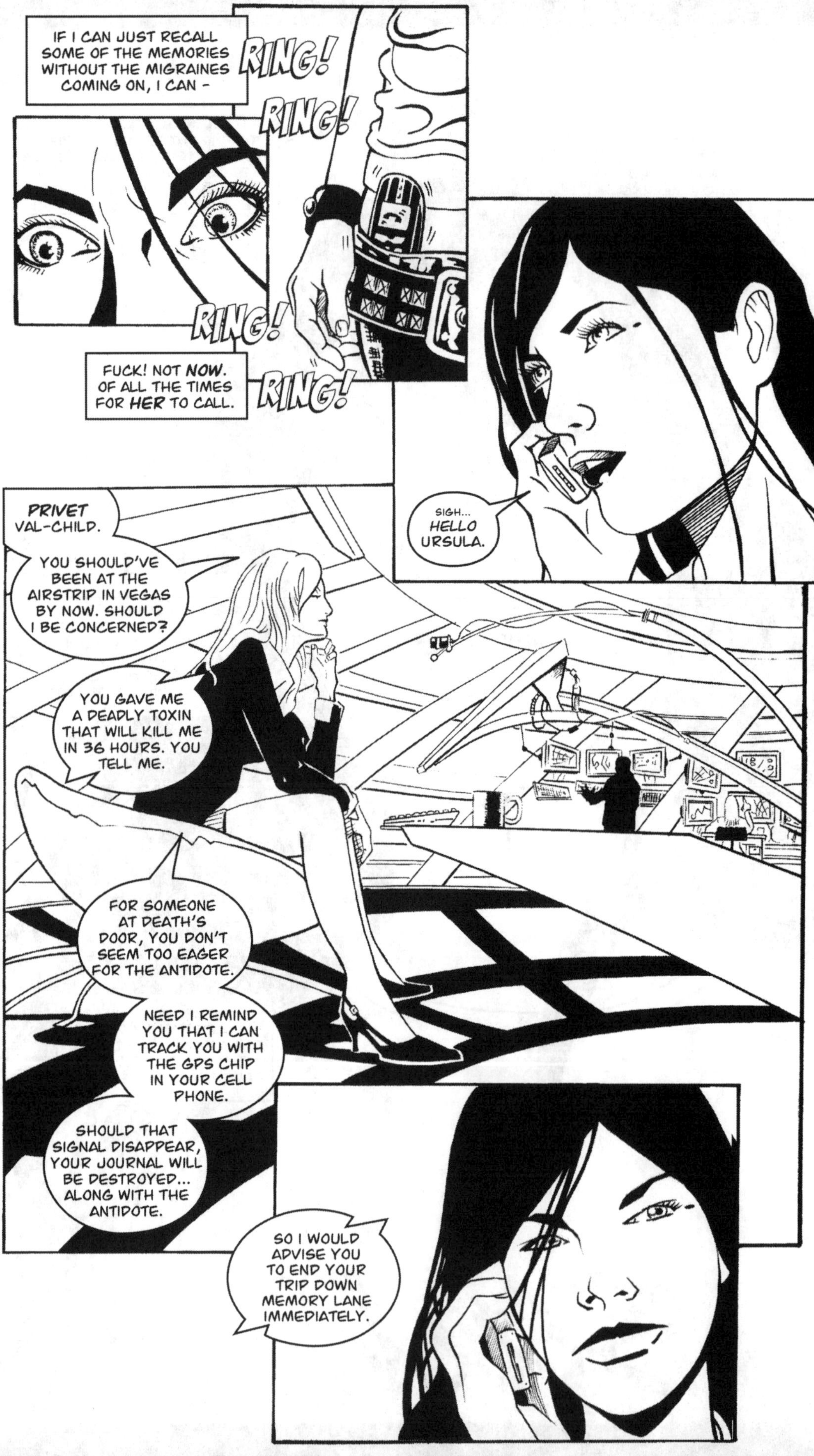
IF I CAN JUST RECALL SOME OF THE MEMORIES WITHOUT THE MIGRAINES COMING ON, I CAN -
RING!
RING!
RING!
FUCK! NOT NOW. OF ALL THE TIMES FOR HER TO CALL.
RING!
SIGH... HELLO URSULA.
PRIVET VAL-CHILD.
YOU SHOULD'VE BEEN AT THE AIRSTRIP IN VEGAS BY NOW. SHOULD I BE CONCERNED?
YOU GAVE ME A DEADLY TOXIN THAT WILL KILL ME IN 36 HOURS. YOU TELL ME.
FOR SOMEONE AT DEATH'S DOOR, YOU DON'T SEEM TOO EAGER FOR THE ANTIDOTE.
NEED I REMIND YOU THAT I CAN TRACK YOU WITH THE GPS CHIP IN YOUR CELL PHONE.
SHOULD THAT SIGNAL DISAPPEAR, YOUR JOURNAL WILL BE DESTROYED... ALONG WITH THE ANTIDOTE.
SO I WOULD ADVISE YOU TO END YOUR TRIP DOWN MEMORY LANE IMMEDIATELY.

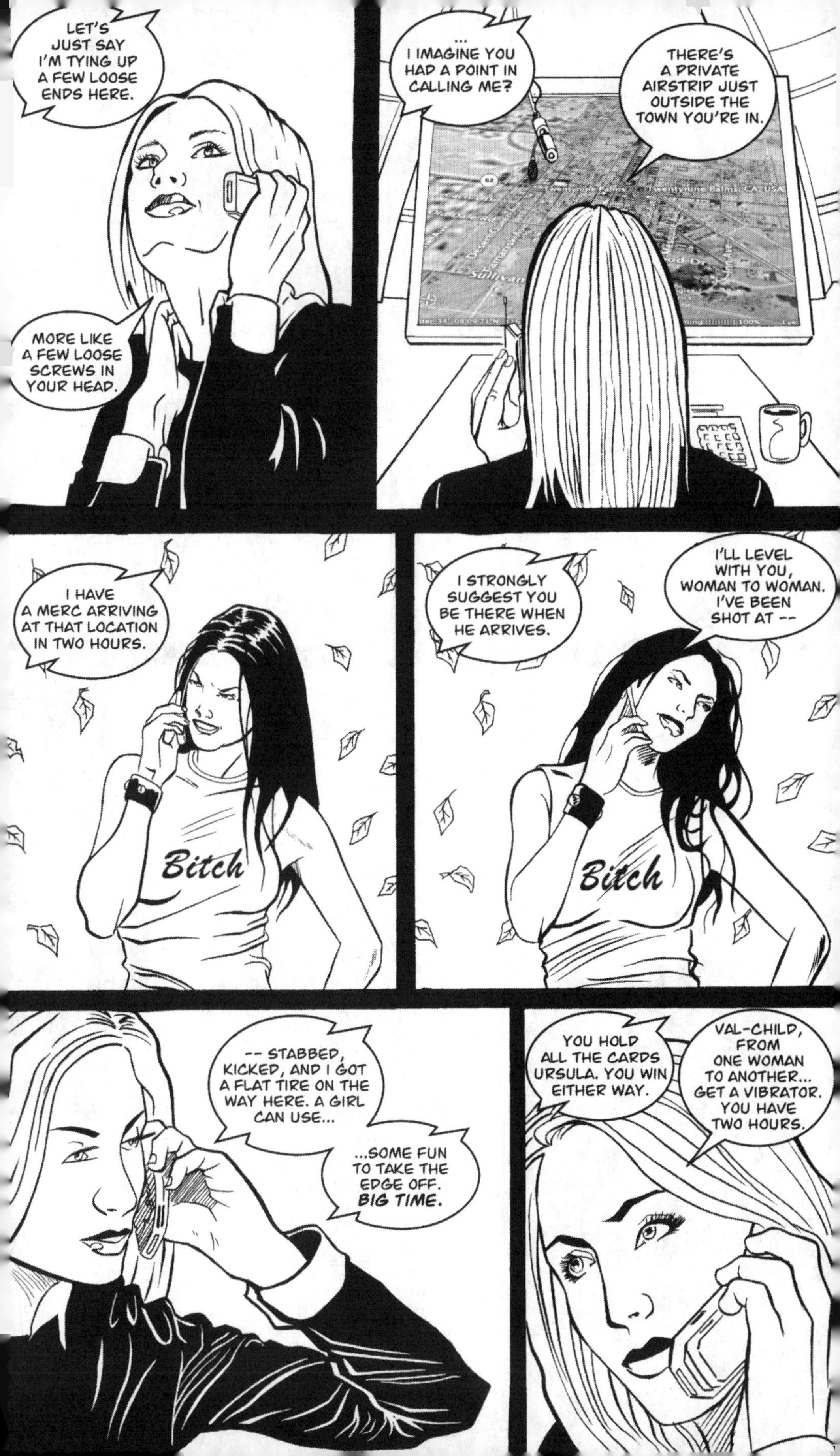

LET'S JUST SAY I'M TYING UP A FEW LOOSE ENDS HERE.
MORE LIKE A FEW LOOSE SCREWS IN YOUR HEAD.
... I IMAGINE YOU HAD A POINT IN CALLING ME?
THERE'S A PRIVATE AIRSTRIP JUST OUTSIDE THE TOWN YOU'RE IN.
I HAVE A MERC ARRIVING AT THAT LOCATION IN TWO HOURS.
Bitch
I STRONGLY SUGGEST YOU BE THERE WHEN HE ARRIVES.
I'LL LEVEL WITH YOU, WOMAN TO WOMAN. I'VE BEEN SHOT AT --
Bitch
-- STABBED, KICKED, AND I GOT A FLAT TIRE ON THE WAY HERE. A GIRL CAN USE...
...SOME FUN TO TAKE THE EDGE OFF. BIG TIME.
YOU HOLD ALL THE CARDS URSULA. YOU WIN EITHER WAY.
VAL-CHILD, FROM ONE WOMAN TO ANOTHER... GET A VIBRATOR. YOU HAVE TWO HOURS.

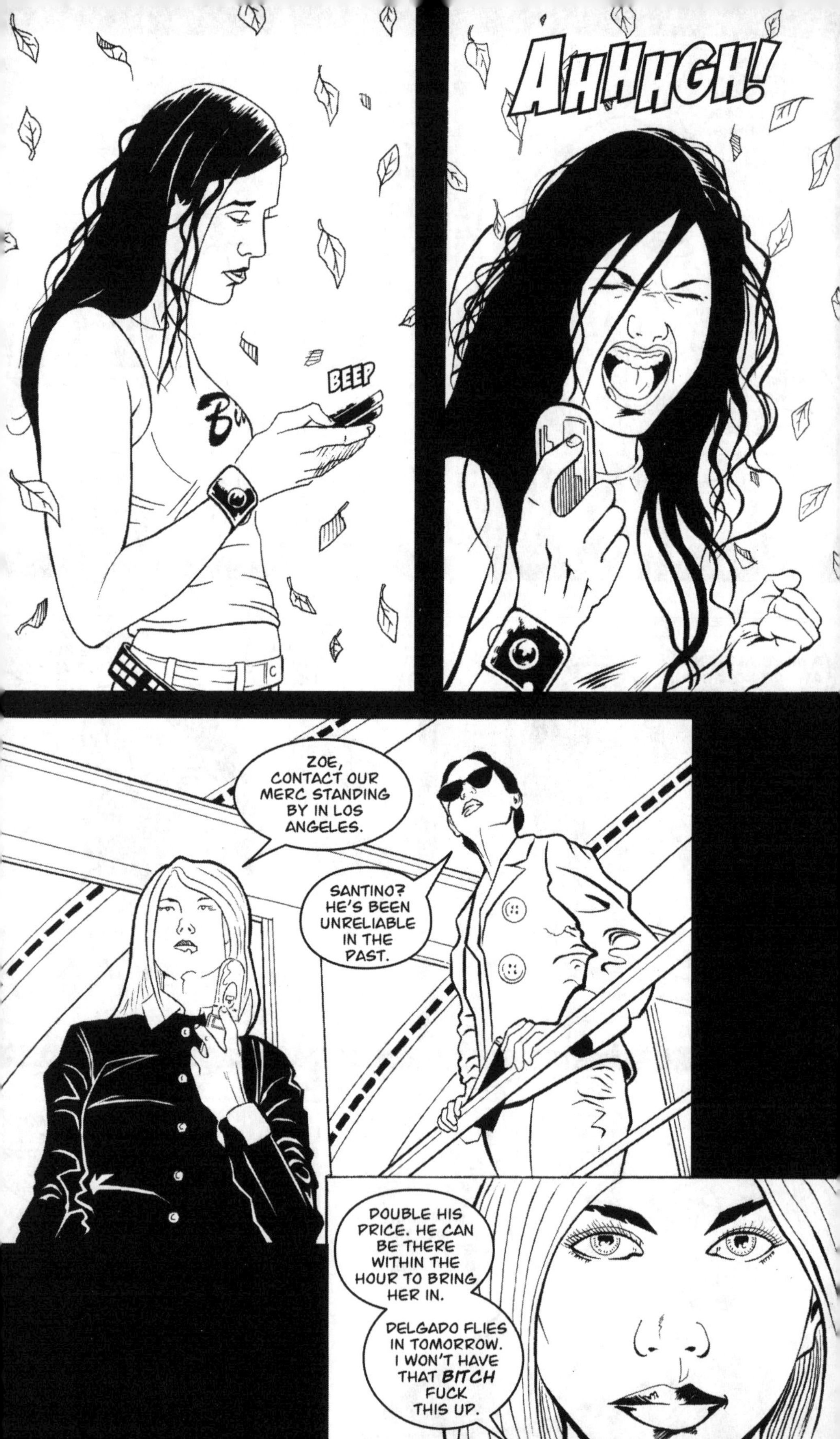
BEEP
AHHHGH!
ZOE, CONTACT OUR MERC STANDING BY IN LOS ANGELES.
SANTINO? HE'S BEEN UNRELIABLE IN THE PAST.
DOUBLE HIS PRICE. HE CAN BE THERE WITHIN THE HOUR TO BRING HER IN.
DELGADO FLIES IN TOMORROW. I WON'T HAVE THAT **BITCH** FUCK THIS UP.

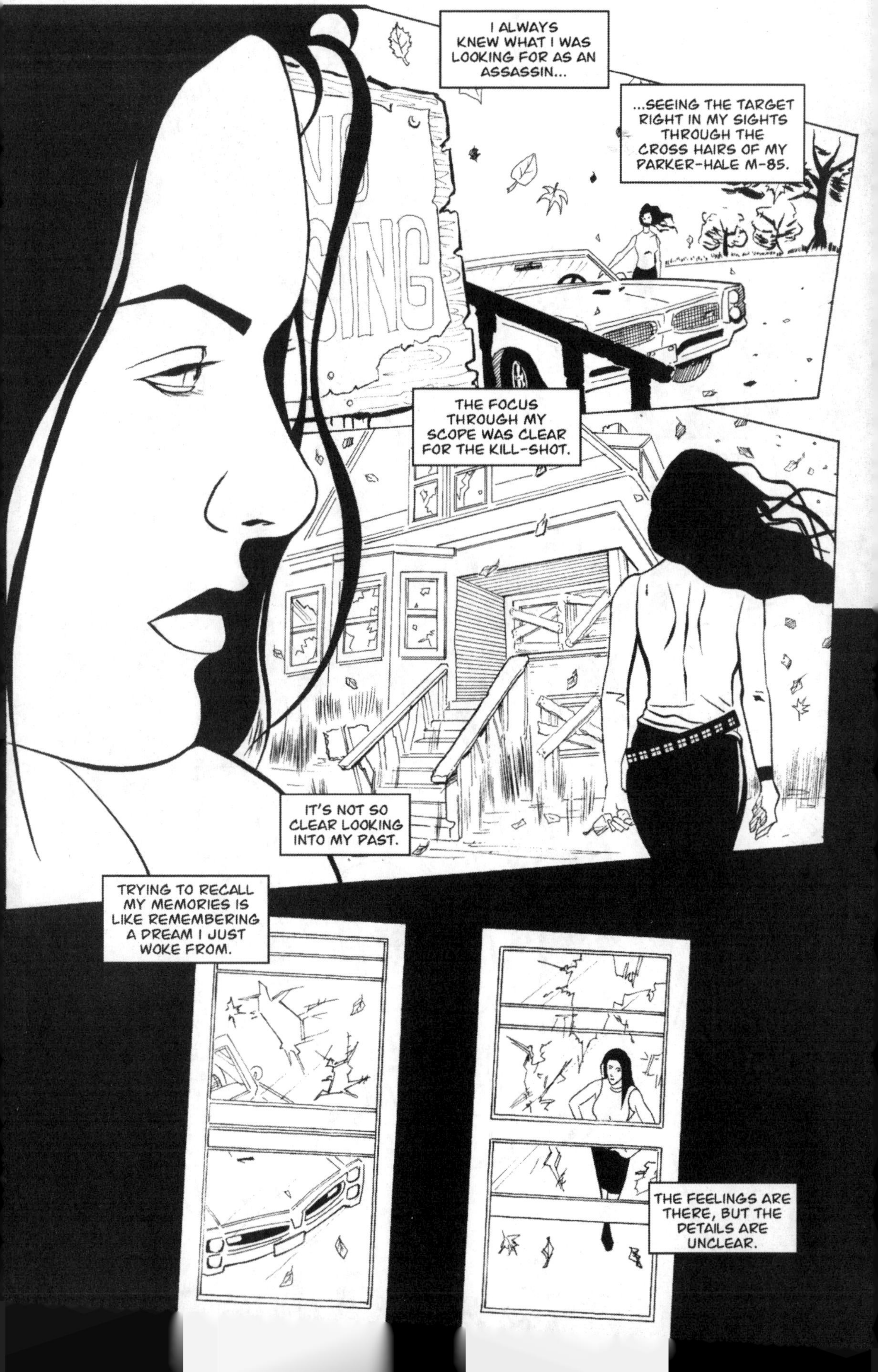
I ALWAYS KNEW WHAT I WAS LOOKING FOR AS AN ASSASSIN...
...SEEING THE TARGET RIGHT IN MY SIGHTS THROUGH THE CROSS HAIRS OF MY PARKER-HALE M-85.
THE FOCUS THROUGH MY SCOPE WAS CLEAR FOR THE KILL-SHOT.
IT'S NOT SO CLEAR LOOKING INTO MY PAST.
TRYING TO RECALL MY MEMORIES IS LIKE REMEMBERING A DREAM I JUST WOKE FROM.
THE FEELINGS ARE THERE, BUT THE DETAILS ARE UNCLEAR.

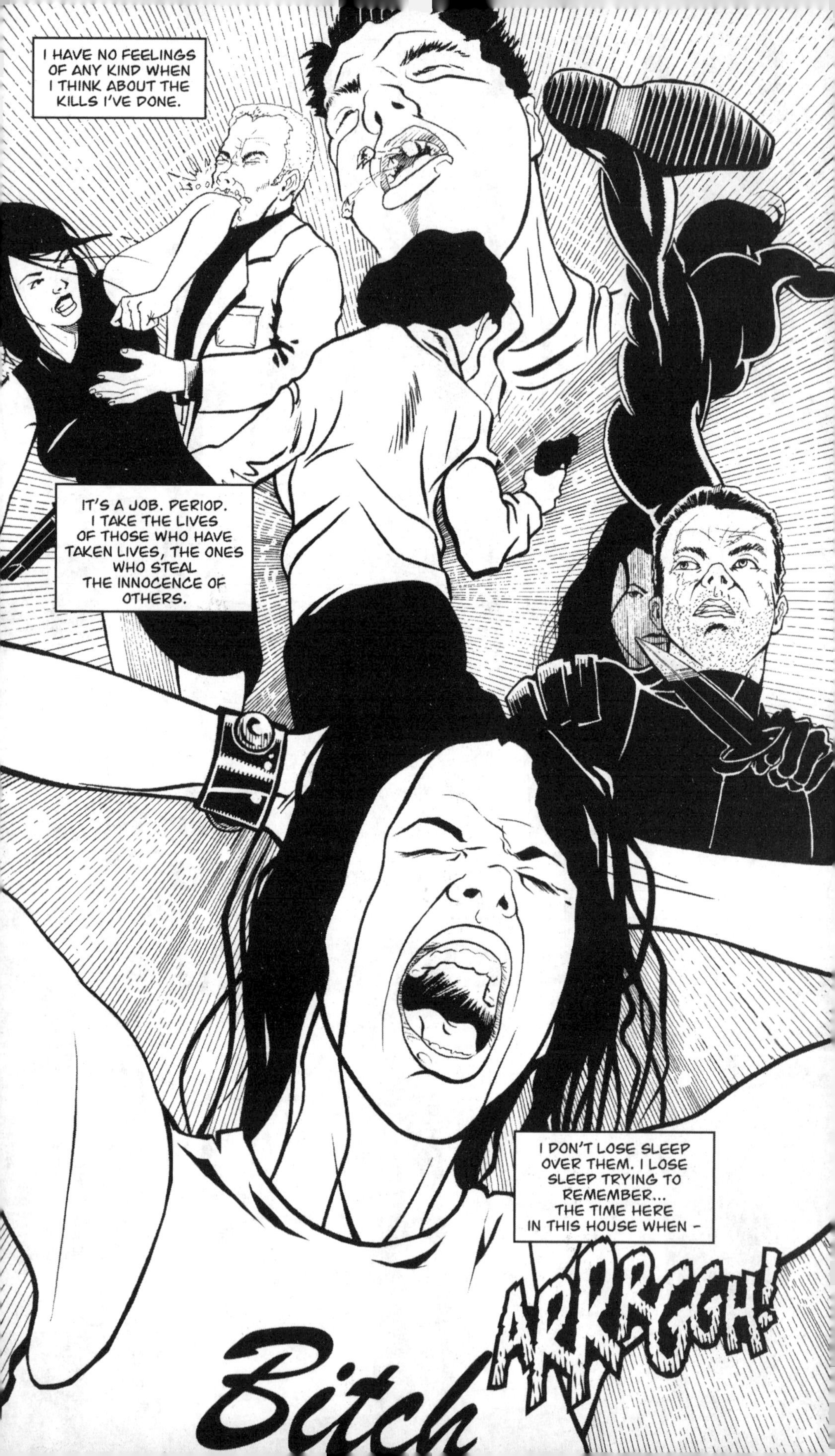
I HAVE NO FEELINGS OF ANY KIND WHEN I THINK ABOUT THE KILLS I'VE DONE.
IT'S A JOB. PERIOD. I TAKE THE LIVES OF THOSE WHO HAVE TAKEN LIVES, THE ONES WHO STEAL THE INNOCENCE OF OTHERS.
I DON'T LOSE SLEEP OVER THEM. I LOSE SLEEP TRYING TO REMEMBER... THE TIME HERE IN THIS HOUSE WHEN -
ARRRGGH!
Bitch

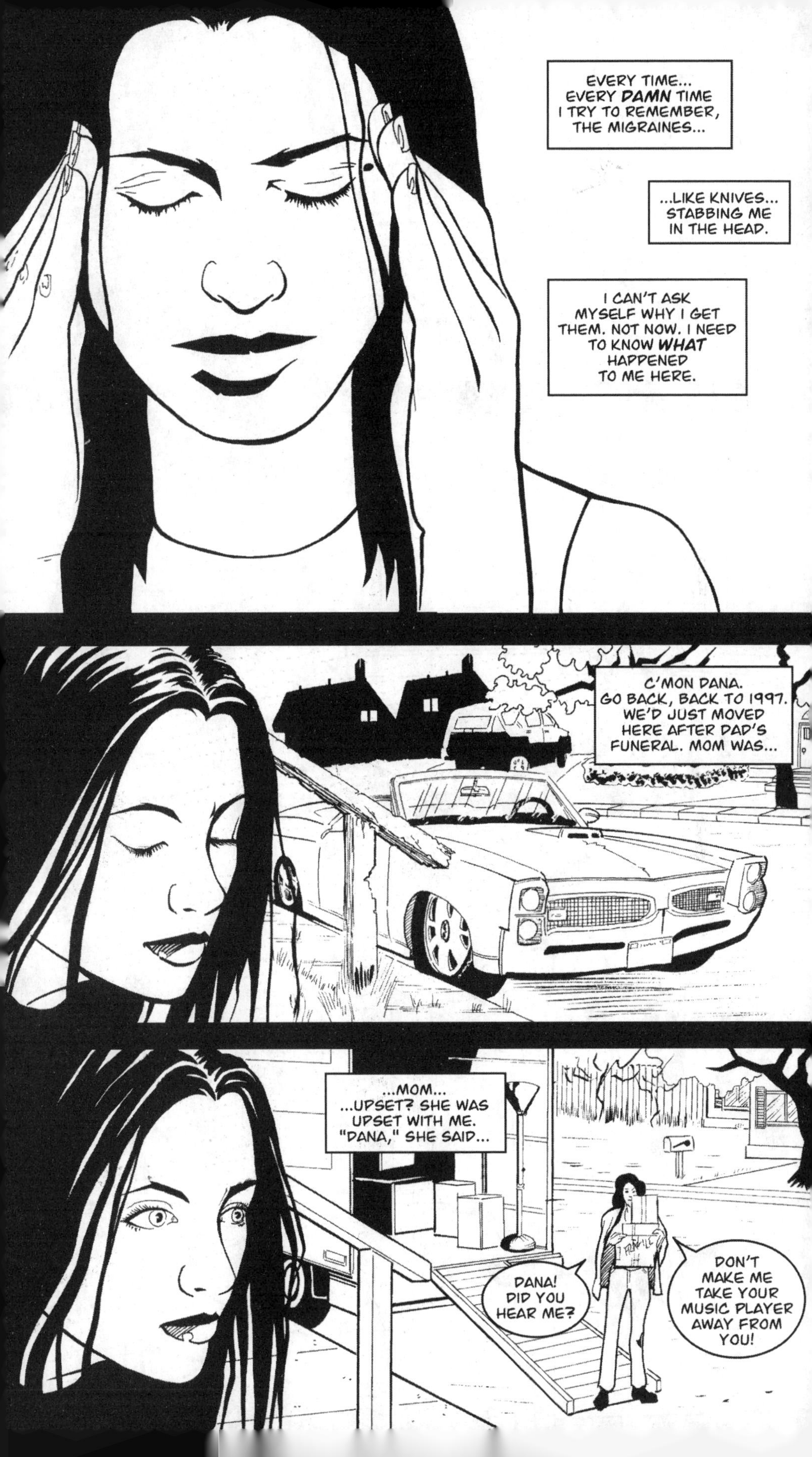
EVERY TIME...
EVERY DAMN TIME I TRY TO REMEMBER, THE MIGRAINES...
...LIKE KNIVES... STABBING ME IN THE HEAD.
I CAN'T ASK MYSELF WHY I GET THEM. NOT NOW. I NEED TO KNOW WHAT HAPPENED TO ME HERE.
C'MON DANA. GO BACK, BACK TO 1997. WE'D JUST MOVED HERE AFTER DAD'S FUNERAL. MOM WAS...
...MOM... ...UPSET? SHE WAS UPSET WITH ME. "DANA," SHE SAID...
DANA! DID YOU HEAR ME?
DON'T MAKE ME TAKE YOUR MUSIC PLAYER AWAY FROM YOU!

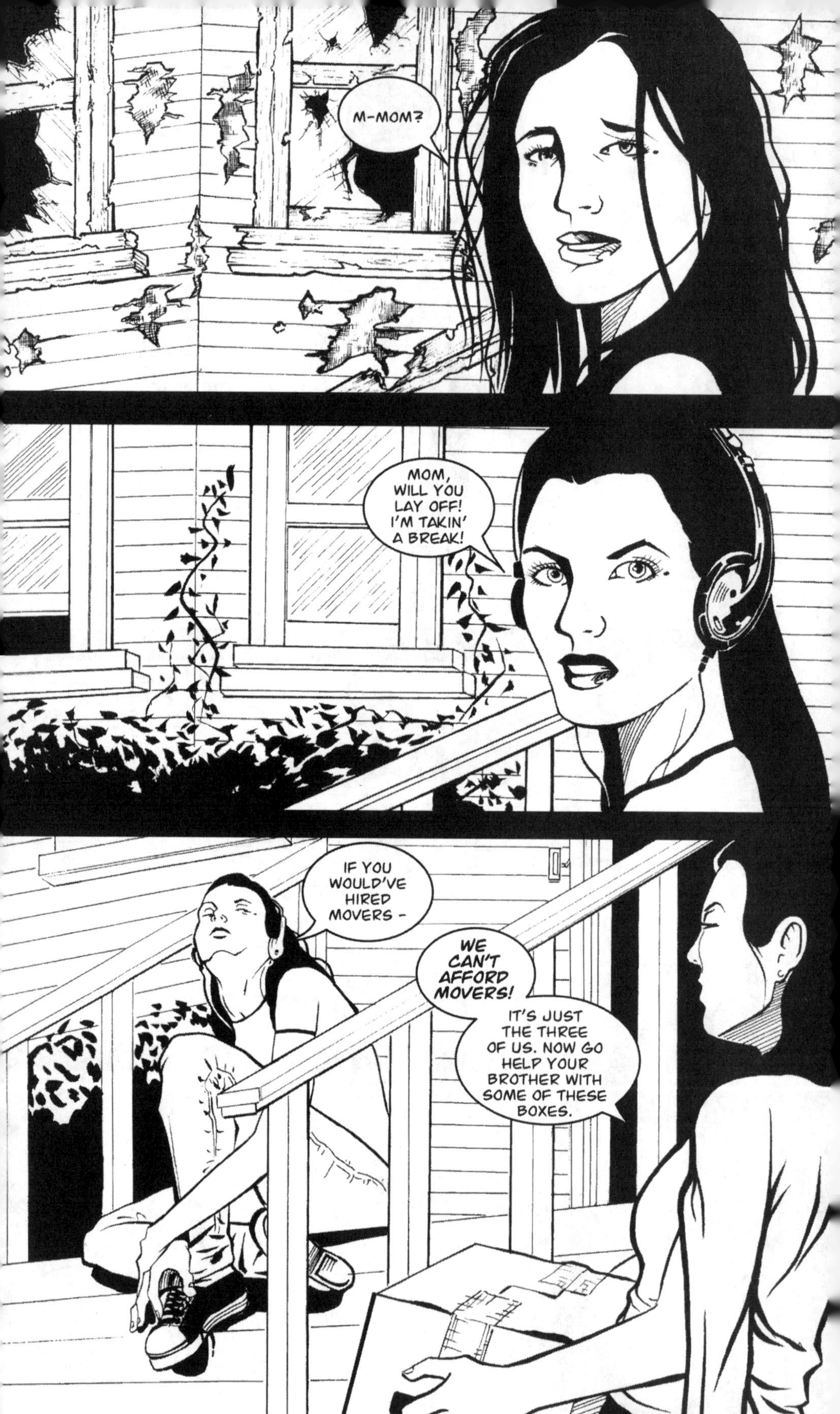
M-MOM?
MOM, WILL YOU LAY OFF! I'M TAKIN' A BREAK!
IF YOU WOULD'VE HIRED MOVERS -
WE CAN'T AFFORD MOVERS!
IT'S JUST THE THREE OF US. NOW GO HELP YOUR BROTHER WITH SOME OF THESE BOXES.

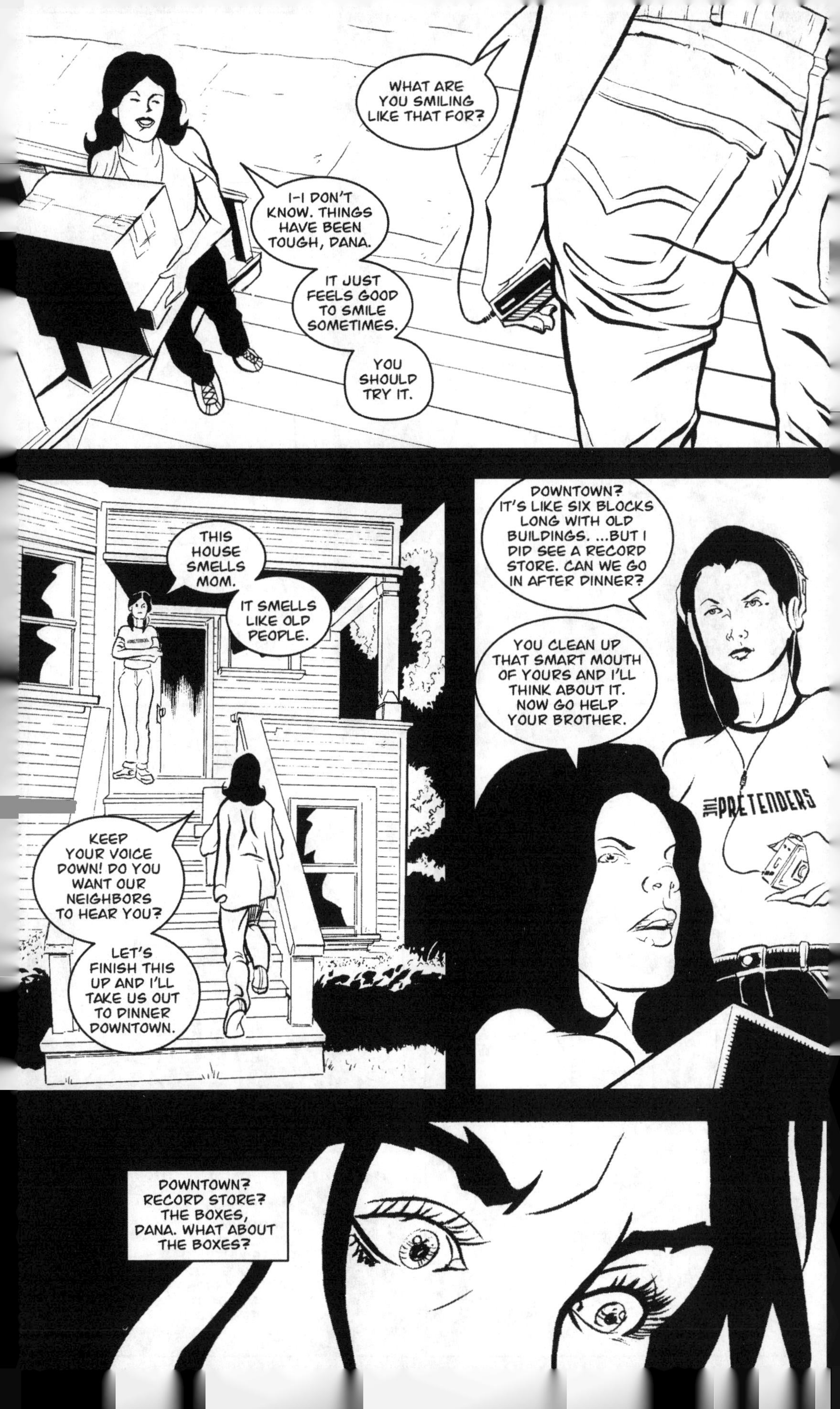
WHAT ARE YOU SMILING LIKE THAT FOR?
I-I DON'T KNOW. THINGS HAVE BEEN TOUGH, DANA.
IT JUST FEELS GOOD TO SMILE SOMETIMES.
YOU SHOULD TRY IT.
THIS HOUSE SMELLS MOM.
IT SMELLS LIKE OLD PEOPLE.
KEEP YOUR VOICE DOWN! DO YOU WANT OUR NEIGHBORS TO HEAR YOU?
LET'S FINISH THIS UP AND I'LL TAKE US OUT TO DINNER DOWNTOWN.
DOWNTOWN? IT'S LIKE SIX BLOCKS LONG WITH OLD BUILDINGS. ...BUT I DID SEE A RECORD STORE. CAN WE GO IN AFTER DINNER?
YOU CLEAN UP THAT SMART MOUTH OF YOURS AND I'LL THINK ABOUT IT. NOW GO HELP YOUR BROTHER.
THE PRETENDERS
DOWNTOWN? RECORD STORE? THE BOXES, DANA. WHAT ABOUT THE BOXES?

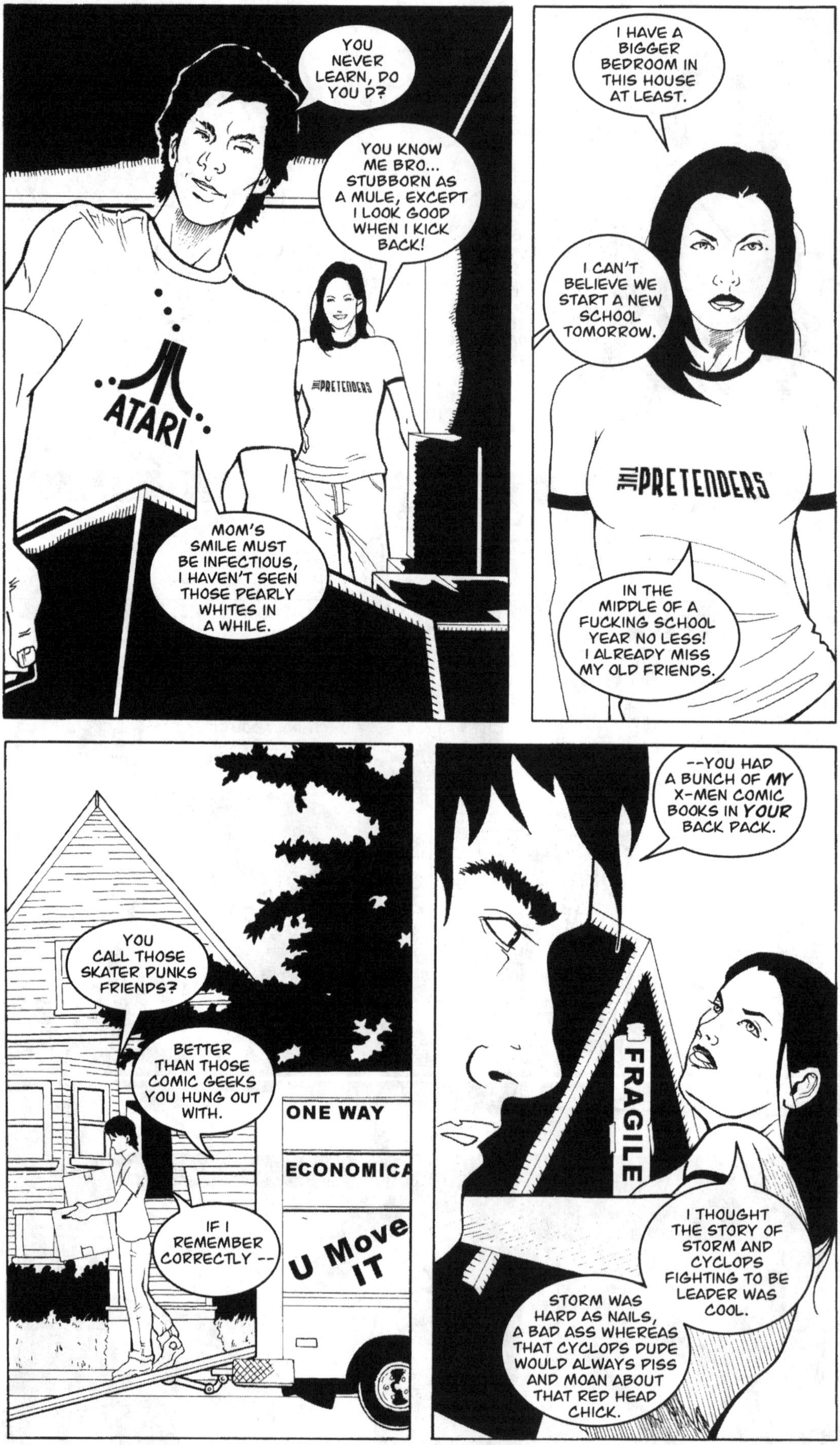
YOU NEVER LEARN, DO YOU D?
YOU KNOW ME BRO... STUBBORN AS A MULE, EXCEPT I LOOK GOOD WHEN I KICK BACK!
ATARI
PRETENDERS
MOM'S SMILE MUST BE INFECTIOUS, I HAVEN'T SEEN THOSE PEARLY WHITES IN A WHILE.
I HAVE A BIGGER BEDROOM IN THIS HOUSE AT LEAST.
I CAN'T BELIEVE WE START A NEW SCHOOL TOMORROW.
PRETENDERS
IN THE MIDDLE OF A FUCKING SCHOOL YEAR NO LESS! I ALREADY MISS MY OLD FRIENDS.
YOU CALL THOSE SKATER PUNKS FRIENDS?
BETTER THAN THOSE COMIC GEEKS YOU HUNG OUT WITH.
ONE WAY
ECONOMICA
IF I REMEMBER CORRECTLY --
U Move IT
--YOU HAD A BUNCH OF MY X-MEN COMIC BOOKS IN YOUR BACK PACK.
FRAGILE
I THOUGHT THE STORY OF STORM AND CYCLOPS FIGHTING TO BE LEADER WAS COOL.
STORM WAS HARD AS NAILS, A BAD ASS WHEREAS THAT CYCLOPS DUDE WOULD ALWAYS PISS AND MOAN ABOUT THAT RED HEAD CHICK.

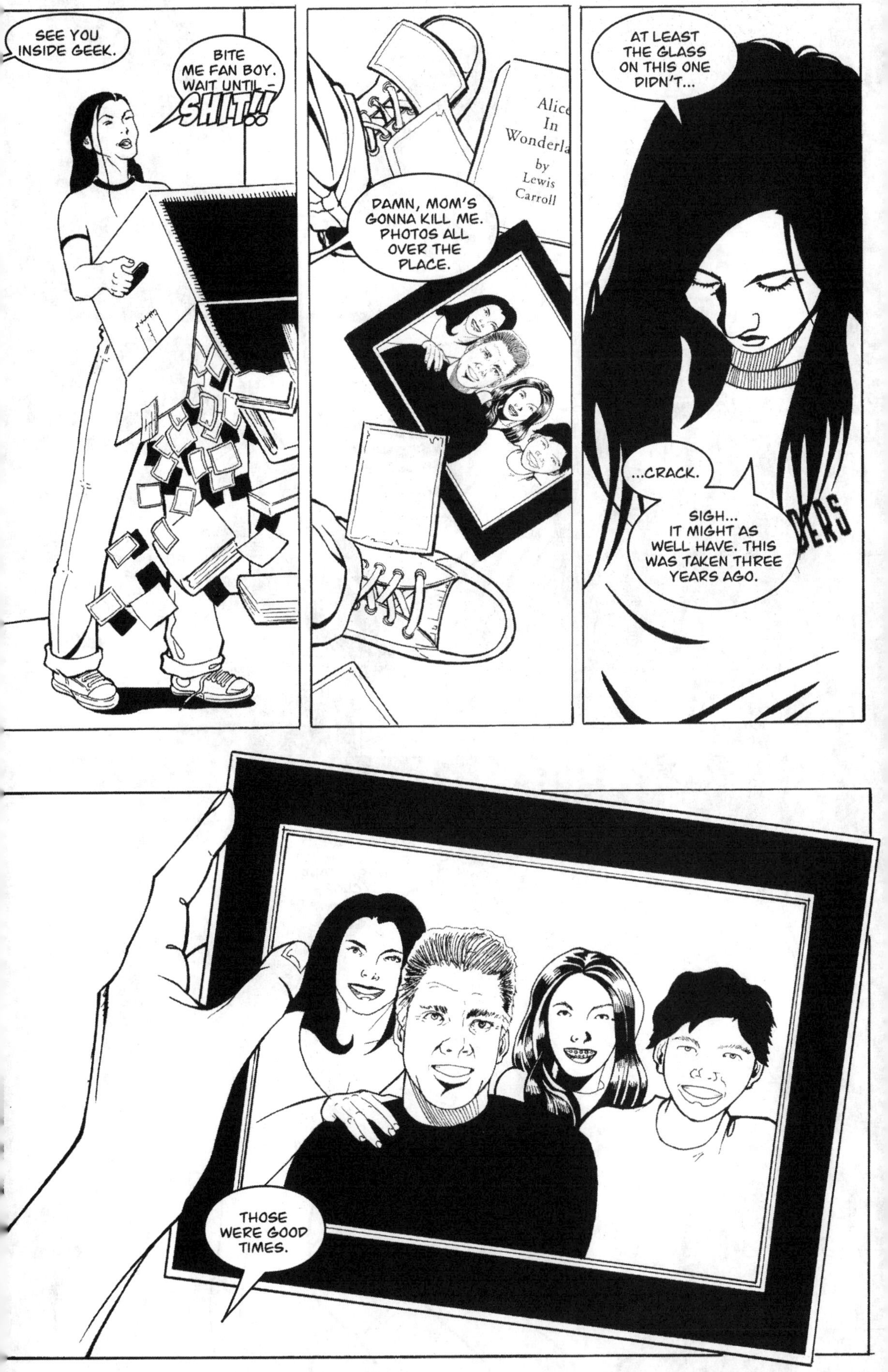
SEE YOU INSIDE GEEK.
BITE ME FAN BOY. WAIT UNTIL –
SHIT!!
Alice In Wonderla by Lewis Carroll
DAMN, MOM'S GONNA KILL ME. PHOTOS ALL OVER THE PLACE.
AT LEAST THE GLASS ON THIS ONE DIDN'T...
...CRACK.
SIGH... IT MIGHT AS WELL HAVE. THIS WAS TAKEN THREE YEARS AGO.
THOSE WERE GOOD TIMES.

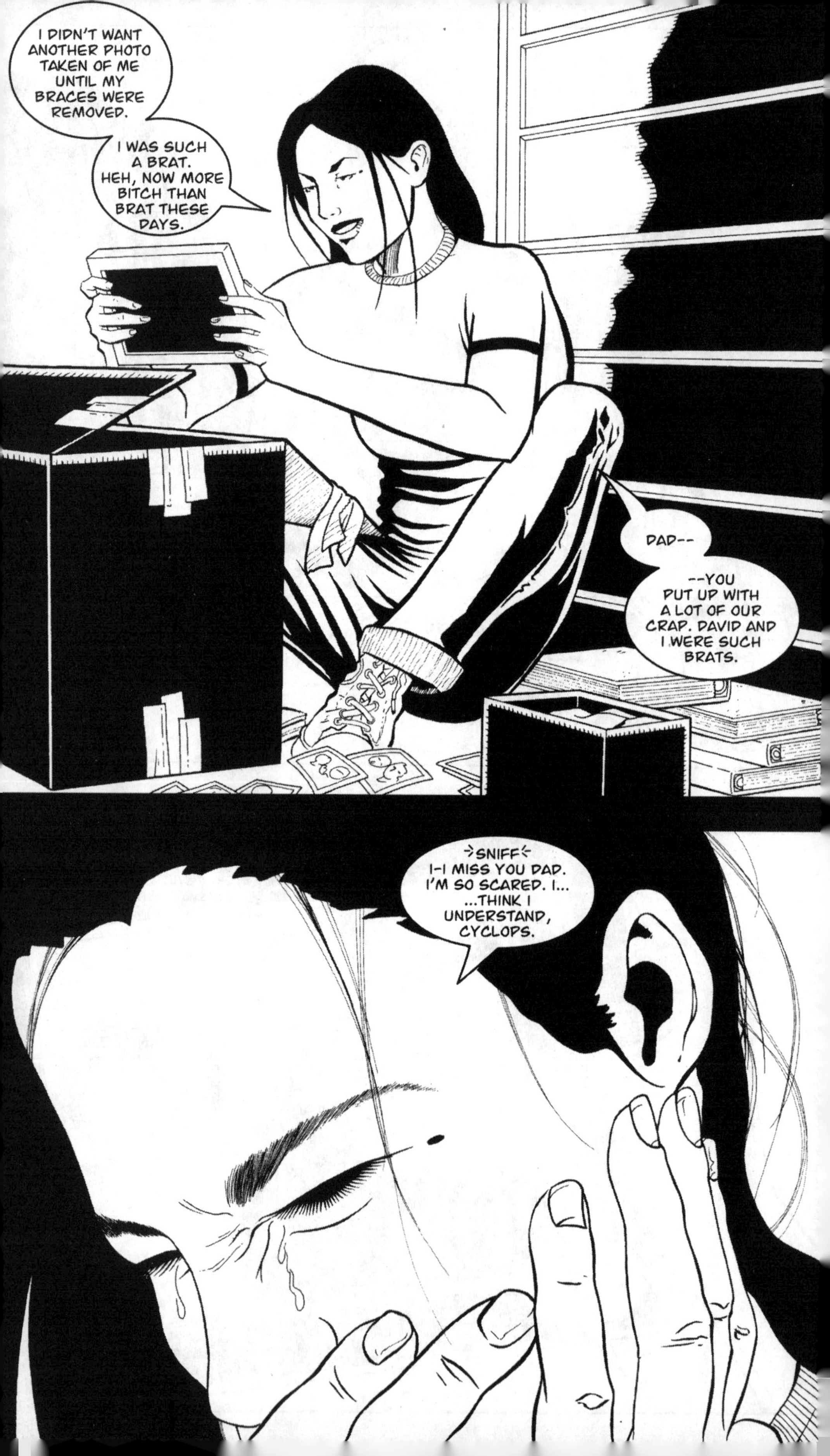
I DIDN'T WANT ANOTHER PHOTO TAKEN OF ME UNTIL MY BRACES WERE REMOVED.
I WAS SUCH A BRAT. HEH, NOW MORE BITCH THAN BRAT THESE DAYS.
DAD--
--YOU PUT UP WITH A LOT OF OUR CRAP. DAVID AND I WERE SUCH BRATS.
SNIFF
I-I MISS YOU DAD. I'M SO SCARED. I... ...THINK I UNDERSTAND, CYCLOPS.

PISS AND MOAN ABOUT LOSING A LOVED ONE INDEED. STUPID COMIC BOOKS! >SNIFF<
FRAGILE
FRAGILE

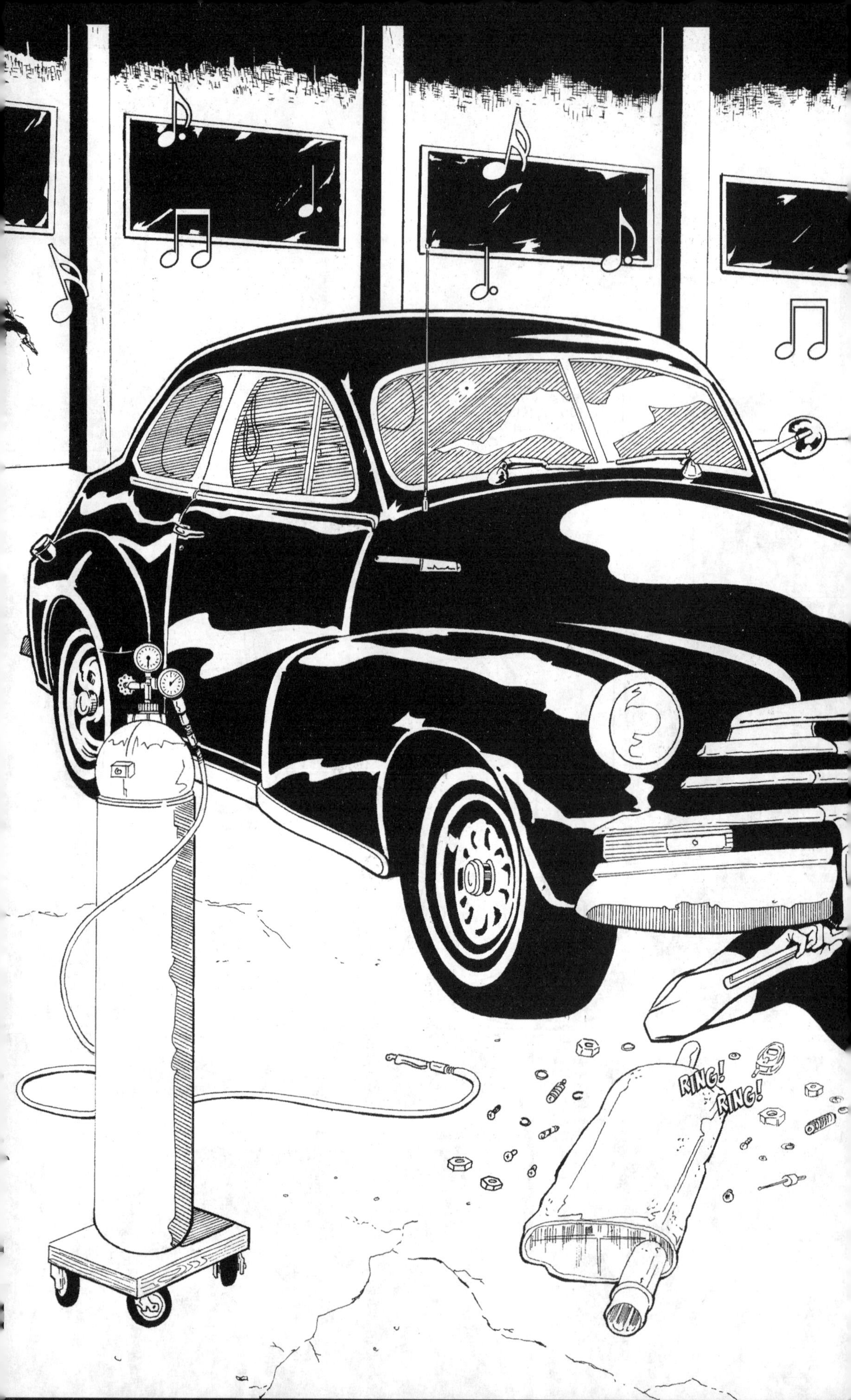
RING!
RING!

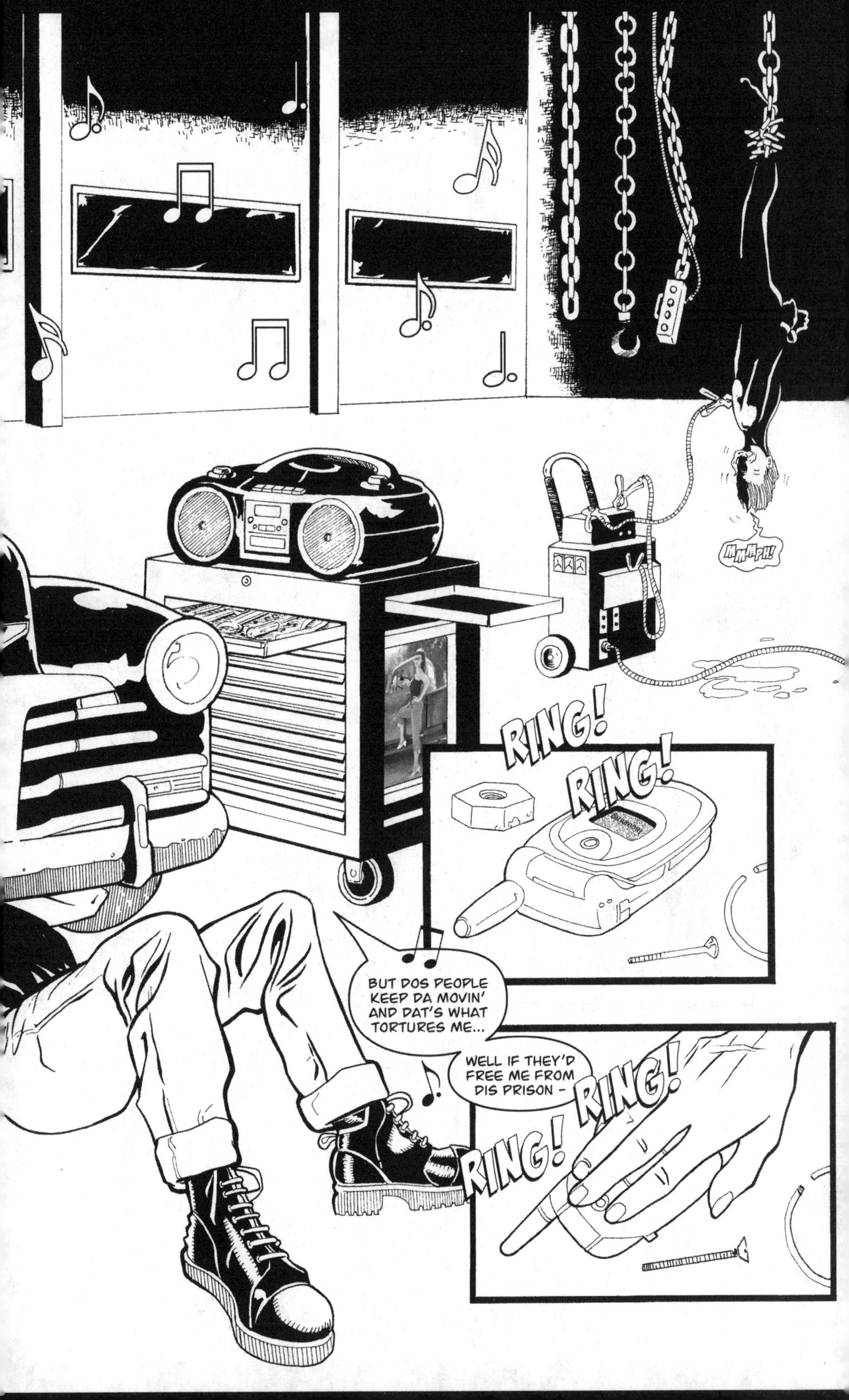

MMMPH!
RING!
RING!
BUT DOS PEOPLE KEEP DA MOVIN' AND DAT'S WHAT TORTURES ME...
WELL IF THEY'D FREE ME FROM DIS PRISON -
RING!
RING!

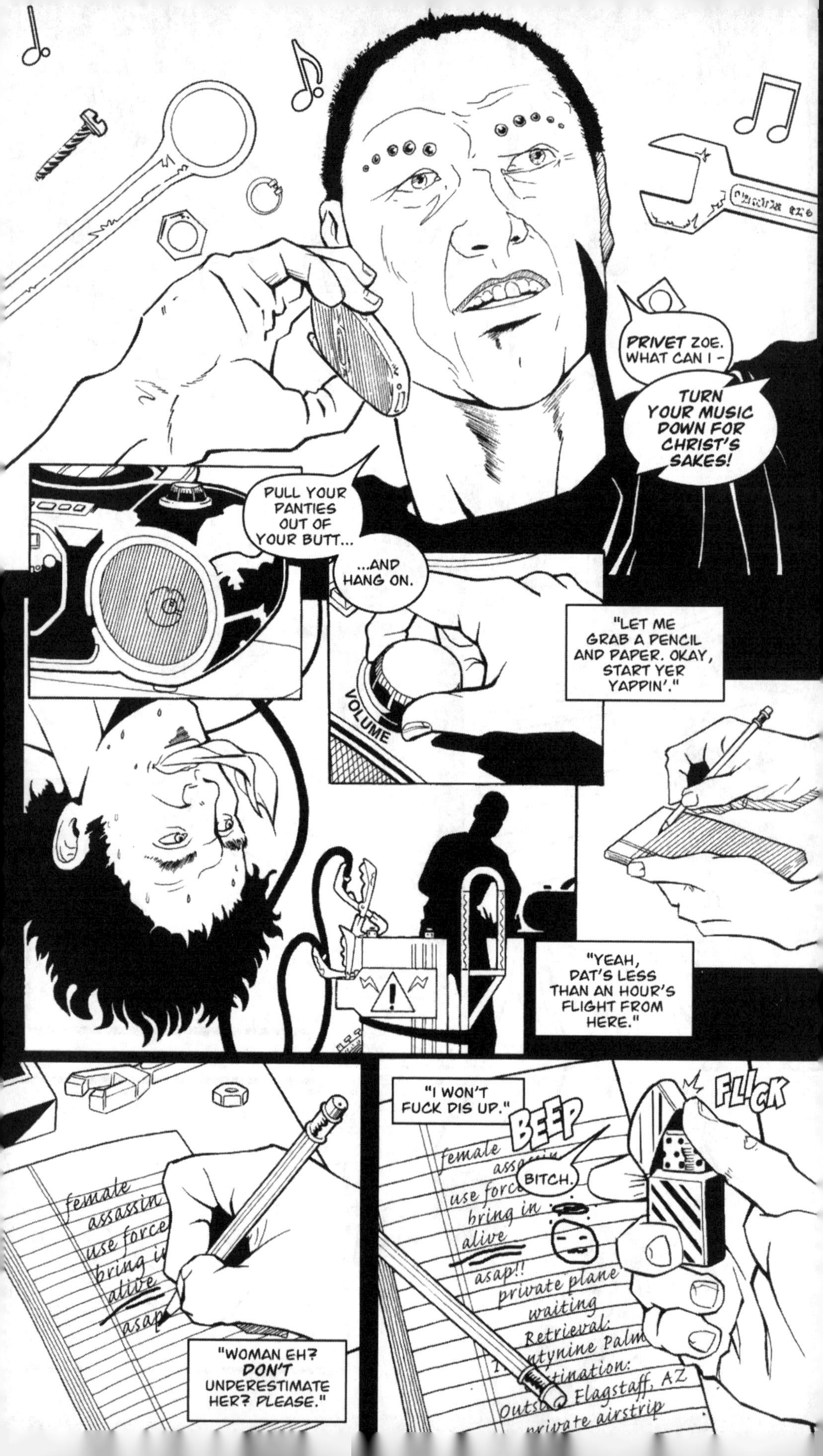

PRIVET ZOE. WHAT CAN I -
TURN YOUR MUSIC DOWN FOR CHRIST'S SAKES!
PULL YOUR PANTIES OUT OF YOUR BUTT...
...AND HANG ON.
VOLUME
"LET ME GRAB A PENCIL AND PAPER. OKAY, START YER YAPPIN'."
"YEAH, DAT'S LESS THAN AN HOUR'S FLIGHT FROM HERE."
female
assassin
use force
alive
"WOMAN EH? DON'T UNDERESTIMATE HER? PLEASE."
"I WON'T FUCK DIS UP."
BEEP
BITCH.
FLICK
female
use force
bring in
alive
asap!!
private plane
waiting
Retrieval:
Flagstaff, AZ
private airstrip

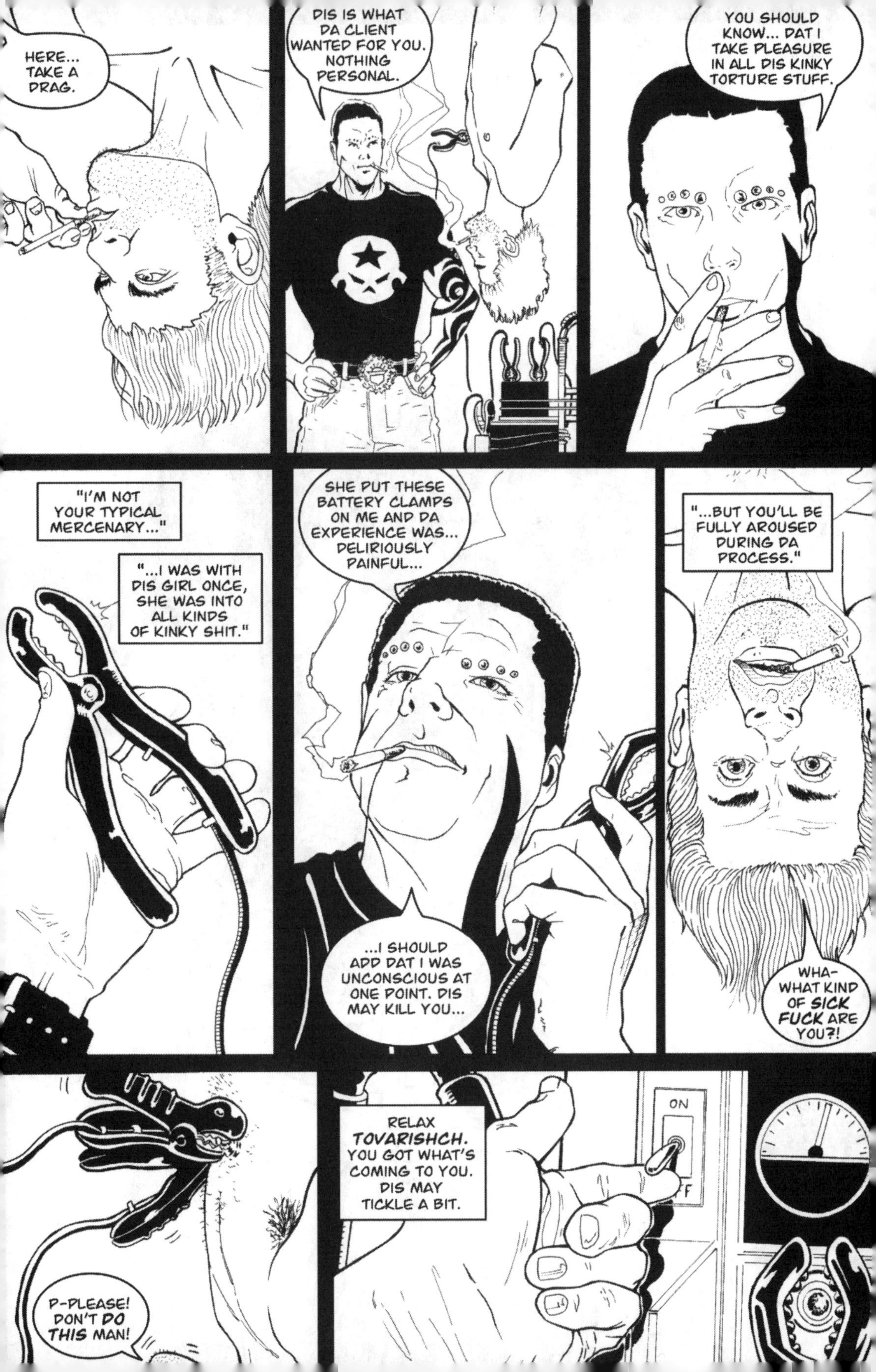
HERE... TAKE A DRAG.
DIS IS WHAT DA CLIENT WANTED FOR YOU. NOTHING PERSONAL.
YOU SHOULD KNOW... DAT I TAKE PLEASURE IN ALL DIS KINKY TORTURE STUFF.
"I'M NOT YOUR TYPICAL MERCENARY..."
"...I WAS WITH DIS GIRL ONCE, SHE WAS INTO ALL KINDS OF KINKY SHIT."
SHE PUT THESE BATTERY CLAMPS ON ME AND DA EXPERIENCE WAS... DELIRIOUSLY PAINFUL...
...I SHOULD ADD DAT I WAS UNCONSCIOUS AT ONE POINT. DIS MAY KILL YOU...
"...BUT YOU'LL BE FULLY AROUSED DURING DA PROCESS."
WHA- WHAT KIND OF SICK FUCK ARE YOU?!
P-PLEASE! DON'T DO THIS MAN!
RELAX TOVARISHCH. YOU GOT WHAT'S COMING TO YOU. DIS MAY TICKLE A BIT.
ON

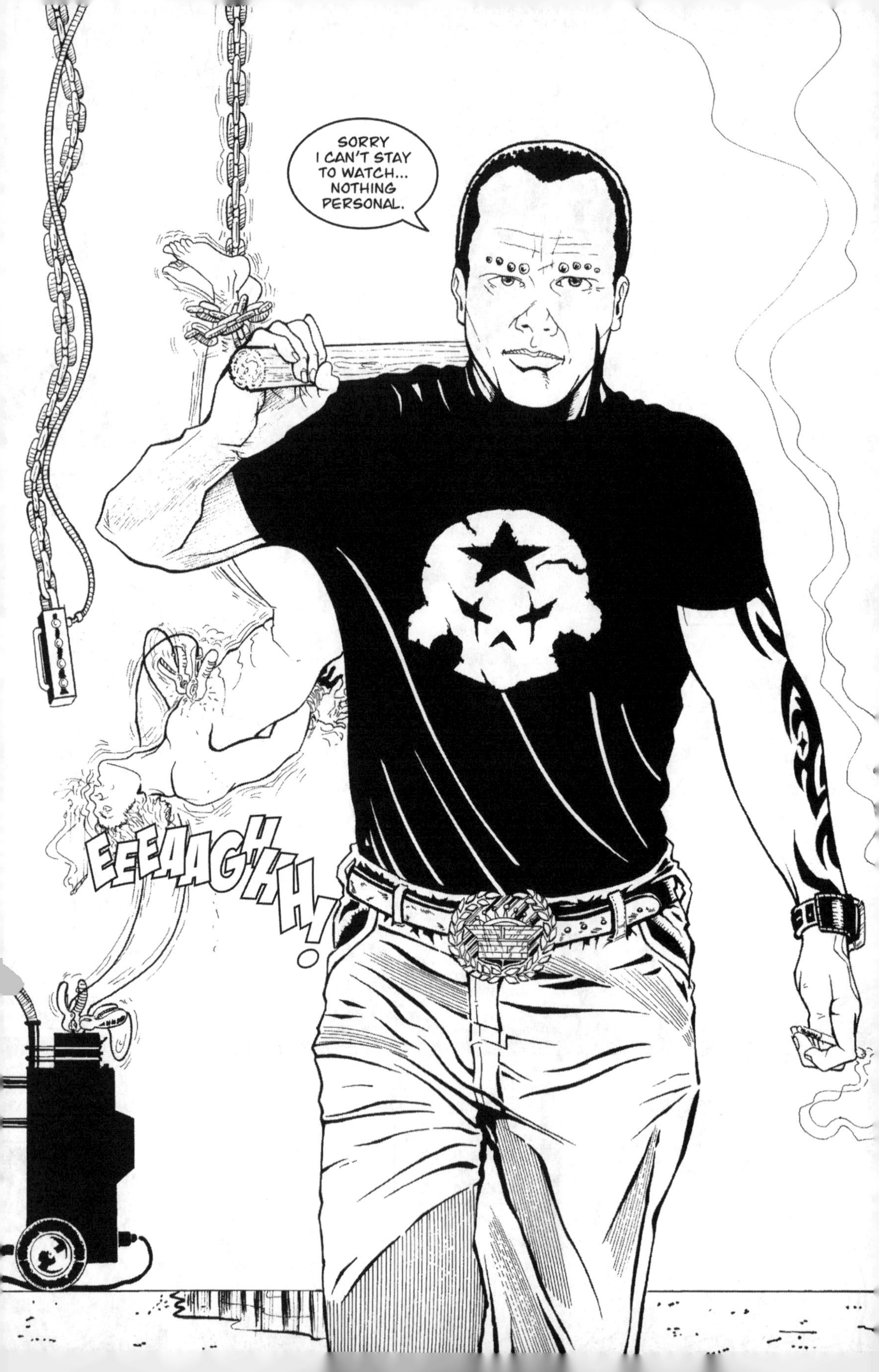
SORRY I CAN'T STAY TO WATCH... NOTHING PERSONAL.
EEEAAGHHH!

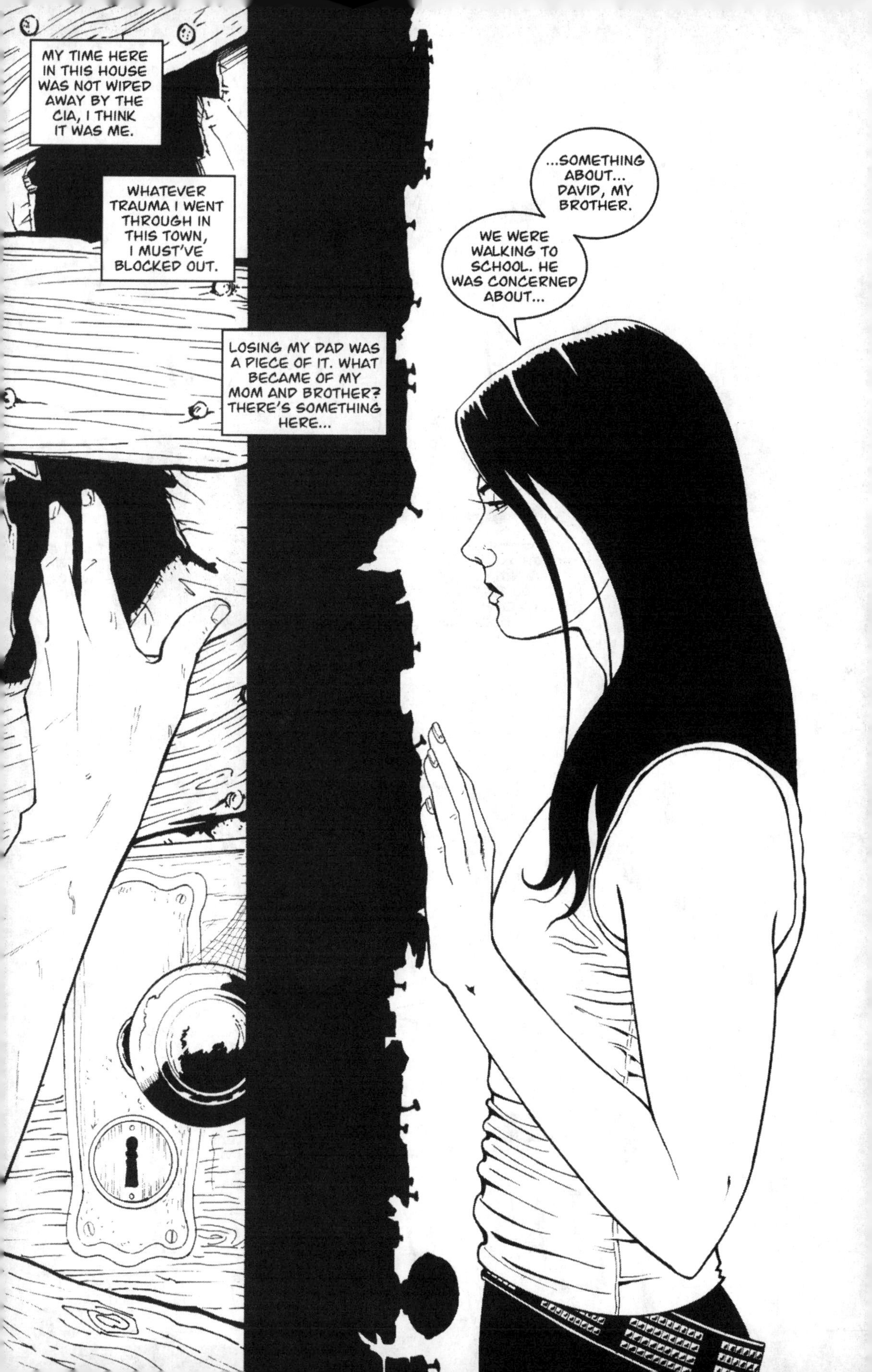
MY TIME HERE IN THIS HOUSE WAS NOT WIPED AWAY BY THE CIA, I THINK IT WAS ME.
WHATEVER TRAUMA I WENT THROUGH IN THIS TOWN, I MUST'VE BLOCKED OUT.
LOSING MY DAD WAS A PIECE OF IT. WHAT BECAME OF MY MOM AND BROTHER? THERE'S SOMETHING HERE...
...SOMETHING ABOUT... DAVID, MY BROTHER.
WE WERE WALKING TO SCHOOL. HE WAS CONCERNED ABOUT...

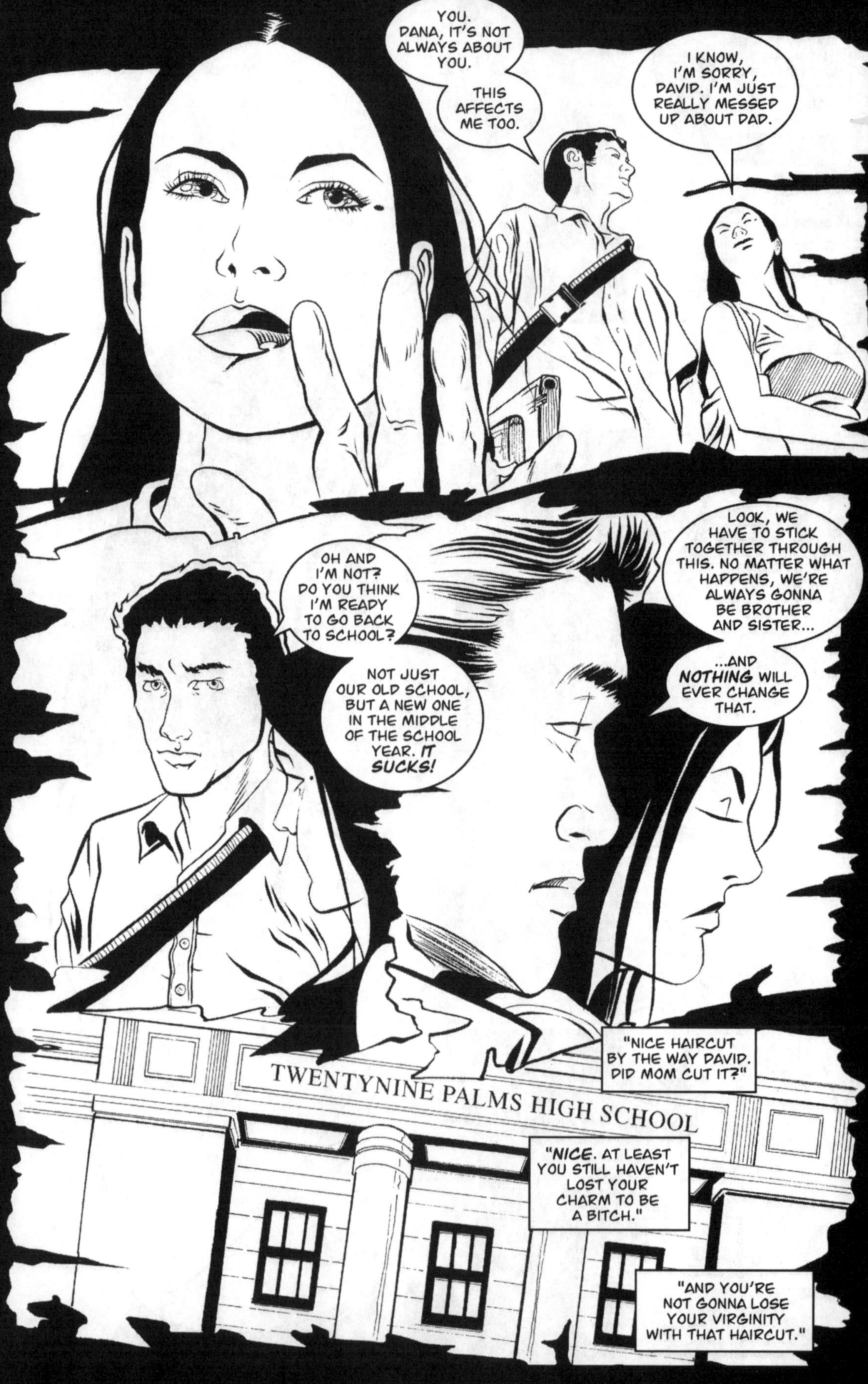
YOU. DANA, IT'S NOT ALWAYS ABOUT YOU.
THIS AFFECTS ME TOO.
I KNOW, I'M SORRY, DAVID. I'M JUST REALLY MESSED UP ABOUT DAD.
OH AND I'M NOT? DO YOU THINK I'M READY TO GO BACK TO SCHOOL?
NOT JUST OUR OLD SCHOOL, BUT A NEW ONE IN THE MIDDLE OF THE SCHOOL YEAR. IT SUCKS!
LOOK, WE HAVE TO STICK TOGETHER THROUGH THIS. NO MATTER WHAT HAPPENS, WE'RE ALWAYS GONNA BE BROTHER AND SISTER...
...AND NOTHING WILL EVER CHANGE THAT.
TWENTYNINE PALMS HIGH SCHOOL
"NICE HAIRCUT BY THE WAY DAVID. DID MOM CUT IT?"
"NICE. AT LEAST YOU STILL HAVEN'T LOST YOUR CHARM TO BE A BITCH."
"AND YOU'RE NOT GONNA LOSE YOUR VIRGINITY WITH THAT HAIRCUT."

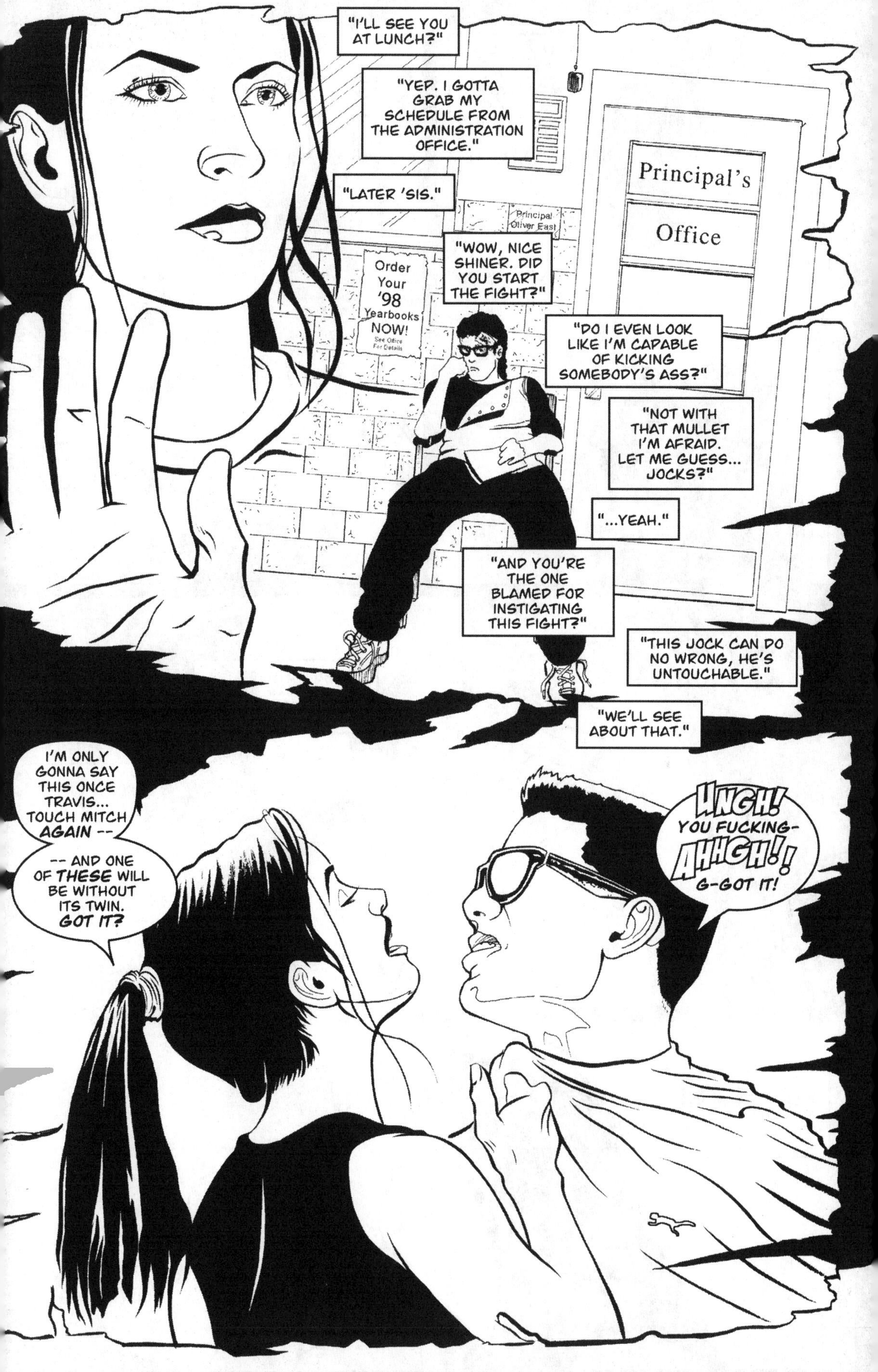
"I'LL SEE YOU AT LUNCH?"
"YEP. I GOTTA GRAB MY SCHEDULE FROM THE ADMINISTRATION OFFICE."
"LATER 'SIS."
Principal's Office
Principal Oliver East
Order Your '98 Yearbooks NOW! See Office For Details
"WOW, NICE SHINER. DID YOU START THE FIGHT?"
"DO I EVEN LOOK LIKE I'M CAPABLE OF KICKING SOMEBODY'S ASS?"
"NOT WITH THAT MULLET I'M AFRAID. LET ME GUESS... JOCKS?"
"...YEAH."
"AND YOU'RE THE ONE BLAMED FOR INSTIGATING THIS FIGHT?"
"THIS JOCK CAN DO NO WRONG, HE'S UNTOUCHABLE."
"WE'LL SEE ABOUT THAT."
I'M ONLY GONNA SAY THIS ONCE TRAVIS... TOUCH MITCH AGAIN --
-- AND ONE OF THESE WILL BE WITHOUT ITS TWIN. GOT IT?
UNGH! YOU FUCKING- AHHGH!! G-GOT IT!

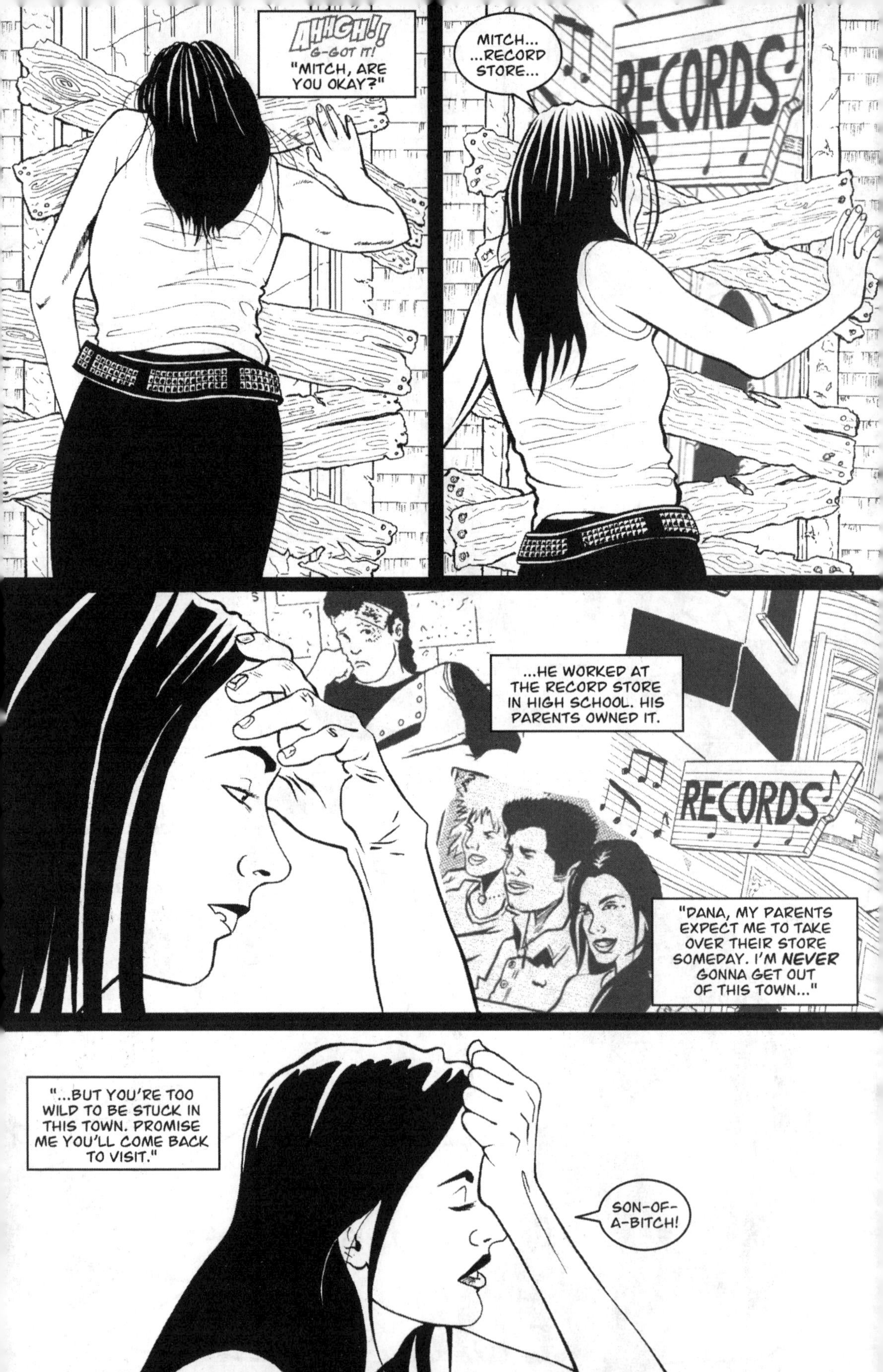
AHHGH!!
G-GOT IT!
"MITCH, ARE YOU OKAY?"
MITCH... ...RECORD STORE...
RECORDS
...HE WORKED AT THE RECORD STORE IN HIGH SCHOOL. HIS PARENTS OWNED IT.
RECORDS
"DANA, MY PARENTS EXPECT ME TO TAKE OVER THEIR STORE SOMEDAY. I'M NEVER GONNA GET OUT OF THIS TOWN..."
"...BUT YOU'RE TOO WILD TO BE STUCK IN THIS TOWN. PROMISE ME YOU'LL COME BACK TO VISIT."
SON-OF-A-BITCH!

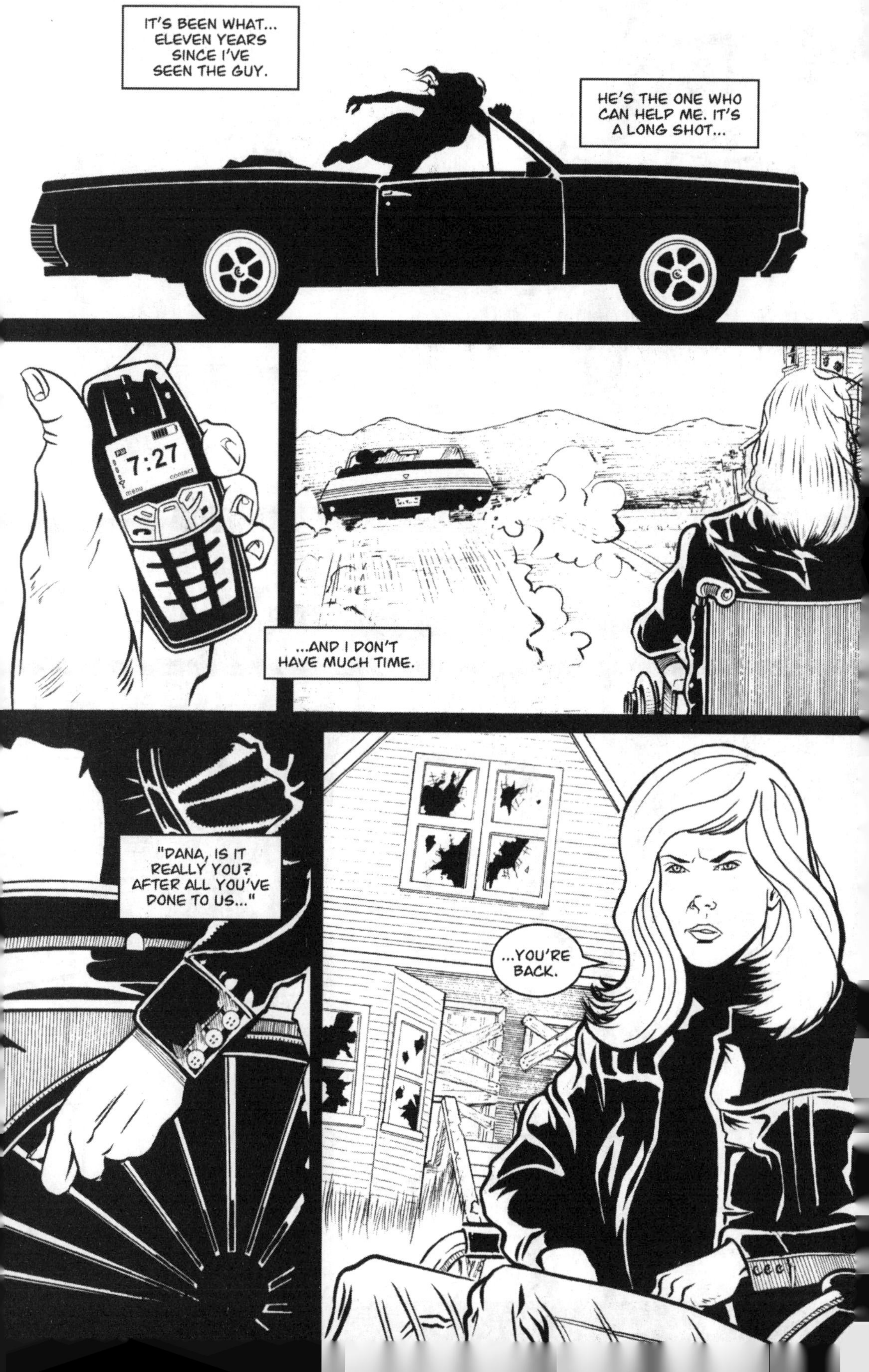
IT'S BEEN WHAT... ELEVEN YEARS SINCE I'VE SEEN THE GUY.
HE'S THE ONE WHO CAN HELP ME. IT'S A LONG SHOT...
7:27
...AND I DON'T HAVE MUCH TIME.
"DANA, IS IT REALLY YOU? AFTER ALL YOU'VE DONE TO US..."
...YOU'RE BACK.

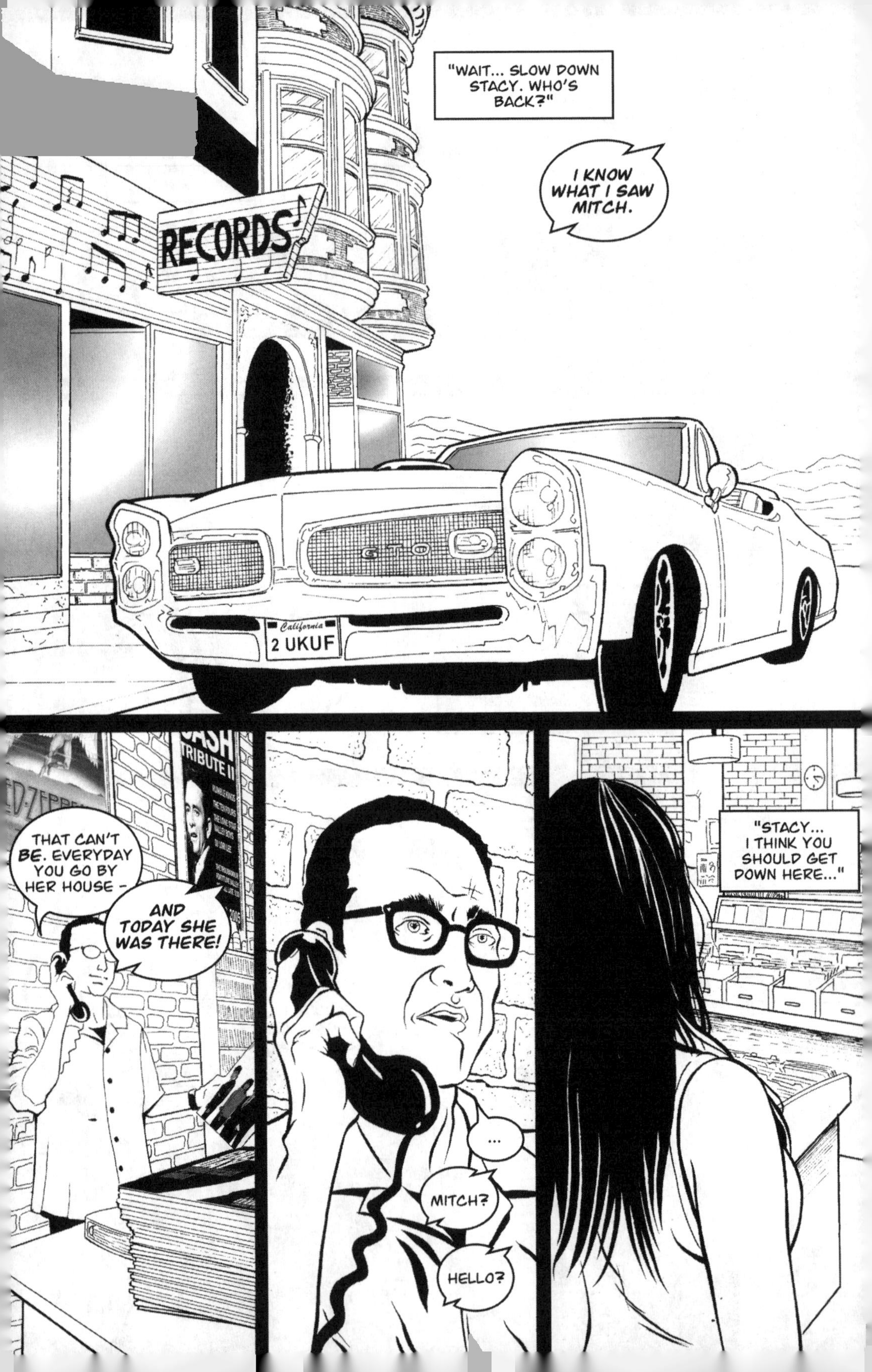
"WAIT... SLOW DOWN STACY. WHO'S BACK?"
I KNOW WHAT I SAW MITCH.
RECORDS
GTO
California
2 UKUF
CASH TRIBUTE II
THAT CAN'T BE. EVERYDAY YOU GO BY HER HOUSE -
AND TODAY SHE WAS THERE!
...
MITCH?
HELLO?
"STACY... I THINK YOU SHOULD GET DOWN HERE..."

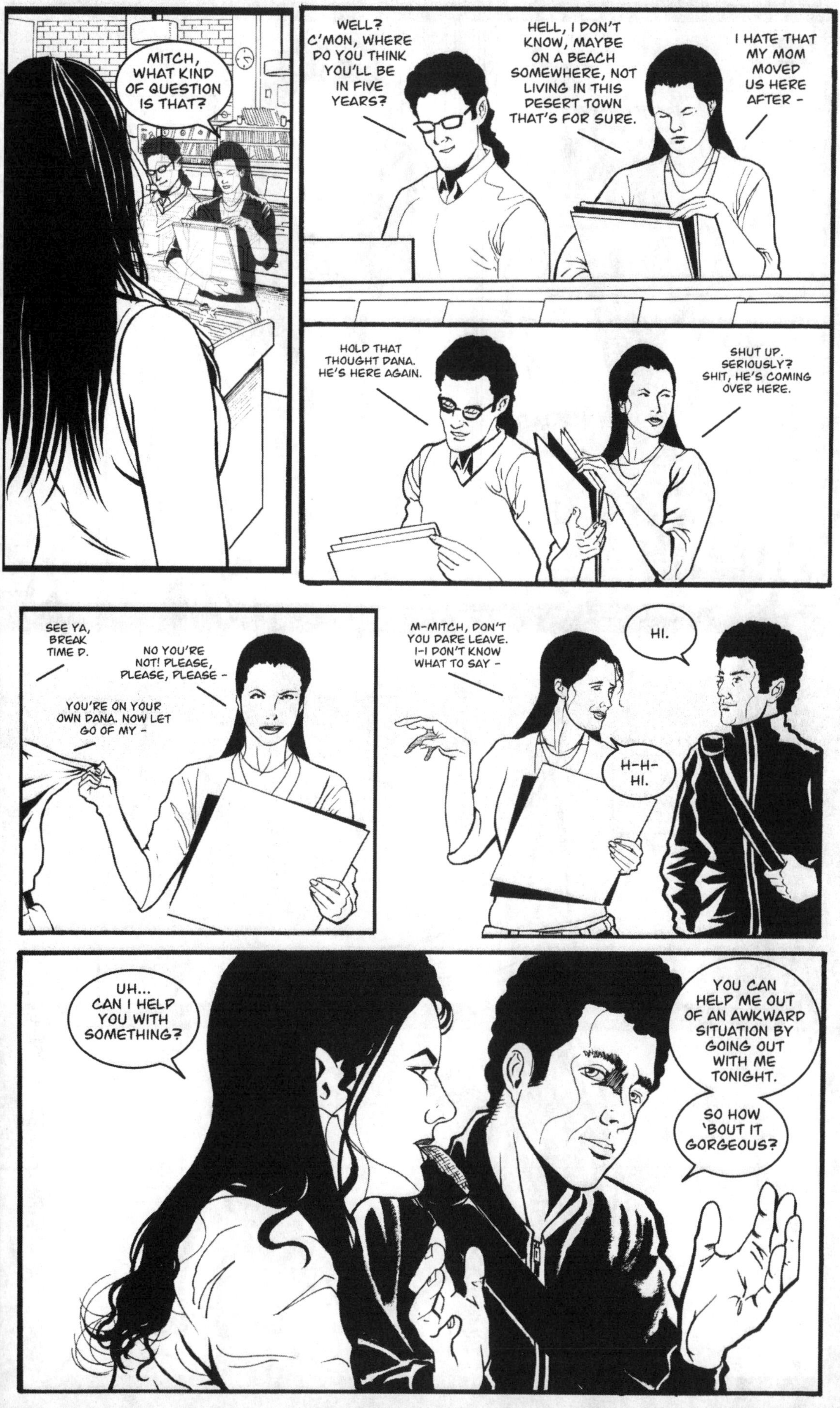
MITCH, WHAT KIND OF QUESTION IS THAT?
WELL? C'MON, WHERE DO YOU THINK YOU'LL BE IN FIVE YEARS?
HELL, I DON'T KNOW, MAYBE ON A BEACH SOMEWHERE, NOT LIVING IN THIS DESERT TOWN THAT'S FOR SURE.
I HATE THAT MY MOM MOVED US HERE AFTER -
HOLD THAT THOUGHT DANA. HE'S HERE AGAIN.
SHUT UP. SERIOUSLY? SHIT, HE'S COMING OVER HERE.
SEE YA, BREAK TIME D.
NO YOU'RE NOT! PLEASE, PLEASE, PLEASE -
YOU'RE ON YOUR OWN DANA. NOW LET GO OF MY -
M-MITCH, DON'T YOU DARE LEAVE. I-I DON'T KNOW WHAT TO SAY -
HI.
H-H-HI.
UH... CAN I HELP YOU WITH SOMETHING?
YOU CAN HELP ME OUT OF AN AWKWARD SITUATION BY GOING OUT WITH ME TONIGHT.
SO HOW 'BOUT IT GORGEOUS?

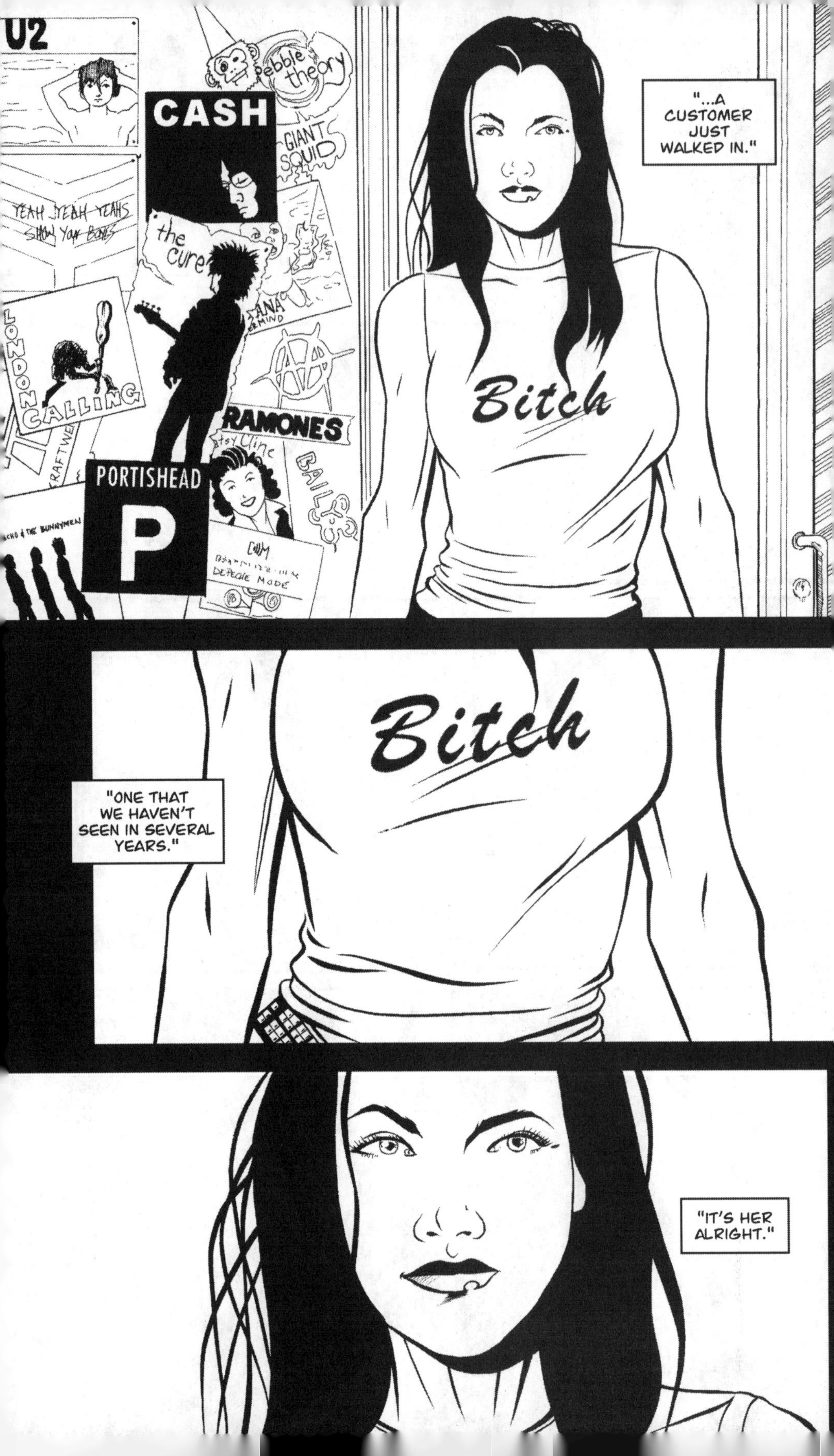
U2
CASH
pebble theory
GIANT SQUID
YEAH YEAH YEAHS
the cure
LONDON CALLING
RAMONES
PORTISHEAD
P
DEPECHE MODE
Bitch
"...A CUSTOMER JUST WALKED IN."
Bitch
"ONE THAT WE HAVEN'T SEEN IN SEVERAL YEARS."
"IT'S HER ALRIGHT."

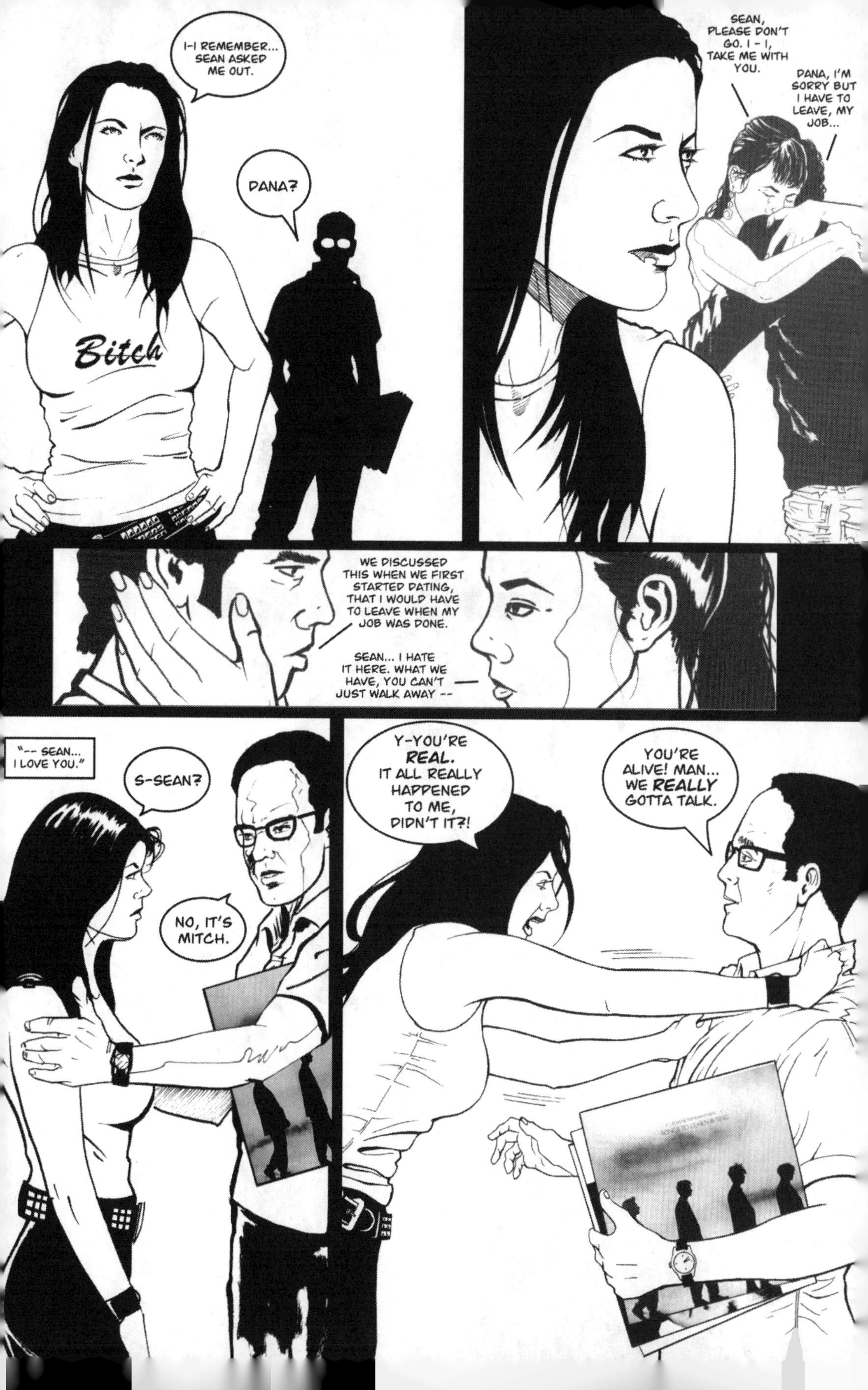

I-I REMEMBER... SEAN ASKED ME OUT.
DANA?
Bitch
SEAN, PLEASE DON'T GO. I - I, TAKE ME WITH YOU.
DANA, I'M SORRY BUT I HAVE TO LEAVE, MY JOB...
WE DISCUSSED THIS WHEN WE FIRST STARTED DATING, THAT I WOULD HAVE TO LEAVE WHEN MY JOB WAS DONE.
SEAN... I HATE IT HERE. WHAT WE HAVE, YOU CAN'T JUST WALK AWAY --
"-- SEAN... I LOVE YOU."
S-SEAN?
NO, IT'S MITCH.
Y-YOU'RE REAL. IT ALL REALLY HAPPENED TO ME, DIDN'T IT?!
YOU'RE ALIVE! MAN... WE REALLY GOTTA TALK.

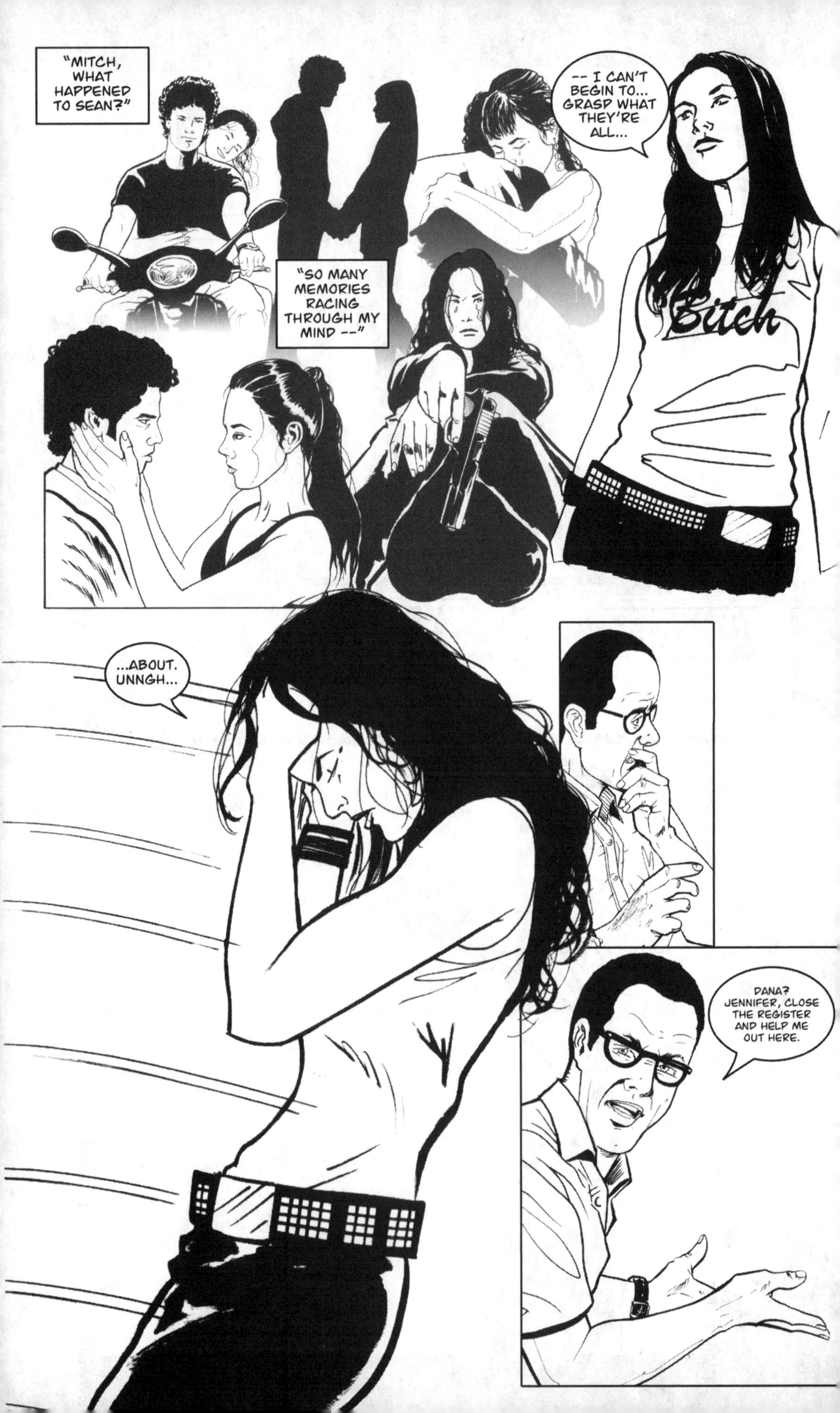
"MITCH, WHAT HAPPENED TO SEAN?"
-- I CAN'T BEGIN TO... GRASP WHAT THEY'RE ALL...
"SO MANY MEMORIES RACING THROUGH MY MIND --"
Bitch
...ABOUT. UNNGH...
DANA? JENNIFER, CLOSE THE REGISTER AND HELP ME OUT HERE.

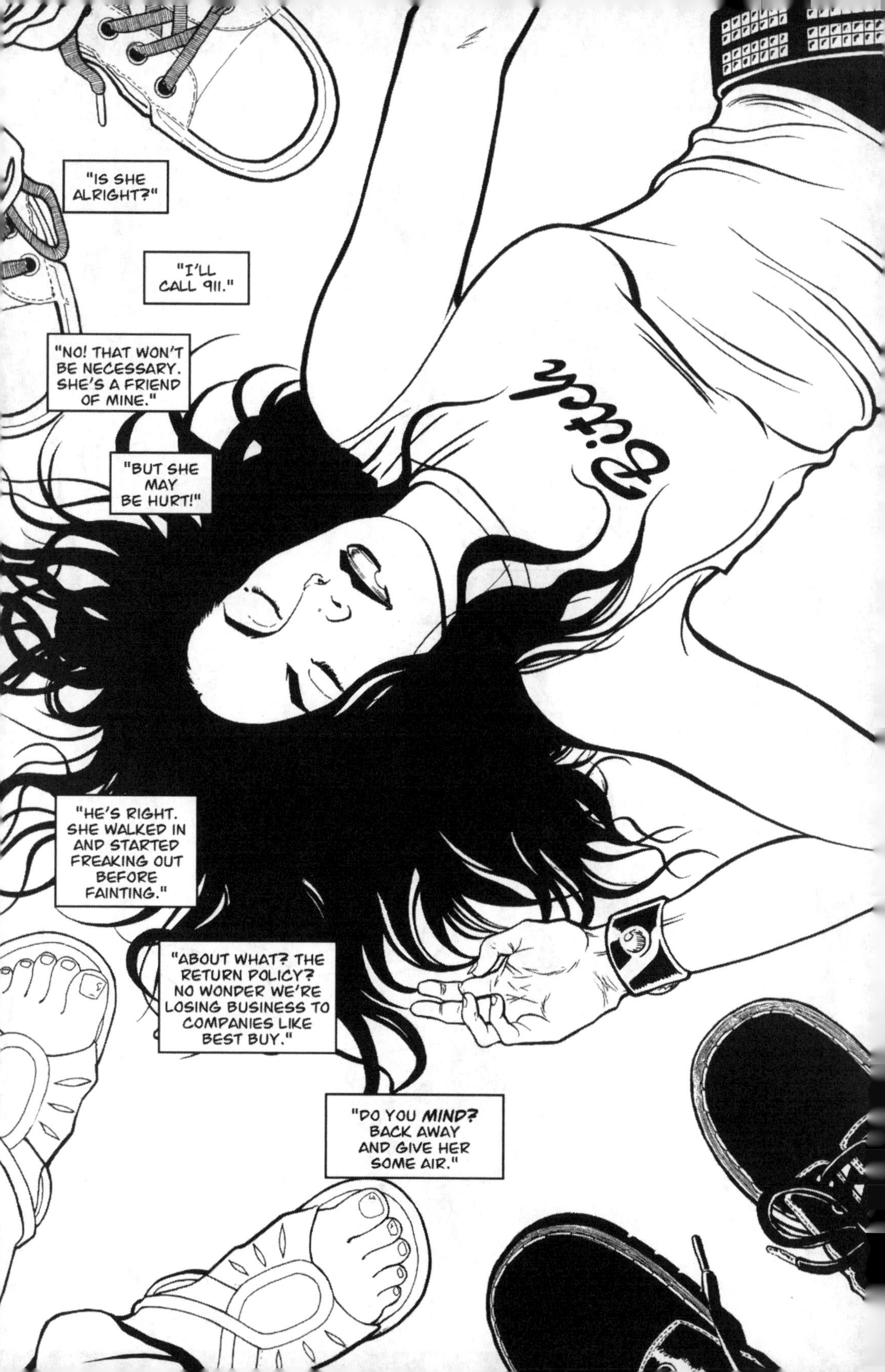
"IS SHE ALRIGHT?"
"I'LL CALL 911."
"NO! THAT WON'T BE NECESSARY. SHE'S A FRIEND OF MINE."
"BUT SHE MAY BE HURT!"
"HE'S RIGHT. SHE WALKED IN AND STARTED FREAKING OUT BEFORE FAINTING."
"ABOUT WHAT? THE RETURN POLICY? NO WONDER WE'RE LOSING BUSINESS TO COMPANIES LIKE BEST BUY."
"DO YOU *MIND?* BACK AWAY AND GIVE HER SOME AIR."
Bitch

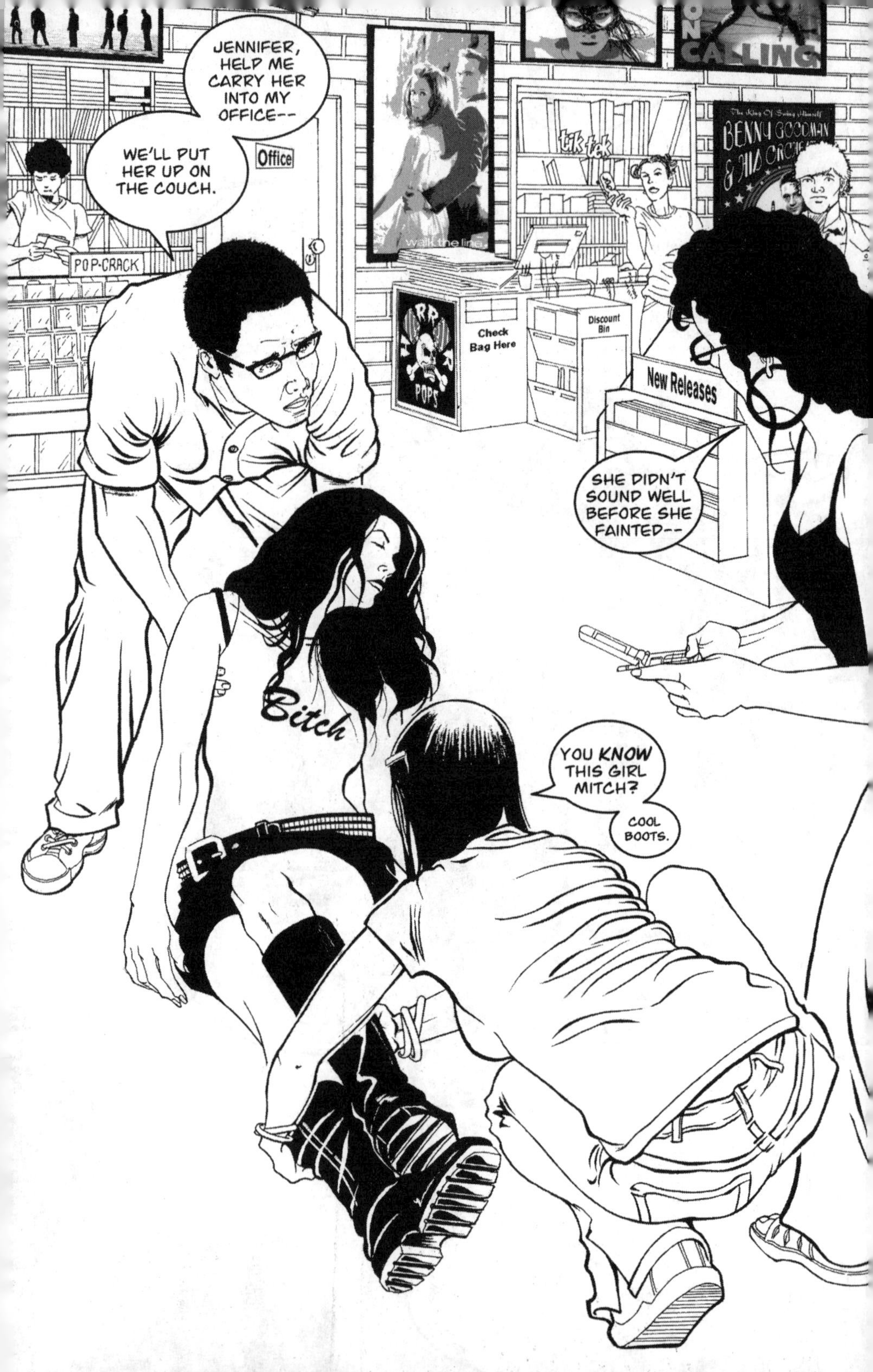
JENNIFER, HELP ME CARRY HER INTO MY OFFICE--
WE'LL PUT HER UP ON THE COUCH.
SHE DIDN'T SOUND WELL BEFORE SHE FAINTED--
YOU KNOW THIS GIRL MITCH?
COOL BOOTS.
Office
POP-CRACK
Check Bag Here
Discount Bin
New Releases
walk the line
Bitch

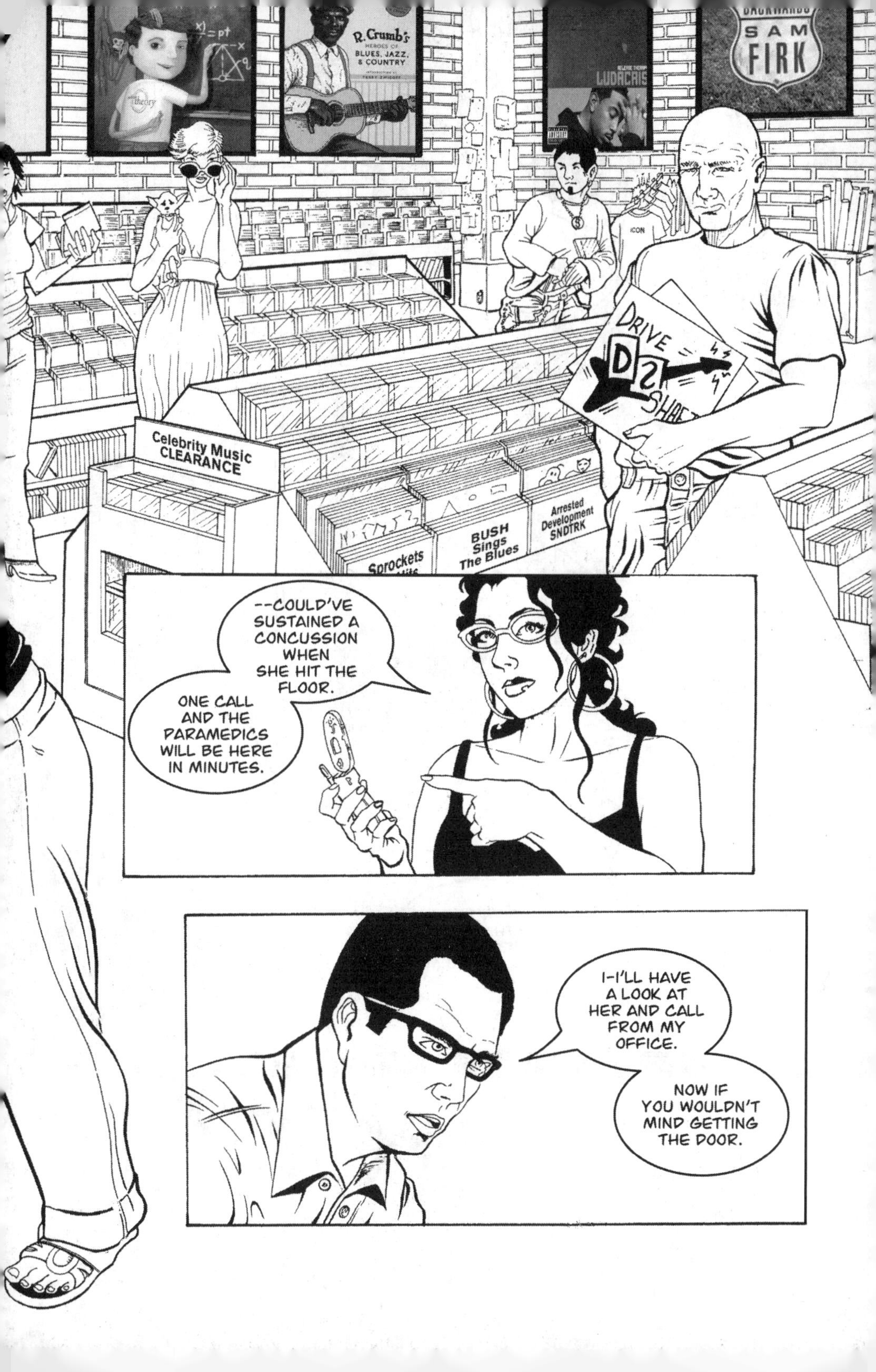
R. Crumb's
HEROES OF BLUES, JAZZ, & COUNTRY
LUDACRIS
SAM FIRK
ICON
DRIVE
Celebrity Music CLEARANCE
Arrested Development SNDTRK
BUSH Sings The Blues
Sprockets
--COULD'VE SUSTAINED A CONCUSSION WHEN SHE HIT THE FLOOR.
ONE CALL AND THE PARAMEDICS WILL BE HERE IN MINUTES.
I-I'LL HAVE A LOOK AT HER AND CALL FROM MY OFFICE.
NOW IF YOU WOULDN'T MIND GETTING THE DOOR.

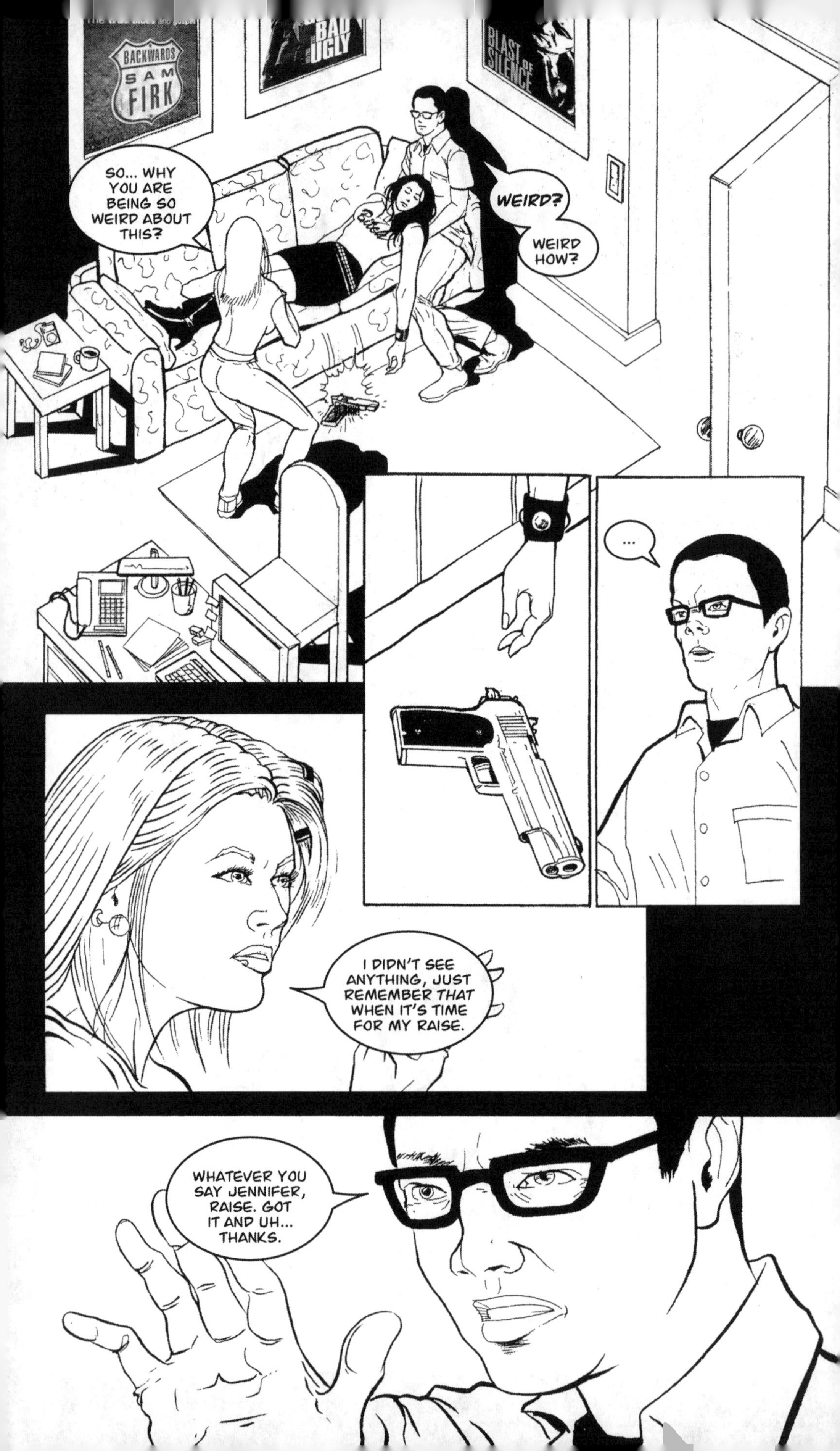
BACKWARDS SAM FIRK
BAD UGLY
BLAST OF SILENCE
SO... WHY YOU ARE BEING SO WEIRD ABOUT THIS?
WEIRD?
WEIRD HOW?
...
I DIDN'T SEE ANYTHING, JUST REMEMBER THAT WHEN IT'S TIME FOR MY RAISE.
WHATEVER YOU SAY JENNIFER, RAISE. GOT IT AND UH... THANKS.

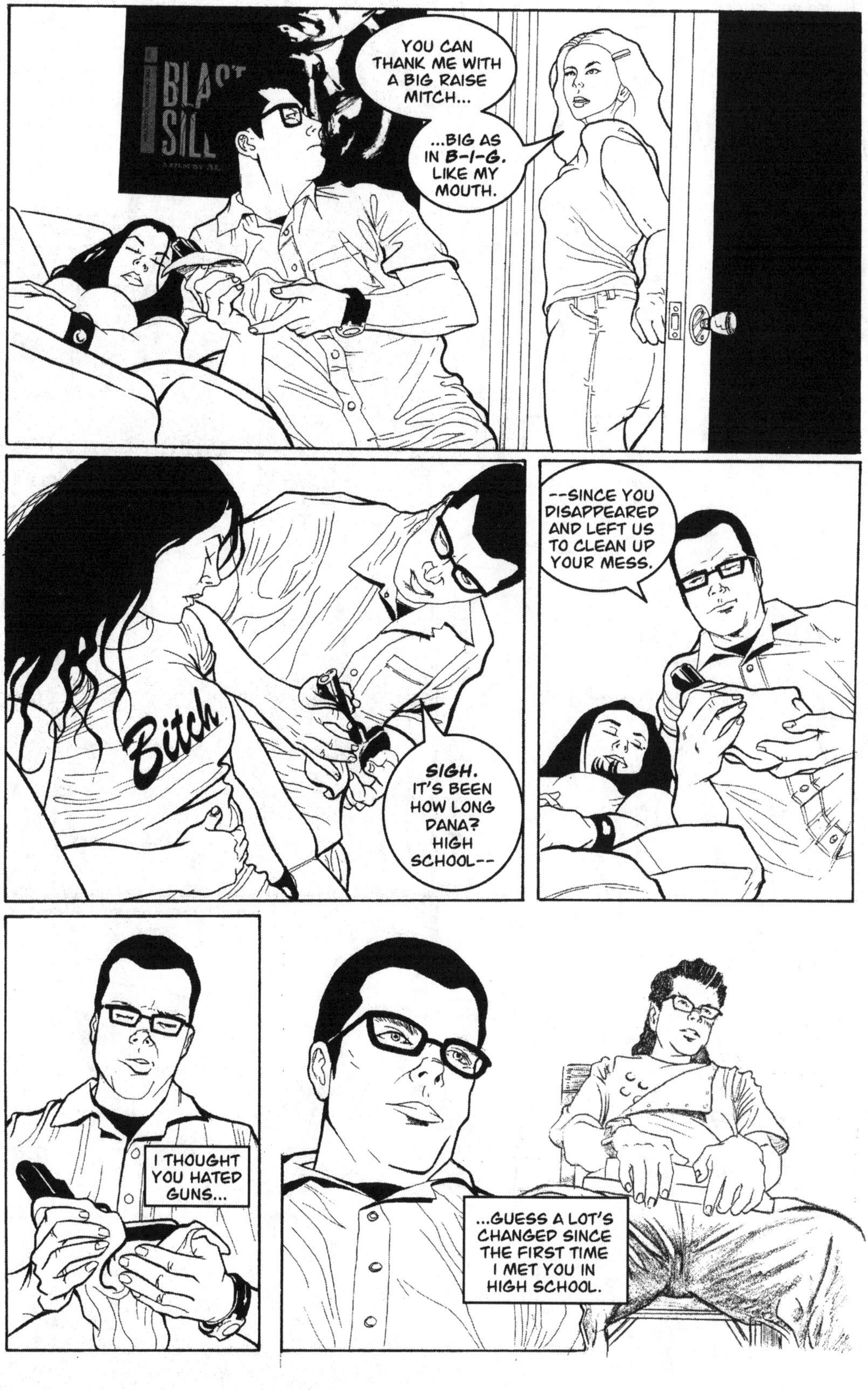

YOU CAN THANK ME WITH A BIG RAISE MITCH...
...BIG AS IN B-I-G. LIKE MY MOUTH.
Bitch
SIGH. IT'S BEEN HOW LONG DANA? HIGH SCHOOL--
--SINCE YOU DISAPPEARED AND LEFT US TO CLEAN UP YOUR MESS.
I THOUGHT YOU HATED GUNS...
...GUESS A LOT'S CHANGED SINCE THE FIRST TIME I MET YOU IN HIGH SCHOOL.

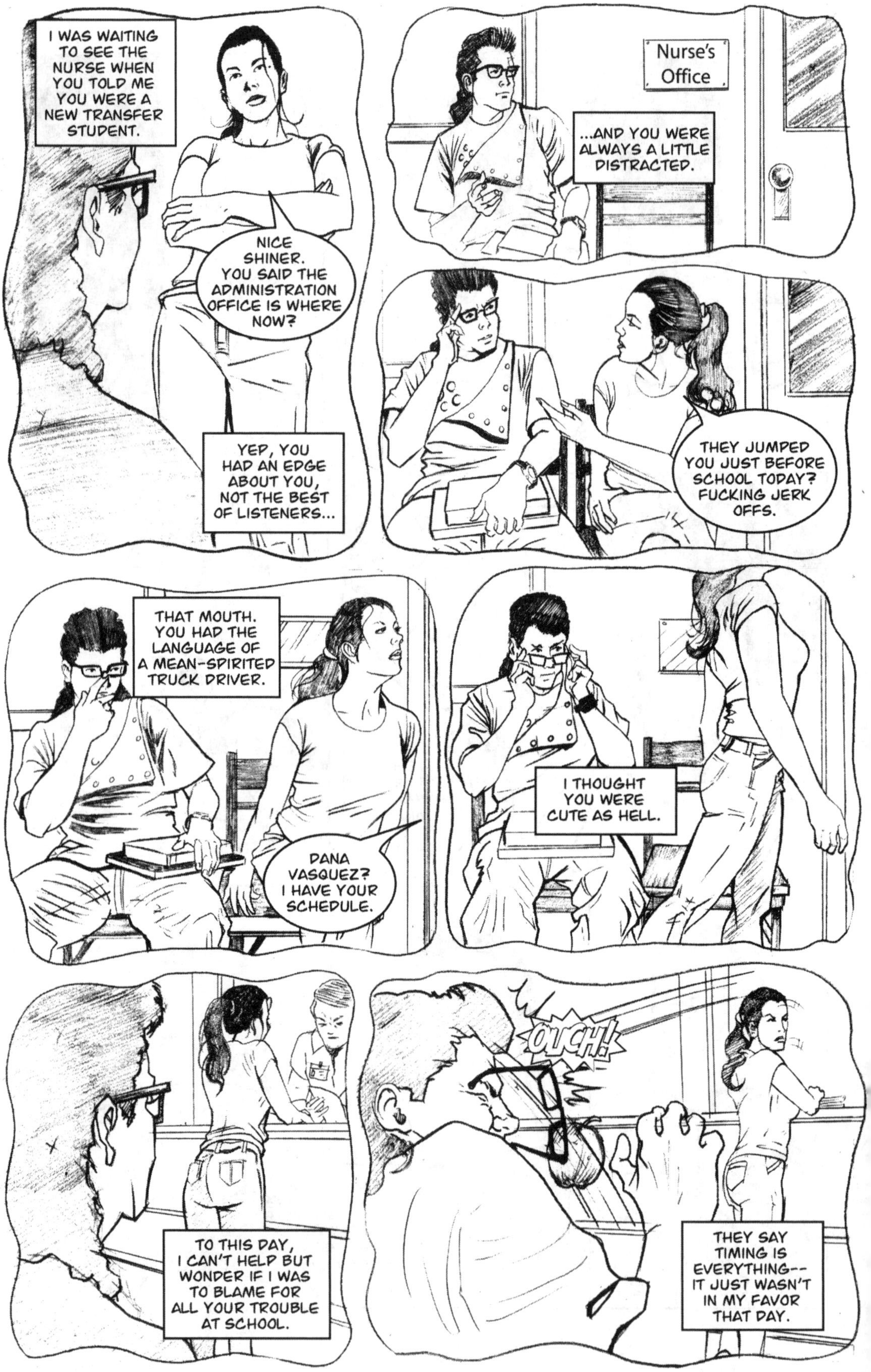

I WAS WAITING TO SEE THE NURSE WHEN YOU TOLD ME YOU WERE A NEW TRANSFER STUDENT.
NICE SHINER. YOU SAID THE ADMINISTRATION OFFICE IS WHERE NOW?
YEP, YOU HAD AN EDGE ABOUT YOU, NOT THE BEST OF LISTENERS...
Nurse's Office
...AND YOU WERE ALWAYS A LITTLE DISTRACTED.
THEY JUMPED YOU JUST BEFORE SCHOOL TODAY? FUCKING JERK OFFS.
THAT MOUTH. YOU HAD THE LANGUAGE OF A MEAN-SPIRITED TRUCK DRIVER.
DANA VASQUEZ? I HAVE YOUR SCHEDULE.
I THOUGHT YOU WERE CUTE AS HELL.
TO THIS DAY, I CAN'T HELP BUT WONDER IF I WAS TO BLAME FOR ALL YOUR TROUBLE AT SCHOOL.
OUCH!
THEY SAY TIMING IS EVERYTHING-- IT JUST WASN'T IN MY FAVOR THAT DAY.

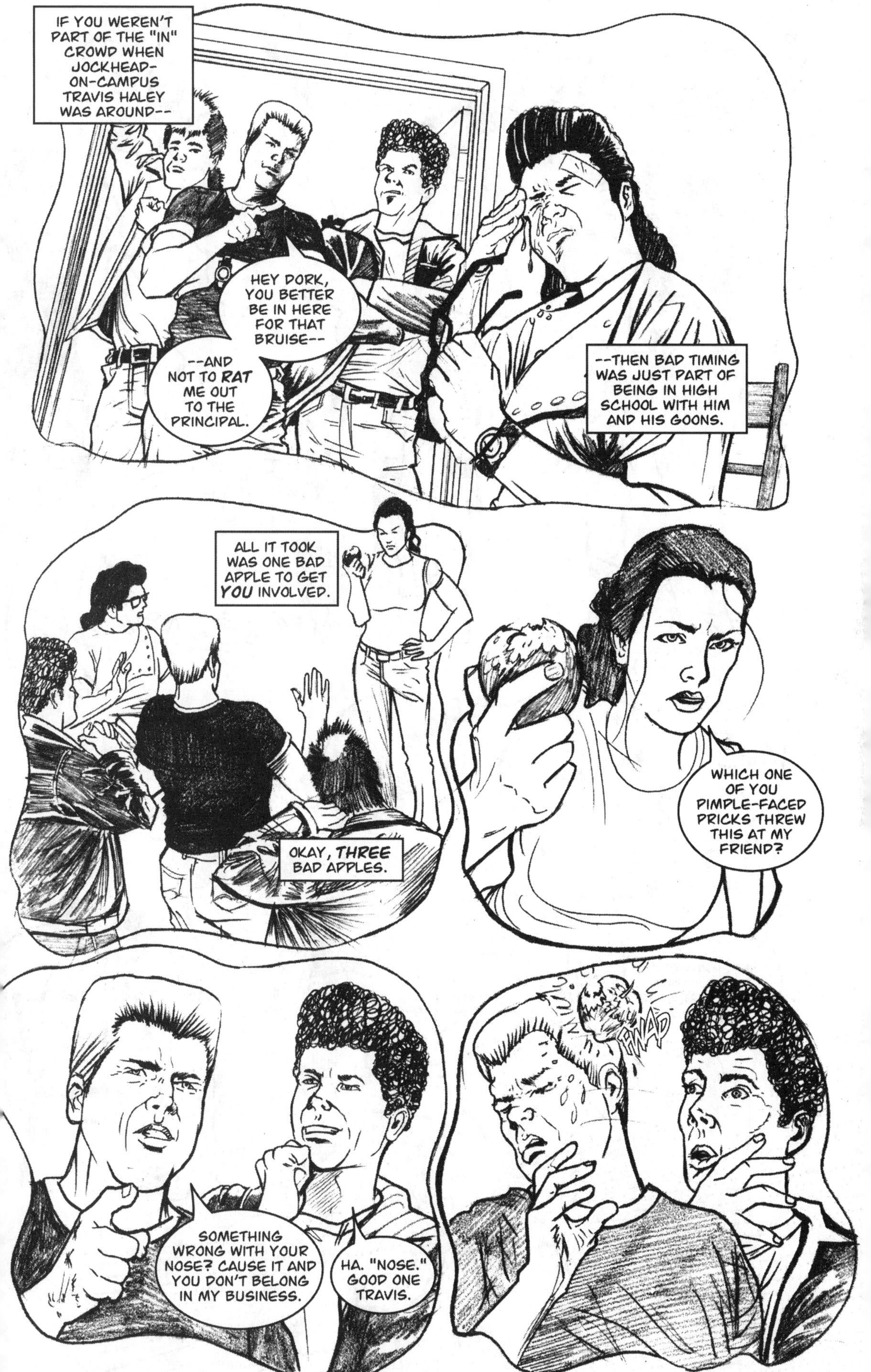
IF YOU WEREN'T PART OF THE "IN" CROWD WHEN JOCKHEAD-ON-CAMPUS TRAVIS HALEY WAS AROUND--
HEY DORK, YOU BETTER BE IN HERE FOR THAT BRUISE--
--AND NOT TO RAT ME OUT TO THE PRINCIPAL.
--THEN BAD TIMING WAS JUST PART OF BEING IN HIGH SCHOOL WITH HIM AND HIS GOONS.
ALL IT TOOK WAS ONE BAD APPLE TO GET YOU INVOLVED.
OKAY, THREE BAD APPLES.
WHICH ONE OF YOU PIMPLE-FACED PRICKS THREW THIS AT MY FRIEND?
SOMETHING WRONG WITH YOUR NOSE? CAUSE IT AND YOU DON'T BELONG IN MY BUSINESS.
HA. "NOSE." GOOD ONE TRAVIS.
THWAP

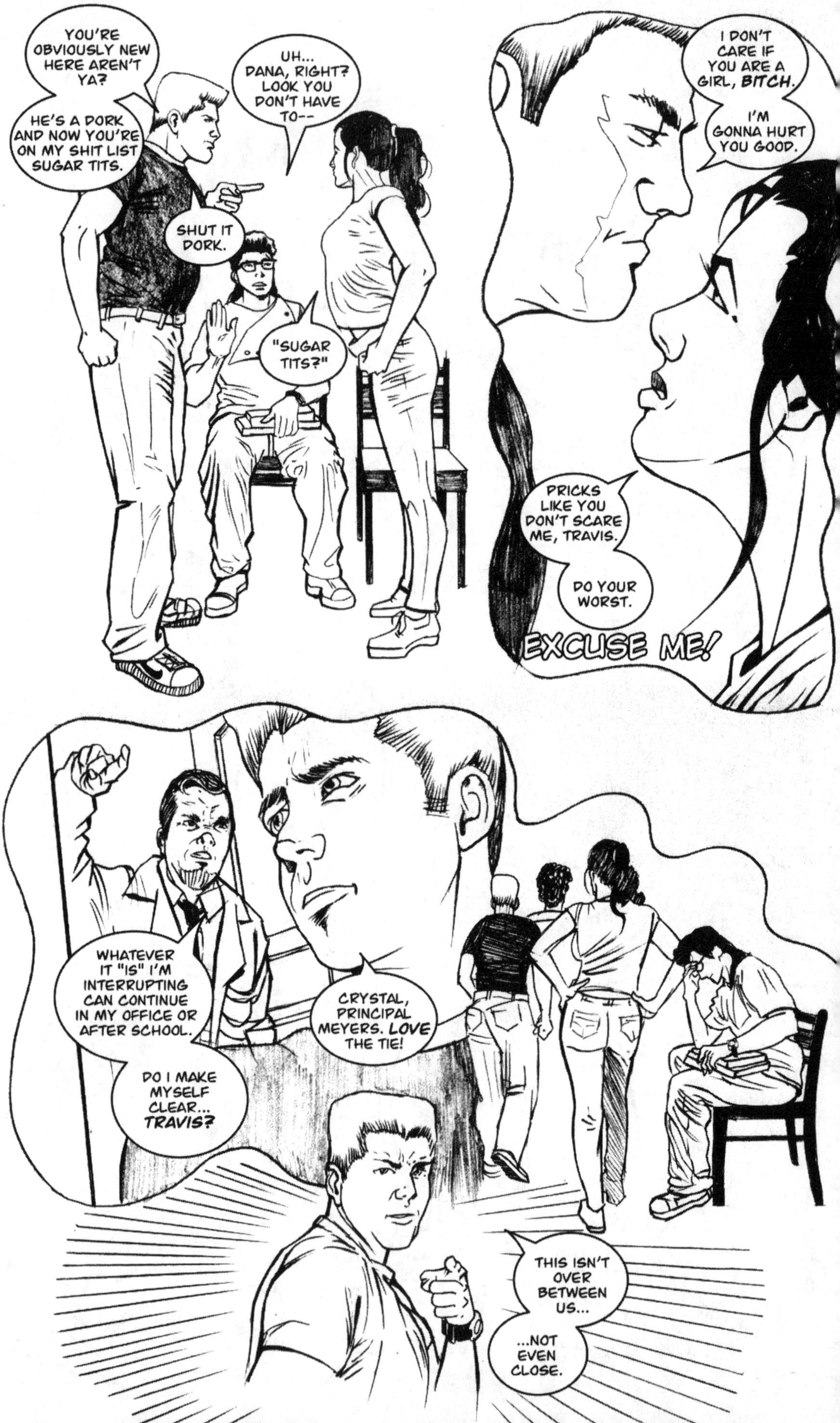
YOU'RE OBVIOUSLY NEW HERE AREN'T YA?
HE'S A DORK AND NOW YOU'RE ON MY SHIT LIST SUGAR TITS.
UH... DANA, RIGHT? LOOK YOU DON'T HAVE TO--
SHUT IT DORK.
"SUGAR TITS?"
I DON'T CARE IF YOU ARE A GIRL, BITCH.
I'M GONNA HURT YOU GOOD.
PRICKS LIKE YOU DON'T SCARE ME, TRAVIS.
DO YOUR WORST.
EXCUSE ME!
WHATEVER IT "IS" I'M INTERRUPTING CAN CONTINUE IN MY OFFICE OR AFTER SCHOOL.
DO I MAKE MYSELF CLEAR... TRAVIS?
CRYSTAL, PRINCIPAL MEYERS. LOVE THE TIE!
THIS ISN'T OVER BETWEEN US...
...NOT EVEN CLOSE.

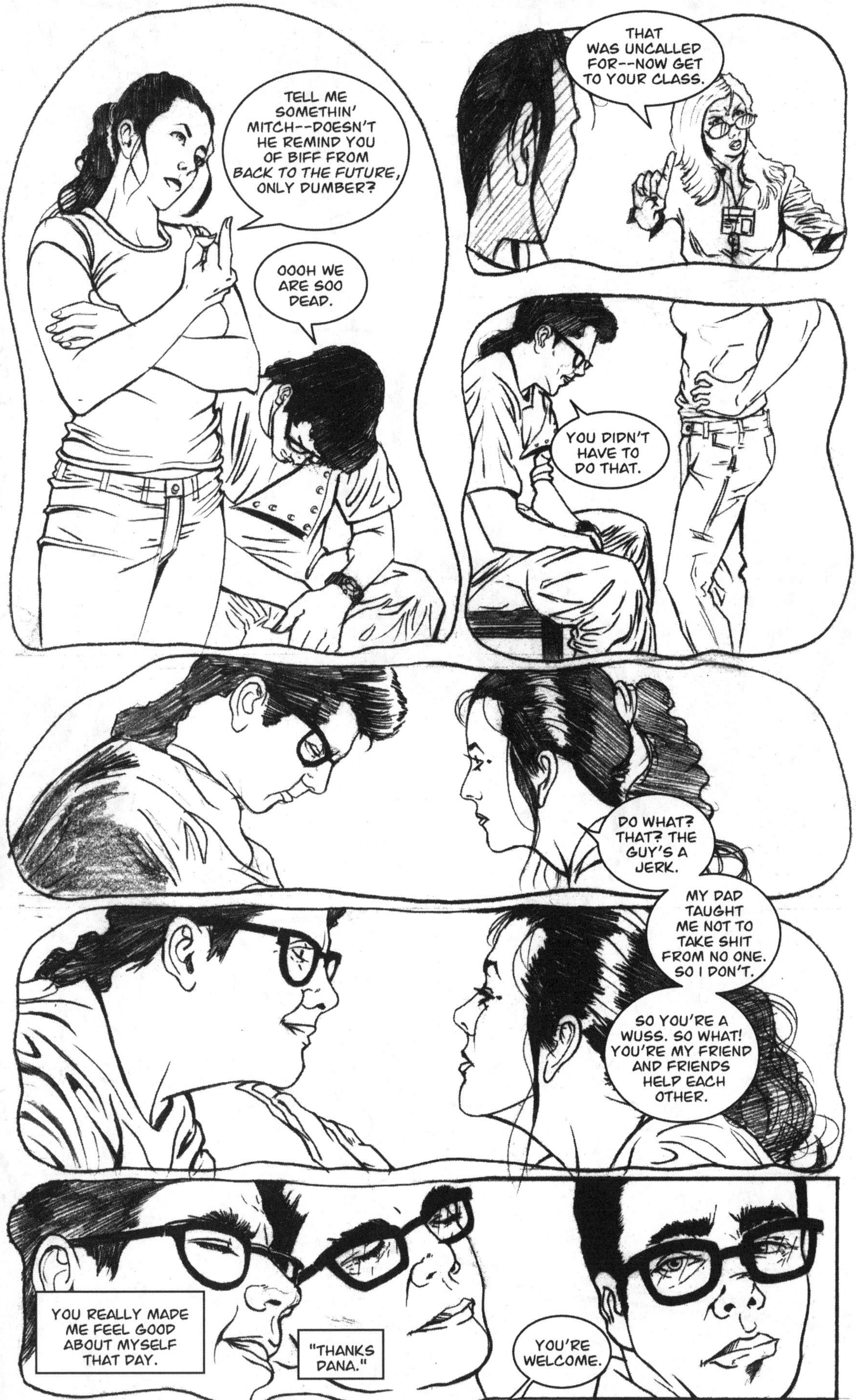
TELL ME SOMETHIN' MITCH--DOESN'T HE REMIND YOU OF BIFF FROM BACK TO THE FUTURE, ONLY DUMBER?
OOOH WE ARE SOO DEAD.
THAT WAS UNCALLED FOR--NOW GET TO YOUR CLASS.
YOU DIDN'T HAVE TO DO THAT.
DO WHAT? THAT? THE GUY'S A JERK.
MY DAD TAUGHT ME NOT TO TAKE SHIT FROM NO ONE. SO I DON'T.
SO YOU'RE A WUSS. SO WHAT! YOU'RE MY FRIEND AND FRIENDS HELP EACH OTHER.
YOU REALLY MADE ME FEEL GOOD ABOUT MYSELF THAT DAY.
"THANKS DANA."
YOU'RE WELCOME.

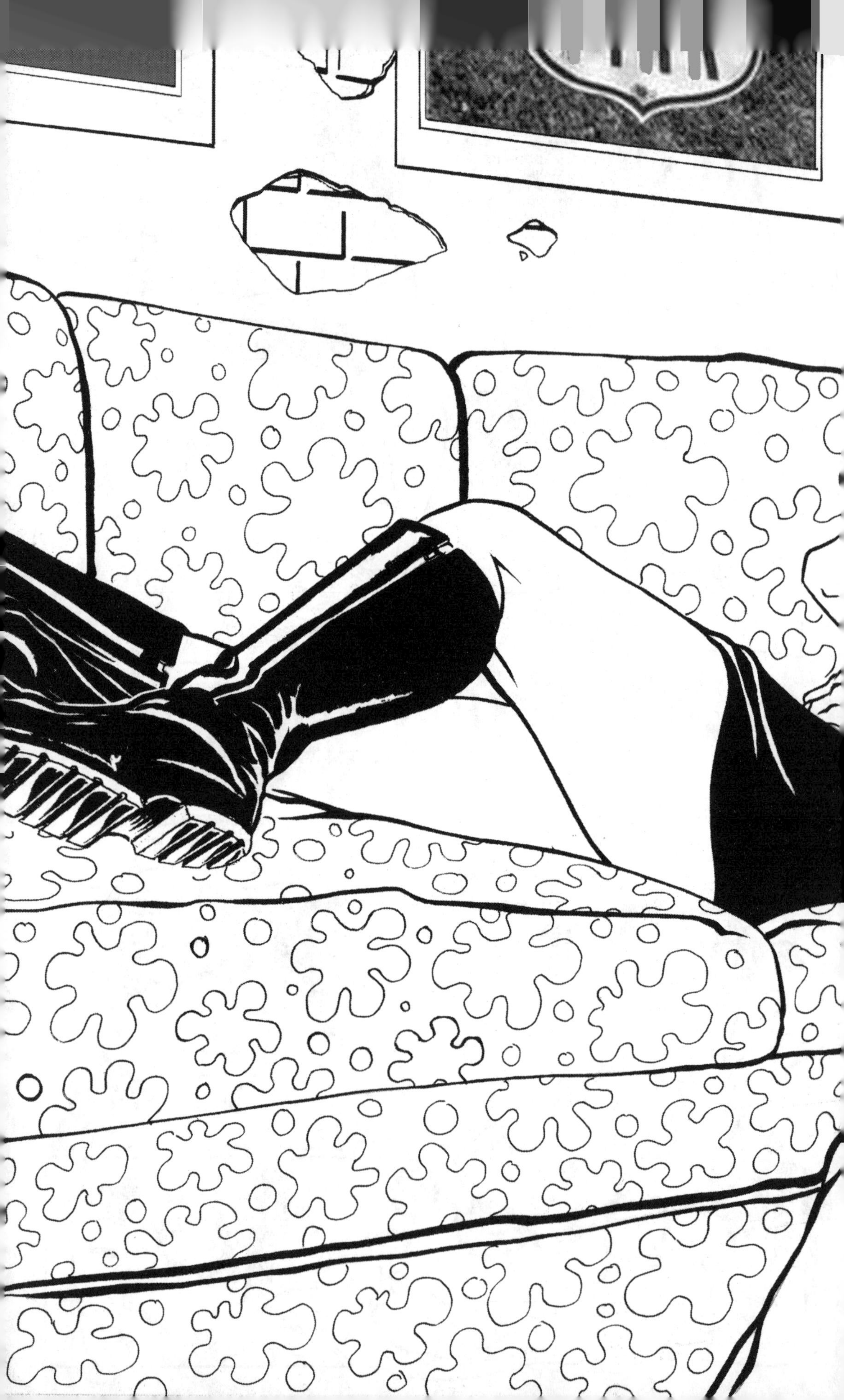

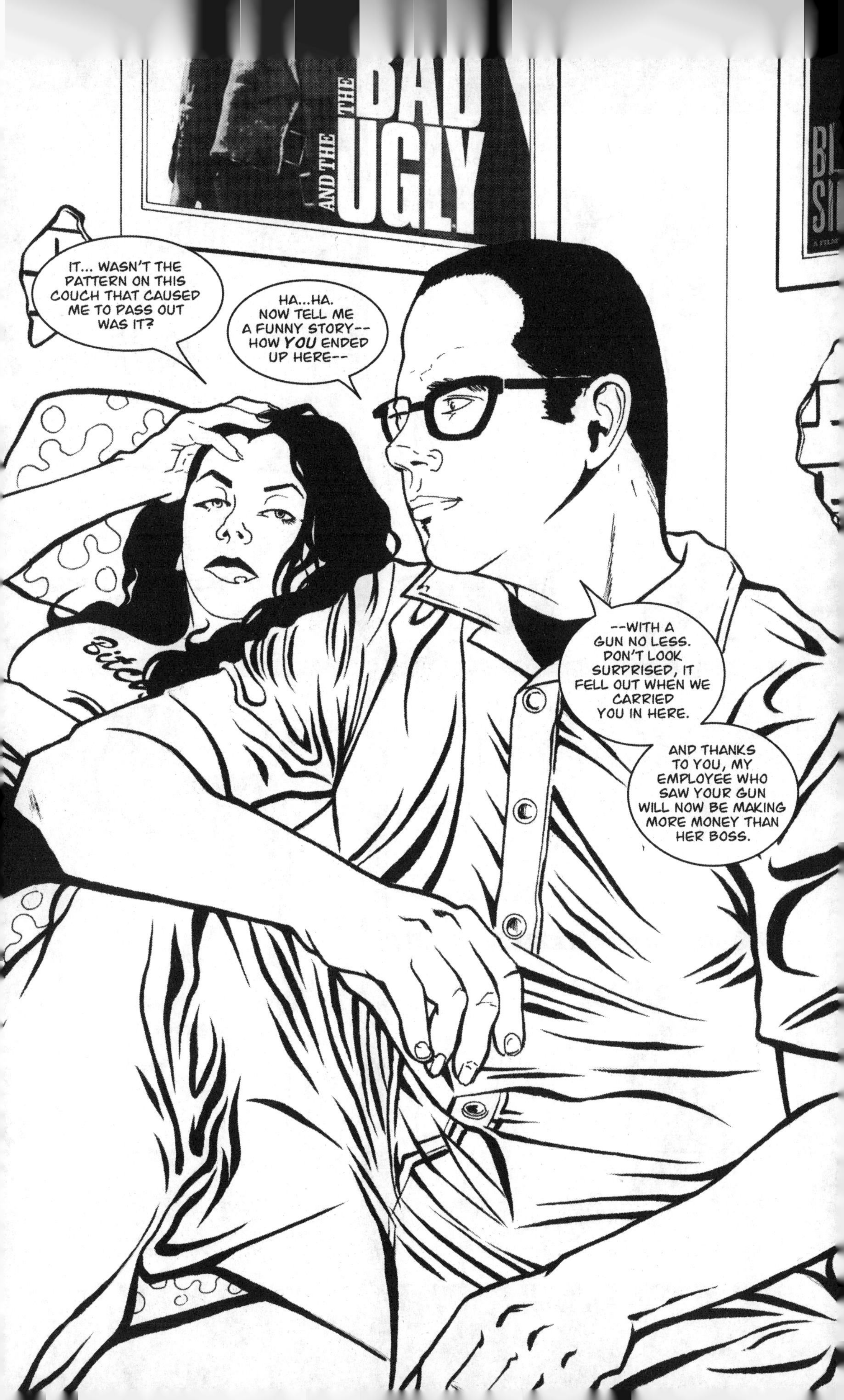
THE BAD AND THE UGLY
IT... WASN'T THE PATTERN ON THIS COUCH THAT CAUSED ME TO PASS OUT WAS IT?
HA...HA. NOW TELL ME A FUNNY STORY-- HOW YOU ENDED UP HERE--
--WITH A GUN NO LESS. DON'T LOOK SURPRISED, IT FELL OUT WHEN WE CARRIED YOU IN HERE.
AND THANKS TO YOU, MY EMPLOYEE WHO SAW YOUR GUN WILL NOW BE MAKING MORE MONEY THAN HER BOSS.

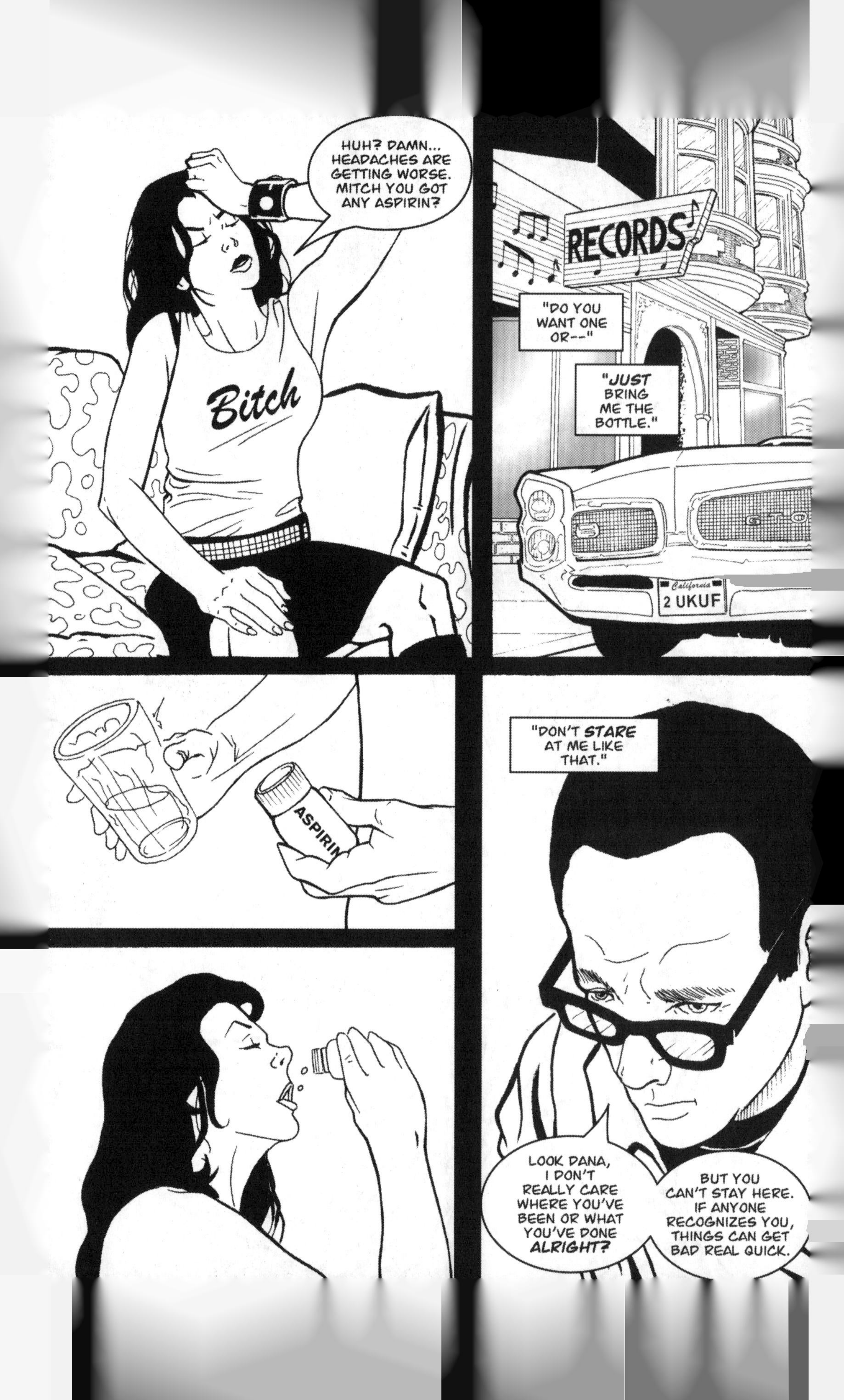
HUH? DAMN... HEADACHES ARE GETTING WORSE. MITCH YOU GOT ANY ASPIRIN?
RECORDS
"DO YOU WANT ONE OR--"
"JUST BRING ME THE BOTTLE."
California
2 UKUF
GTO
ASPIRIN
"DON'T STARE AT ME LIKE THAT."
LOOK DANA, I DON'T REALLY CARE WHERE YOU'VE BEEN OR WHAT YOU'VE DONE ALRIGHT?
BUT YOU CAN'T STAY HERE. IF ANYONE RECOGNIZES YOU, THINGS CAN GET BAD REAL QUICK.

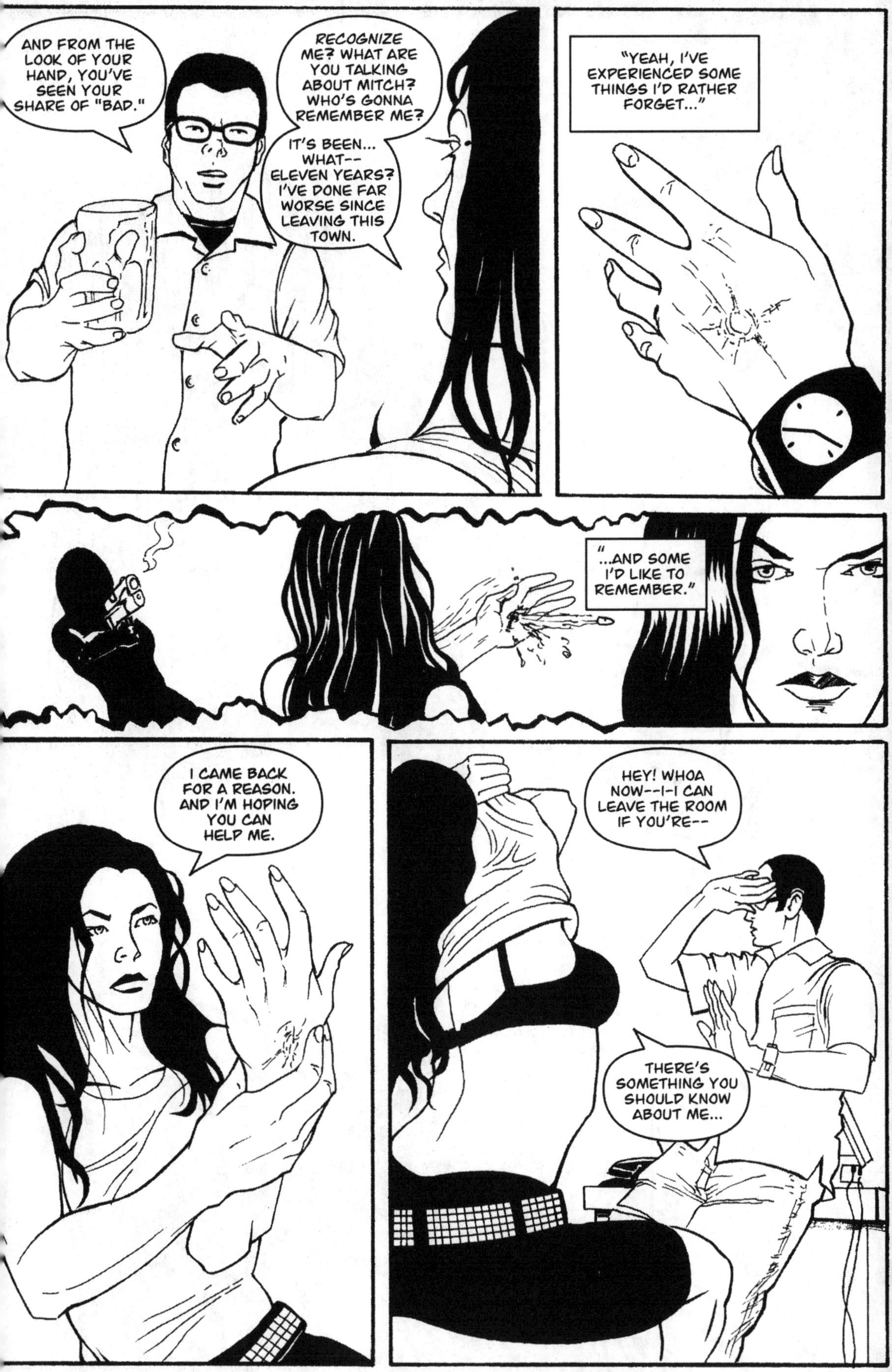
AND FROM THE LOOK OF YOUR HAND, YOU'VE SEEN YOUR SHARE OF "BAD."
RECOGNIZE ME? WHAT ARE YOU TALKING ABOUT MITCH? WHO'S GONNA REMEMBER ME?
IT'S BEEN... WHAT-- ELEVEN YEARS? I'VE DONE FAR WORSE SINCE LEAVING THIS TOWN.
"YEAH, I'VE EXPERIENCED SOME THINGS I'D RATHER FORGET..."
"...AND SOME I'D LIKE TO REMEMBER."
I CAME BACK FOR A REASON. AND I'M HOPING YOU CAN HELP ME.
HEY! WHOA NOW--I-I CAN LEAVE THE ROOM IF YOU'RE--
THERE'S SOMETHING YOU SHOULD KNOW ABOUT ME...

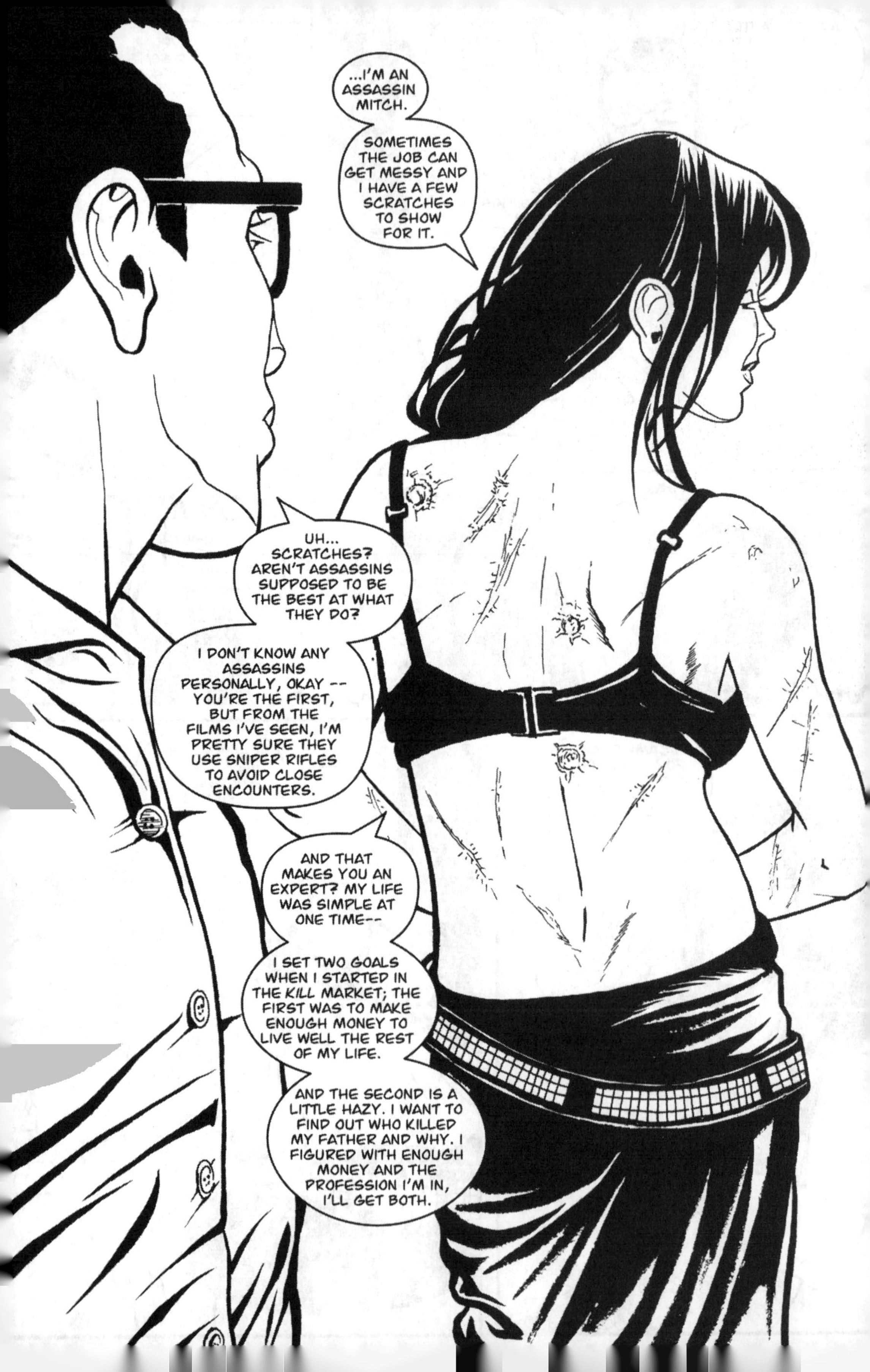
...I'M AN ASSASSIN MITCH.
SOMETIMES THE JOB CAN GET MESSY AND I HAVE A FEW SCRATCHES TO SHOW FOR IT.
UH... SCRATCHES? AREN'T ASSASSINS SUPPOSED TO BE THE BEST AT WHAT THEY DO?
I DON'T KNOW ANY ASSASSINS PERSONALLY, OKAY -- YOU'RE THE FIRST, BUT FROM THE FILMS I'VE SEEN, I'M PRETTY SURE THEY USE SNIPER RIFLES TO AVOID CLOSE ENCOUNTERS.
AND THAT MAKES YOU AN EXPERT? MY LIFE WAS SIMPLE AT ONE TIME--
I SET TWO GOALS WHEN I STARTED IN THE KILL MARKET; THE FIRST WAS TO MAKE ENOUGH MONEY TO LIVE WELL THE REST OF MY LIFE.
AND THE SECOND IS A LITTLE HAZY. I WANT TO FIND OUT WHO KILLED MY FATHER AND WHY. I FIGURED WITH ENOUGH MONEY AND THE PROFESSION I'M IN, I'LL GET BOTH.

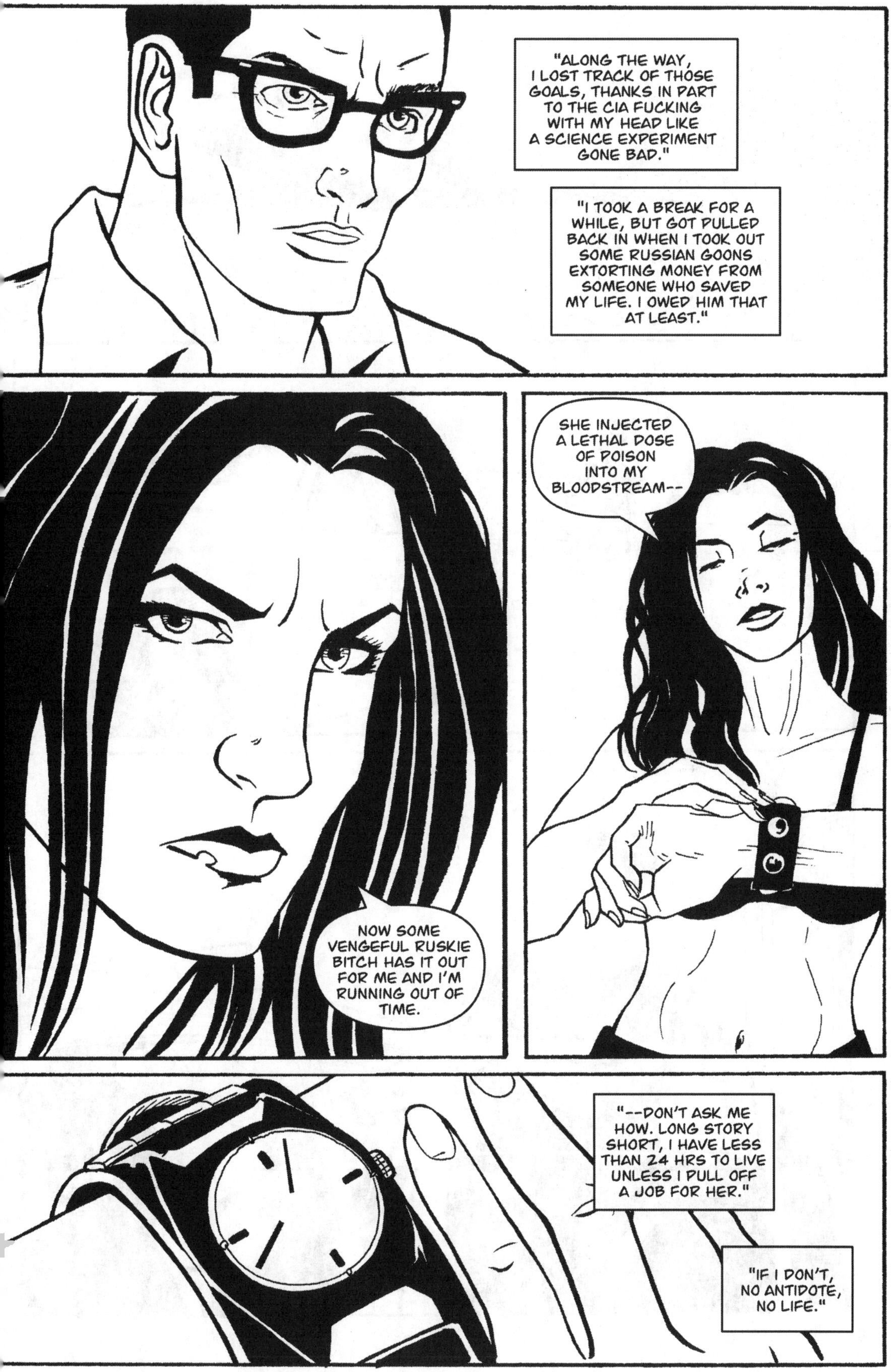
"ALONG THE WAY, I LOST TRACK OF THOSE GOALS, THANKS IN PART TO THE CIA FUCKING WITH MY HEAD LIKE A SCIENCE EXPERIMENT GONE BAD."
"I TOOK A BREAK FOR A WHILE, BUT GOT PULLED BACK IN WHEN I TOOK OUT SOME RUSSIAN GOONS EXTORTING MONEY FROM SOMEONE WHO SAVED MY LIFE. I OWED HIM THAT AT LEAST."
NOW SOME VENGEFUL RUSKIE BITCH HAS IT OUT FOR ME AND I'M RUNNING OUT OF TIME.
SHE INJECTED A LETHAL DOSE OF POISON INTO MY BLOODSTREAM--
"--DON'T ASK ME HOW. LONG STORY SHORT, I HAVE LESS THAN 24 HRS TO LIVE UNLESS I PULL OFF A JOB FOR HER."
"IF I DON'T, NO ANTIDOTE, NO LIFE."

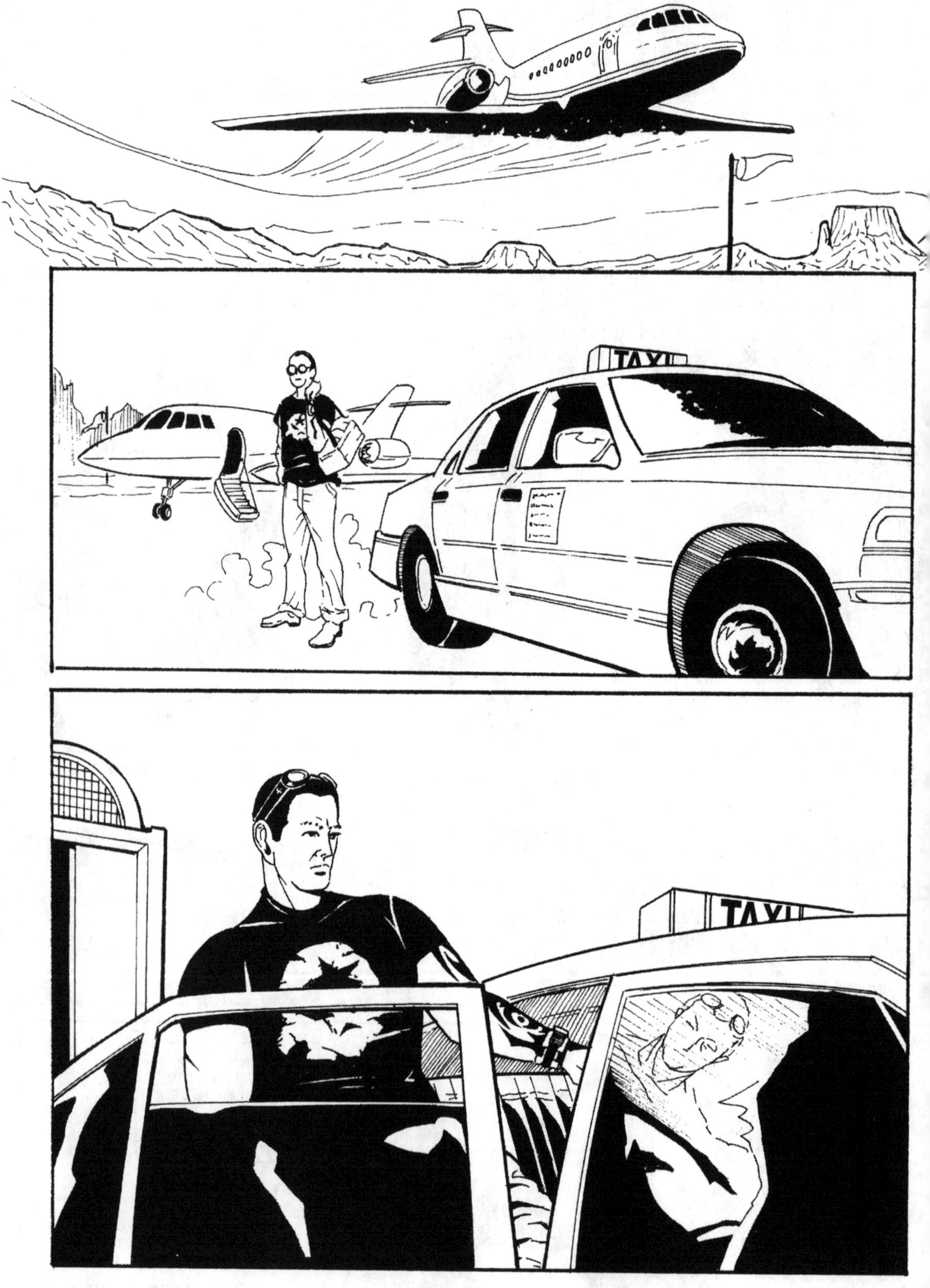

TAXI
TAXI

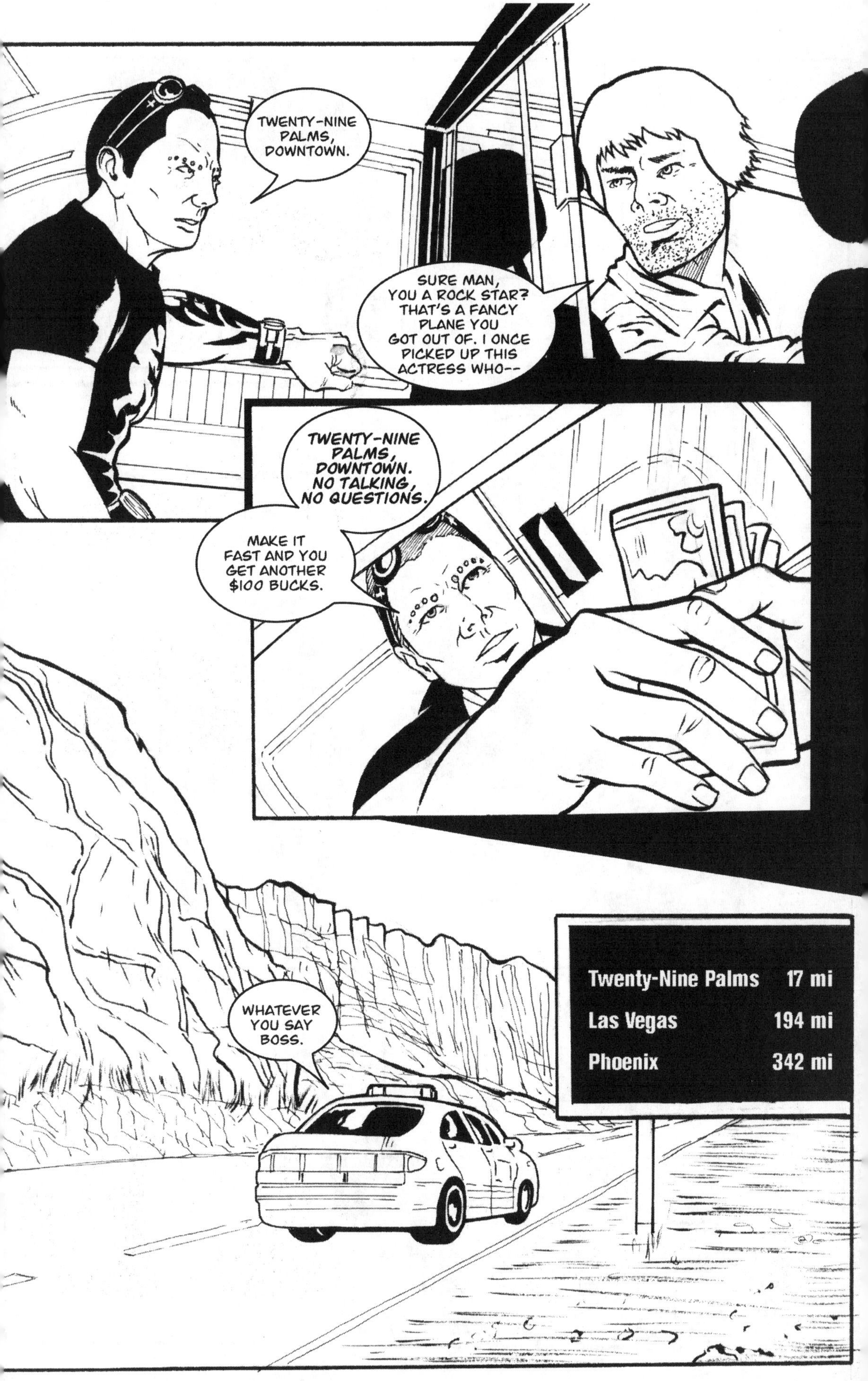
TWENTY-NINE PALMS, DOWNTOWN.
SURE MAN, YOU A ROCK STAR? THAT'S A FANCY PLANE YOU GOT OUT OF. I ONCE PICKED UP THIS ACTRESS WHO--
TWENTY-NINE PALMS, DOWNTOWN. NO TALKING, NO QUESTIONS.
MAKE IT FAST AND YOU GET ANOTHER $100 BUCKS.
Twenty-Nine Palms 17 mi
Las Vegas 194 mi
Phoenix 342 mi
WHATEVER YOU SAY BOSS.

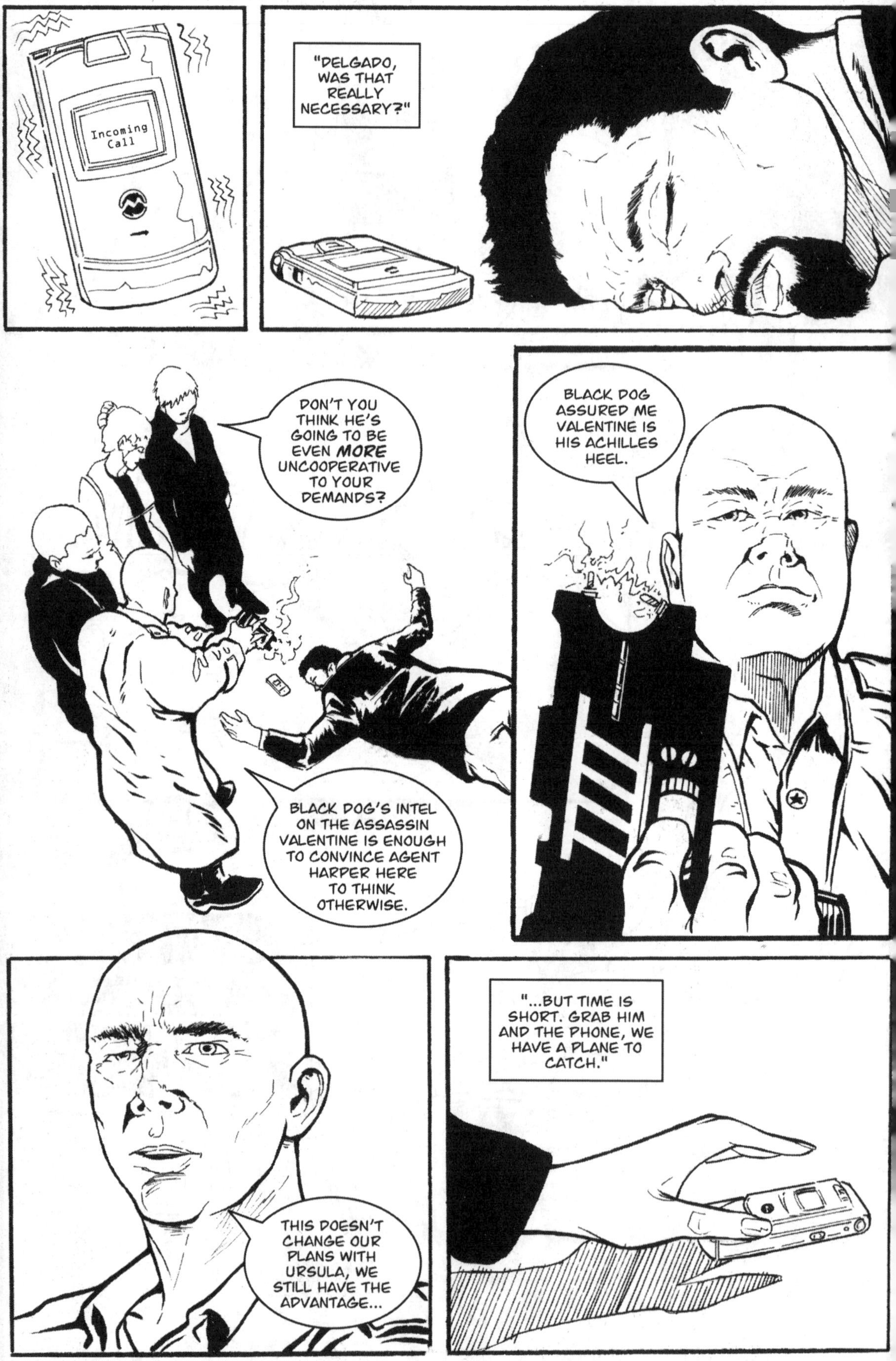
Incoming Call
"DELGADO, WAS THAT REALLY NECESSARY?"
DON'T YOU THINK HE'S GOING TO BE EVEN MORE UNCOOPERATIVE TO YOUR DEMANDS?
BLACK DOG'S INTEL ON THE ASSASSIN VALENTINE IS ENOUGH TO CONVINCE AGENT HARPER HERE TO THINK OTHERWISE.
BLACK DOG ASSURED ME VALENTINE IS HIS ACHILLES HEEL.
THIS DOESN'T CHANGE OUR PLANS WITH URSULA, WE STILL HAVE THE ADVANTAGE...
"...BUT TIME IS SHORT. GRAB HIM AND THE PHONE, WE HAVE A PLANE TO CATCH."

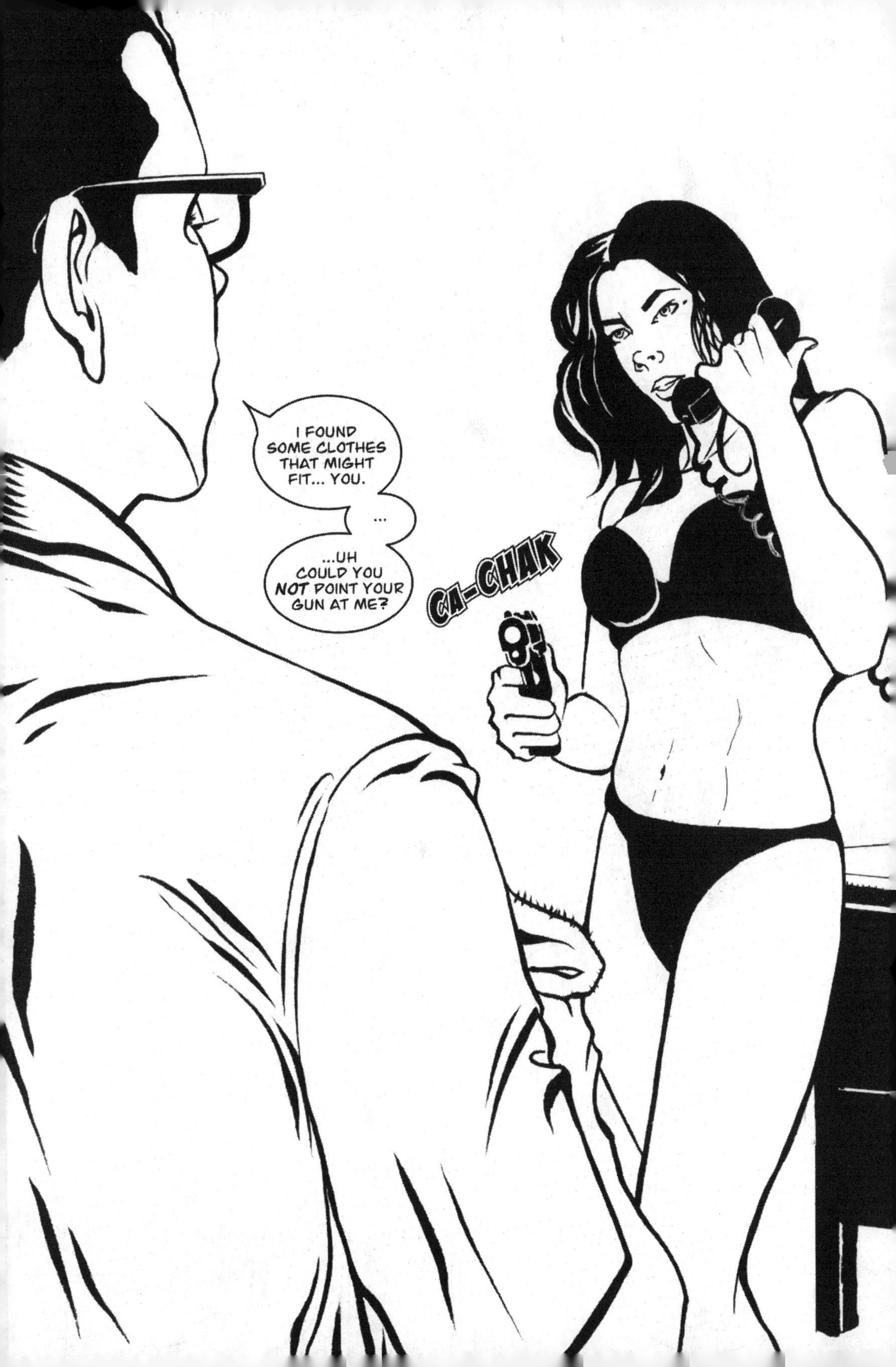
I FOUND SOME CLOTHES THAT MIGHT FIT... YOU.
...
...UH COULD YOU NOT POINT YOUR GUN AT ME?
CA-CHAK

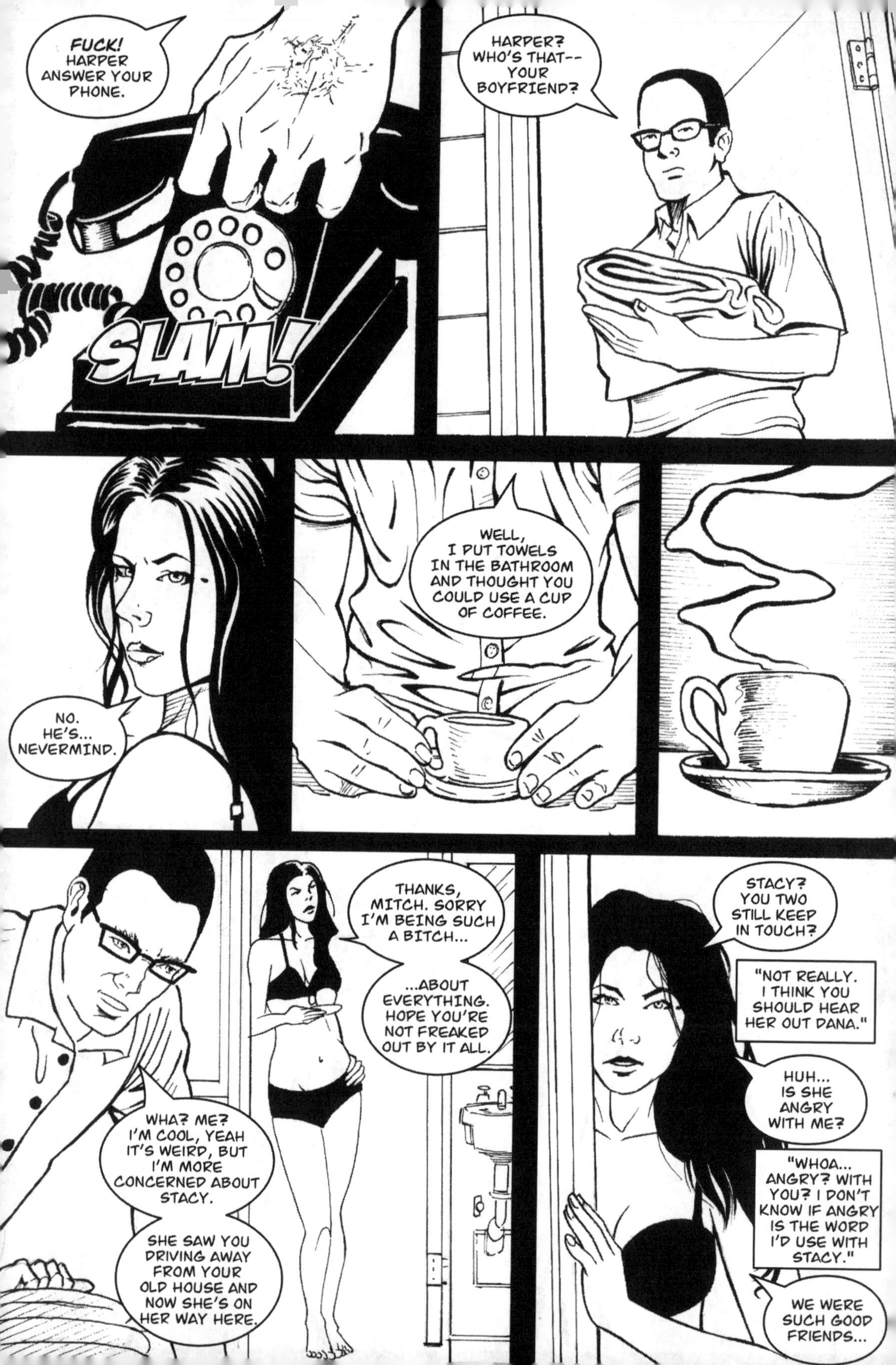
FUCK! HARPER ANSWER YOUR PHONE.
SLAM!
HARPER? WHO'S THAT-- YOUR BOYFRIEND?
NO. HE'S... NEVERMIND.
WELL, I PUT TOWELS IN THE BATHROOM AND THOUGHT YOU COULD USE A CUP OF COFFEE.
THANKS, MITCH. SORRY I'M BEING SUCH A BITCH...
...ABOUT EVERYTHING. HOPE YOU'RE NOT FREAKED OUT BY IT ALL.
WHA? ME? I'M COOL, YEAH IT'S WEIRD, BUT I'M MORE CONCERNED ABOUT STACY.
SHE SAW YOU DRIVING AWAY FROM YOUR OLD HOUSE AND NOW SHE'S ON HER WAY HERE.
STACY? YOU TWO STILL KEEP IN TOUCH?
"NOT REALLY. I THINK YOU SHOULD HEAR HER OUT DANA."
HUH... IS SHE ANGRY WITH ME?
"WHOA... ANGRY? WITH YOU? I DON'T KNOW IF ANGRY IS THE WORD I'D USE WITH STACY."
WE WERE SUCH GOOD FRIENDS...

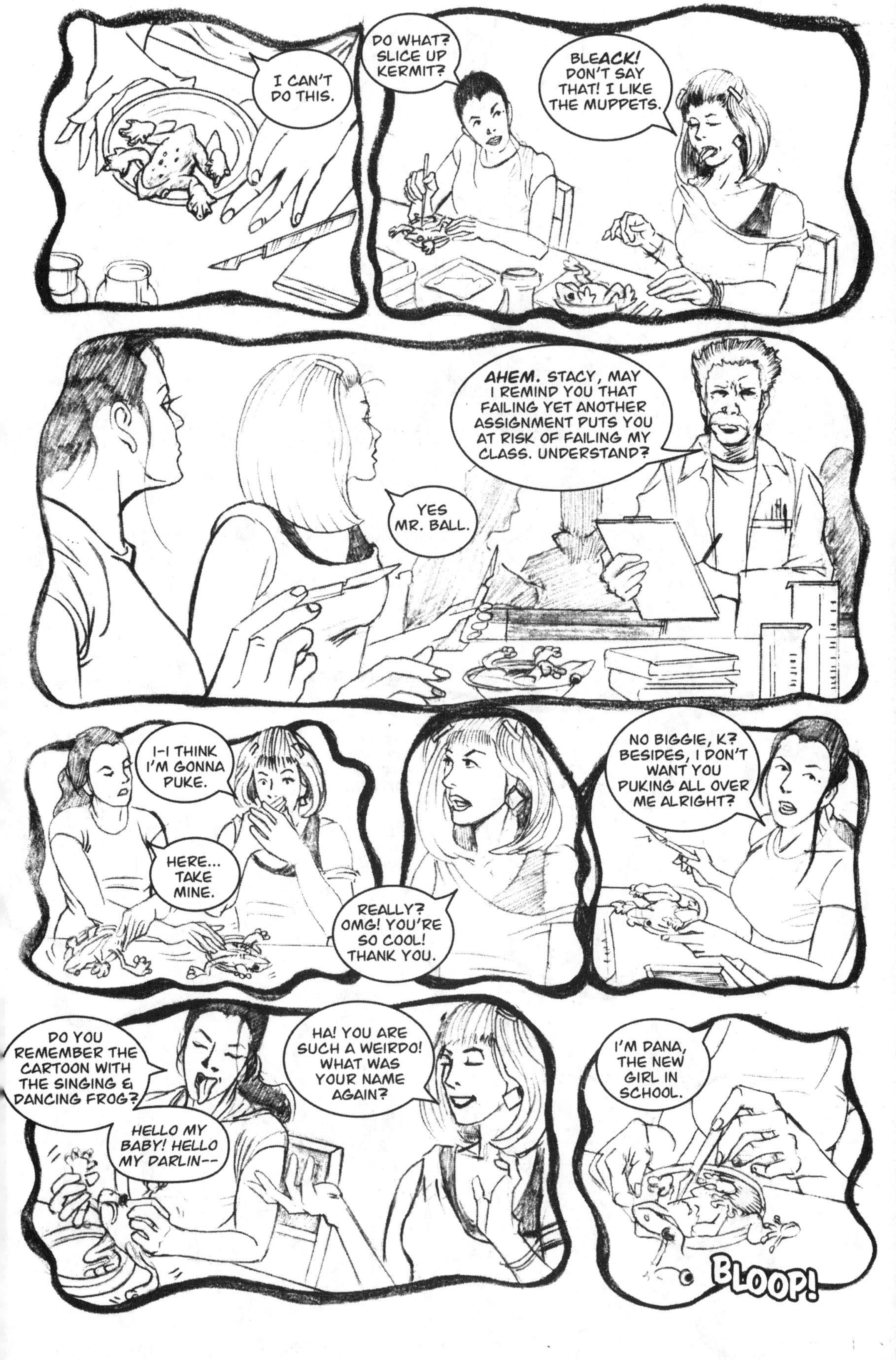
I CAN'T DO THIS.
DO WHAT? SLICE UP KERMIT?
BLEACK! DON'T SAY THAT! I LIKE THE MUPPETS.
AHEM. STACY, MAY I REMIND YOU THAT FAILING YET ANOTHER ASSIGNMENT PUTS YOU AT RISK OF FAILING MY CLASS. UNDERSTAND?
YES MR. BALL.
I-I THINK I'M GONNA PUKE.
HERE... TAKE MINE.
REALLY? OMG! YOU'RE SO COOL! THANK YOU.
NO BIGGIE, K? BESIDES, I DON'T WANT YOU PUKING ALL OVER ME ALRIGHT?
DO YOU REMEMBER THE CARTOON WITH THE SINGING & DANCING FROG?
HELLO MY BABY! HELLO MY DARLIN--
HA! YOU ARE SUCH A WEIRDO! WHAT WAS YOUR NAME AGAIN?
I'M DANA, THE NEW GIRL IN SCHOOL.
BLOOP!

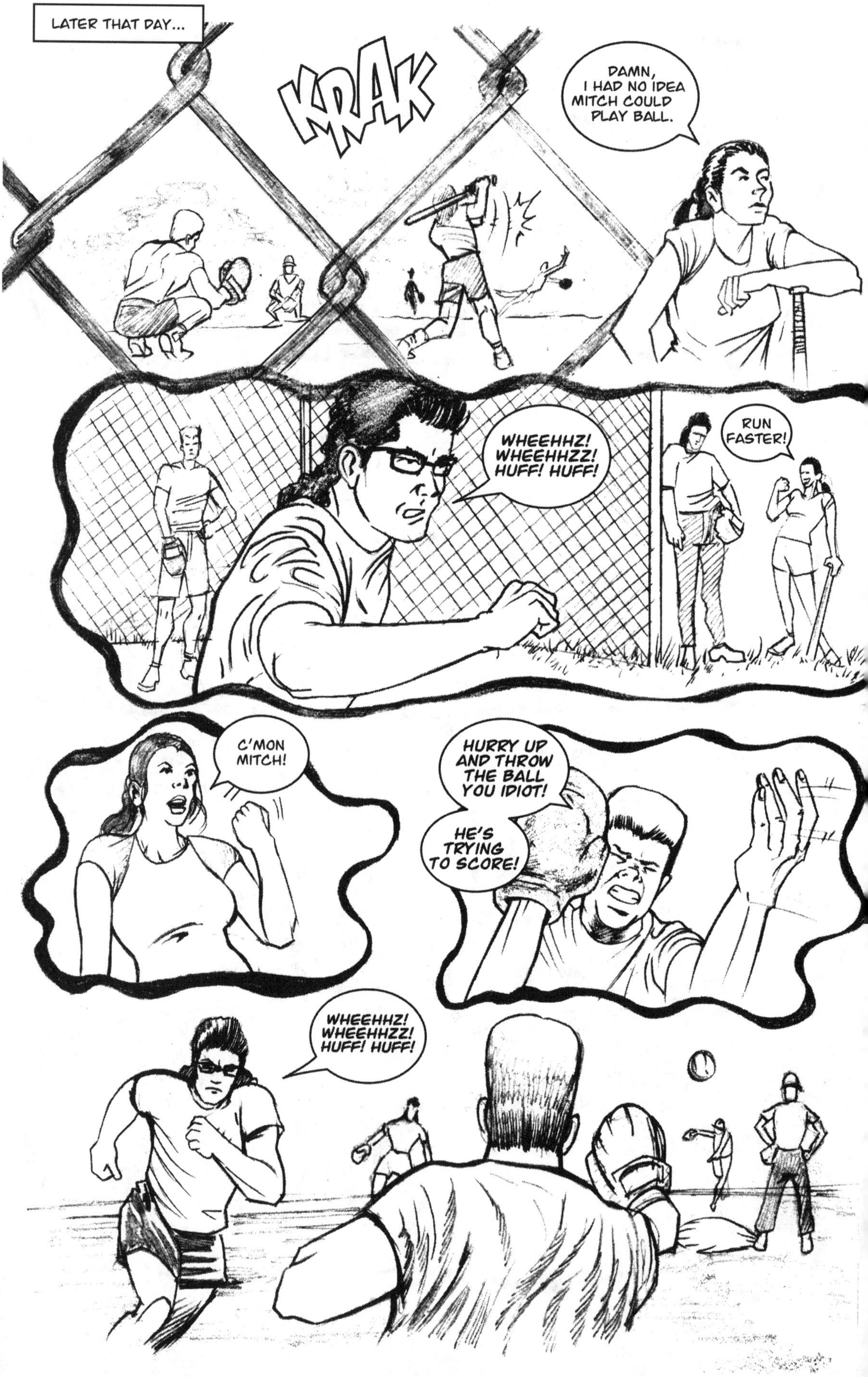
LATER THAT DAY...
KRAK
DAMN, I HAD NO IDEA MITCH COULD PLAY BALL.
WHEEHHZ! WHEEHHZZ! HUFF! HUFF!
RUN FASTER!
C'MON MITCH!
HURRY UP AND THROW THE BALL YOU IDIOT!
HE'S TRYING TO SCORE!
WHEEHHZ! WHEEHHZZ! HUFF! HUFF!

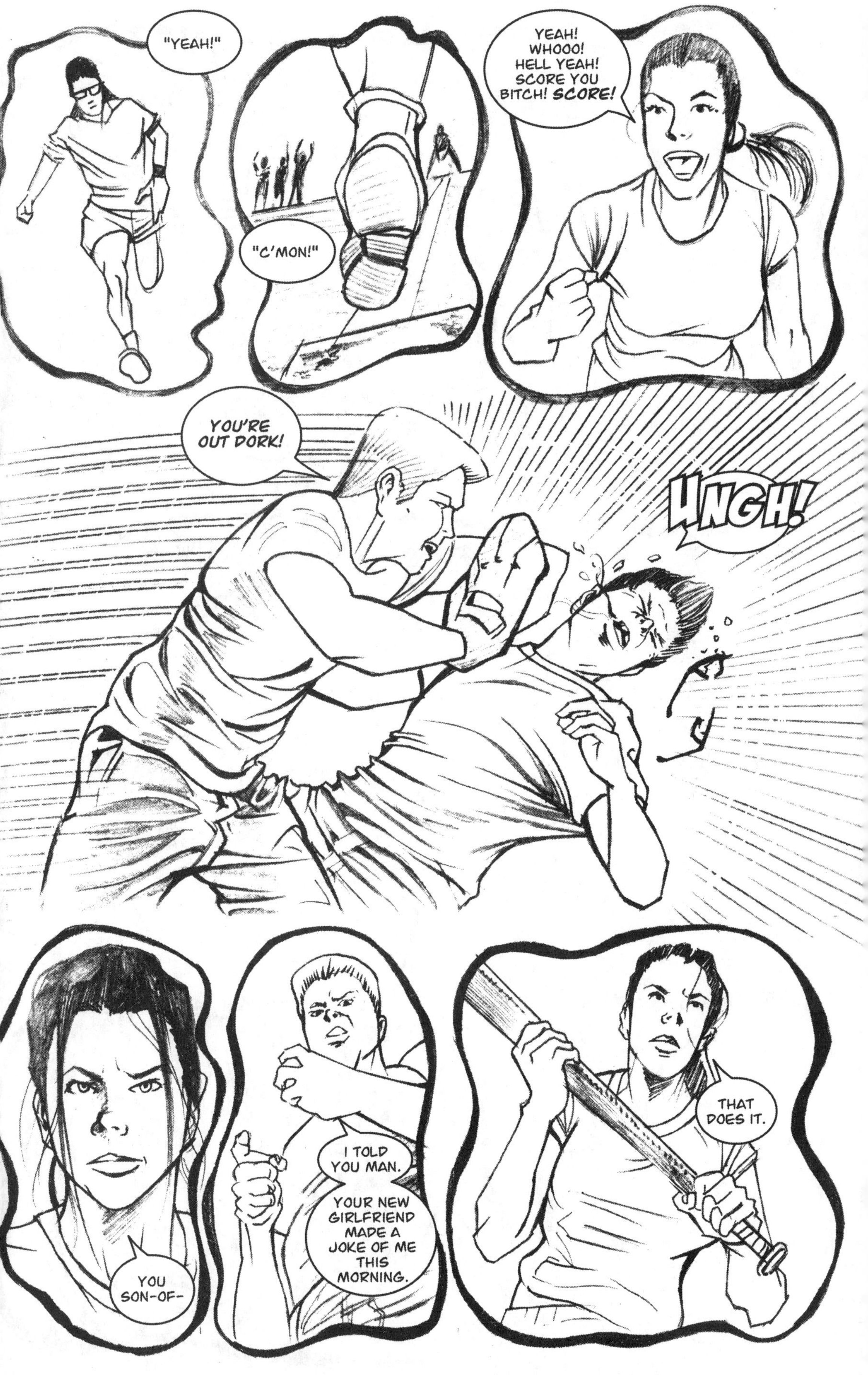
"YEAH!"
"C'MON!"
YEAH! WHOOO! HELL YEAH! SCORE YOU BITCH! SCORE!
YOU'RE OUT DORK!
UNGH!
YOU SON-OF-
I TOLD YOU MAN.
YOUR NEW GIRLFRIEND MADE A JOKE OF ME THIS MORNING.
THAT DOES IT.

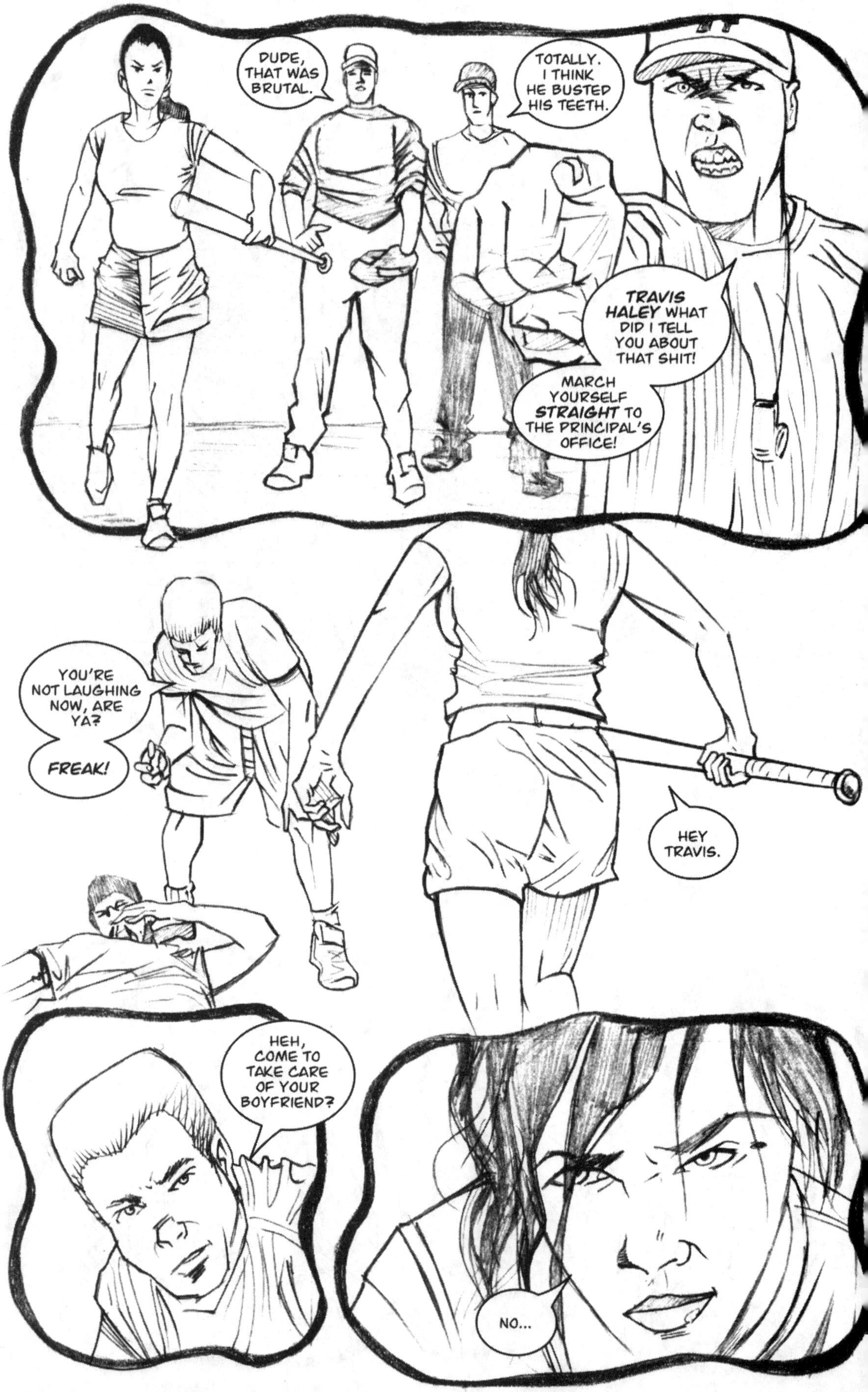

DUDE, THAT WAS BRUTAL.
TOTALLY. I THINK HE BUSTED HIS TEETH.
TRAVIS HALEY WHAT DID I TELL YOU ABOUT THAT SHIT!
MARCH YOURSELF STRAIGHT TO THE PRINCIPAL'S OFFICE!
YOU'RE NOT LAUGHING NOW, ARE YA?
FREAK!
HEY TRAVIS.
HEH, COME TO TAKE CARE OF YOUR BOYFRIEND?
NO...

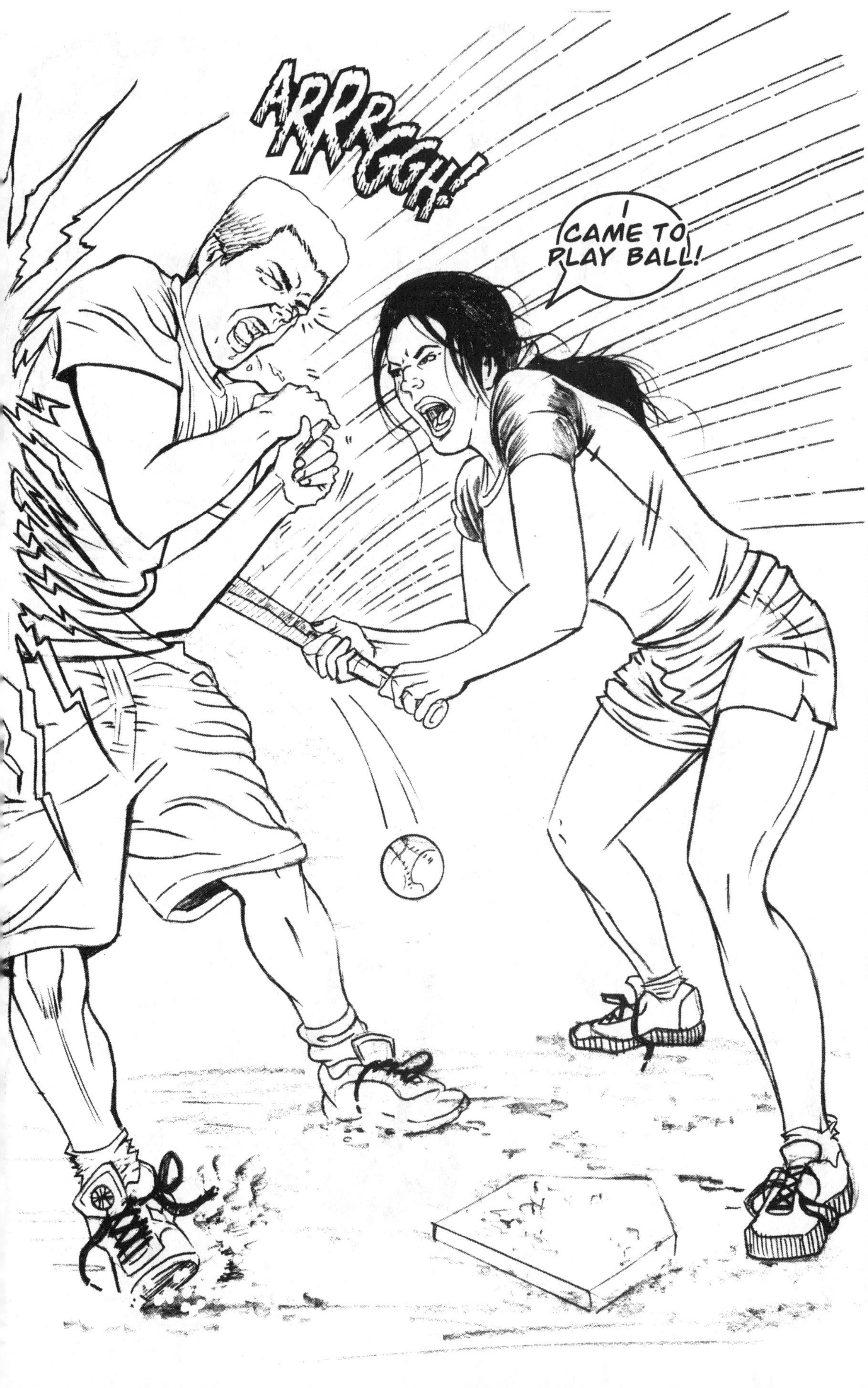
ARRRGGH!
I CAME TO PLAY BALL!

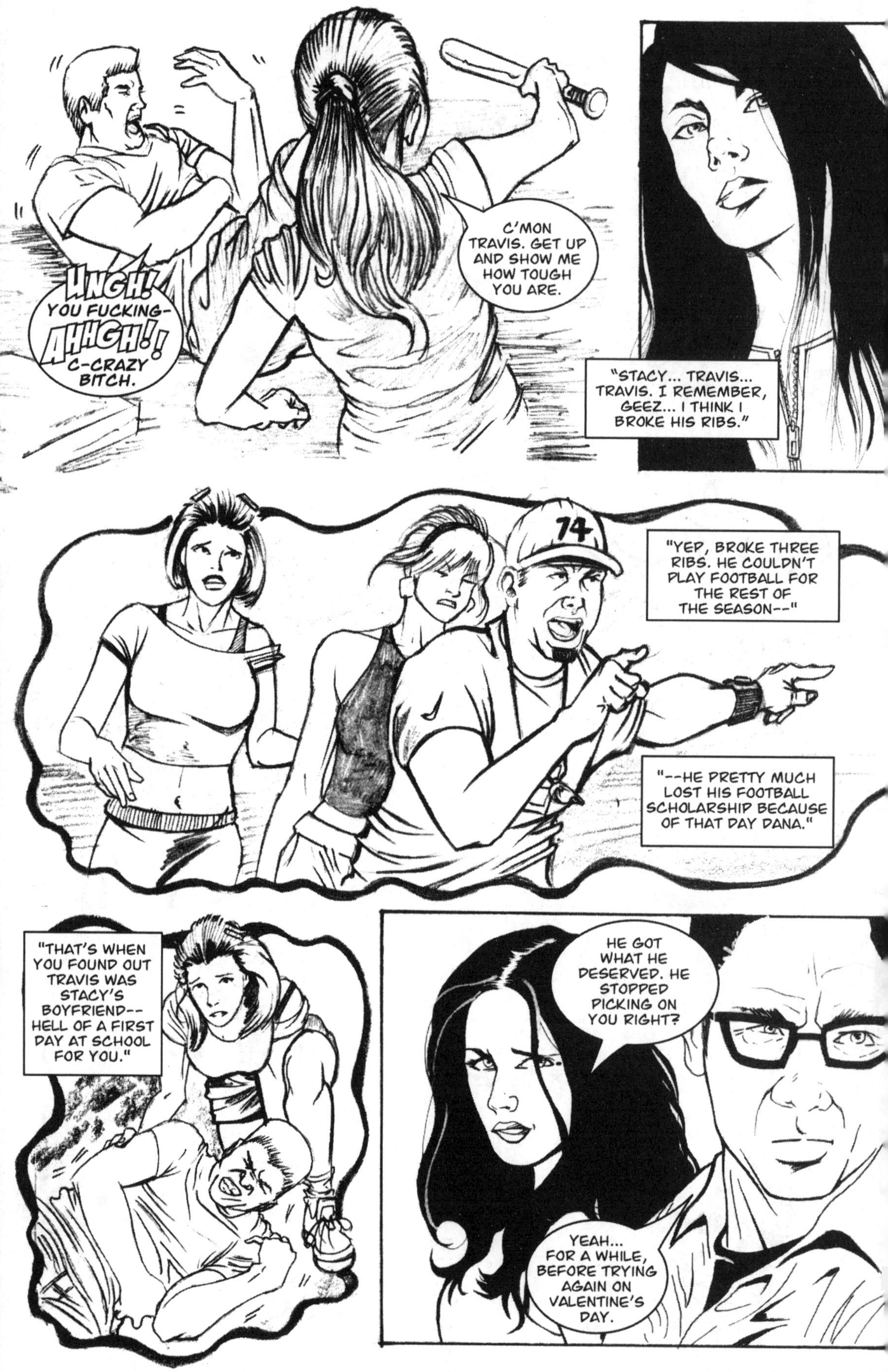
UNGH! YOU FUCKING- AHHGH!! C-CRAZY BITCH.
C'MON TRAVIS. GET UP AND SHOW ME HOW TOUGH YOU ARE.
"STACY... TRAVIS... TRAVIS. I REMEMBER, GEEZ... I THINK I BROKE HIS RIBS."
74
"YEP, BROKE THREE RIBS. HE COULDN'T PLAY FOOTBALL FOR THE REST OF THE SEASON--"
"--HE PRETTY MUCH LOST HIS FOOTBALL SCHOLARSHIP BECAUSE OF THAT DAY DANA."
"THAT'S WHEN YOU FOUND OUT TRAVIS WAS STACY'S BOYFRIEND-- HELL OF A FIRST DAY AT SCHOOL FOR YOU."
HE GOT WHAT HE DESERVED. HE STOPPED PICKING ON YOU RIGHT?
YEAH... FOR A WHILE, BEFORE TRYING AGAIN ON VALENTINE'S DAY.

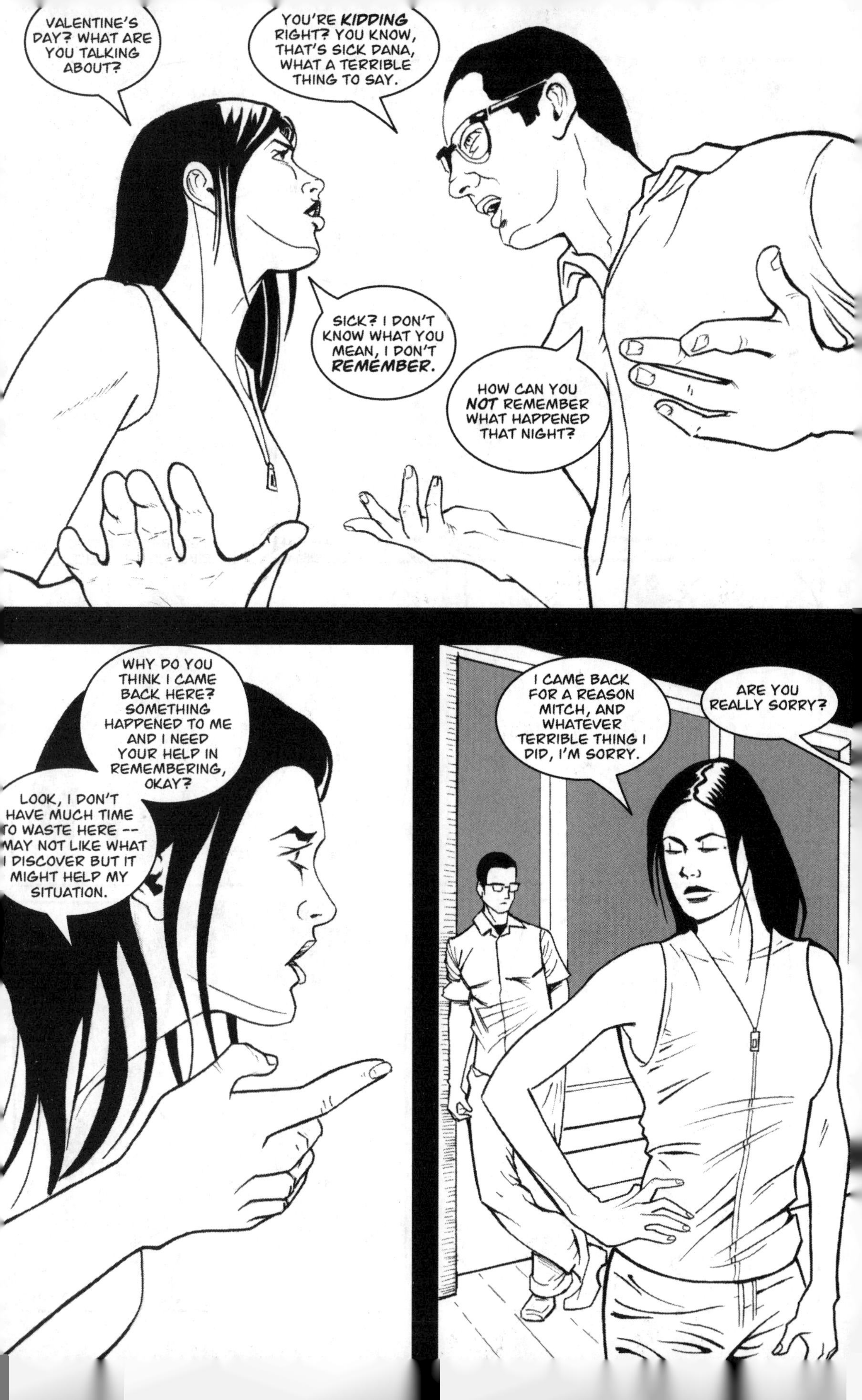
VALENTINE'S DAY? WHAT ARE YOU TALKING ABOUT?
YOU'RE KIDDING RIGHT? YOU KNOW, THAT'S SICK DANA, WHAT A TERRIBLE THING TO SAY.
SICK? I DON'T KNOW WHAT YOU MEAN, I DON'T REMEMBER.
HOW CAN YOU NOT REMEMBER WHAT HAPPENED THAT NIGHT?
WHY DO YOU THINK I CAME BACK HERE? SOMETHING HAPPENED TO ME AND I NEED YOUR HELP IN REMEMBERING, OKAY?
LOOK, I DON'T HAVE MUCH TIME TO WASTE HERE -- MAY NOT LIKE WHAT I DISCOVER BUT IT MIGHT HELP MY SITUATION.
I CAME BACK FOR A REASON MITCH, AND WHATEVER TERRIBLE THING I DID, I'M SORRY.
ARE YOU REALLY SORRY?

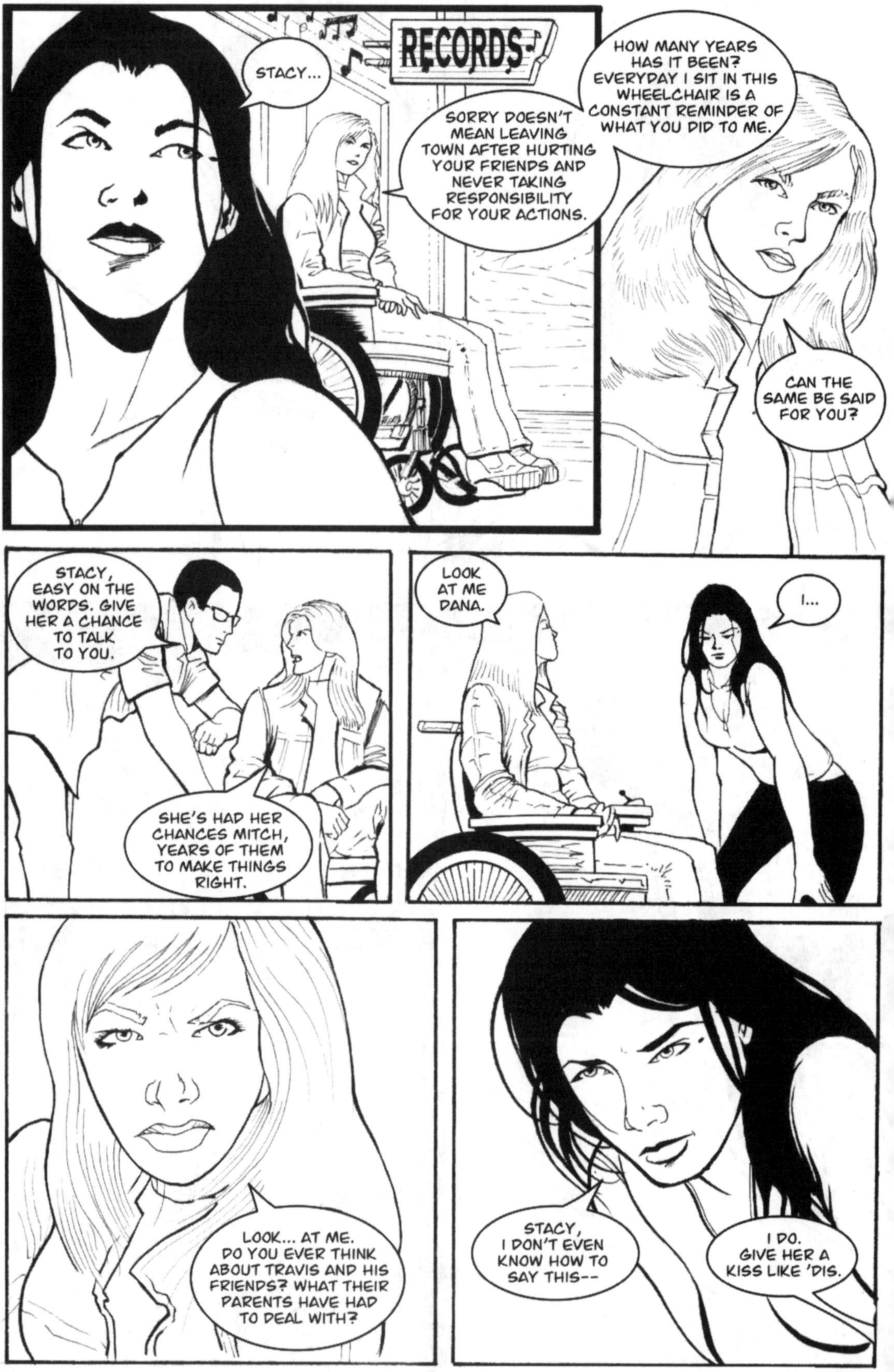
RECORDS
STACY...
SORRY DOESN'T MEAN LEAVING TOWN AFTER HURTING YOUR FRIENDS AND NEVER TAKING RESPONSIBILITY FOR YOUR ACTIONS.
HOW MANY YEARS HAS IT BEEN? EVERYDAY I SIT IN THIS WHEELCHAIR IS A CONSTANT REMINDER OF WHAT YOU DID TO ME.
CAN THE SAME BE SAID FOR YOU?
STACY, EASY ON THE WORDS. GIVE HER A CHANCE TO TALK TO YOU.
SHE'S HAD HER CHANCES MITCH, YEARS OF THEM TO MAKE THINGS RIGHT.
LOOK AT ME DANA.
I...
LOOK... AT ME. DO YOU EVER THINK ABOUT TRAVIS AND HIS FRIENDS? WHAT THEIR PARENTS HAVE HAD TO DEAL WITH?
STACY, I DON'T EVEN KNOW HOW TO SAY THIS--
I DO. GIVE HER A KISS LIKE 'DIS.

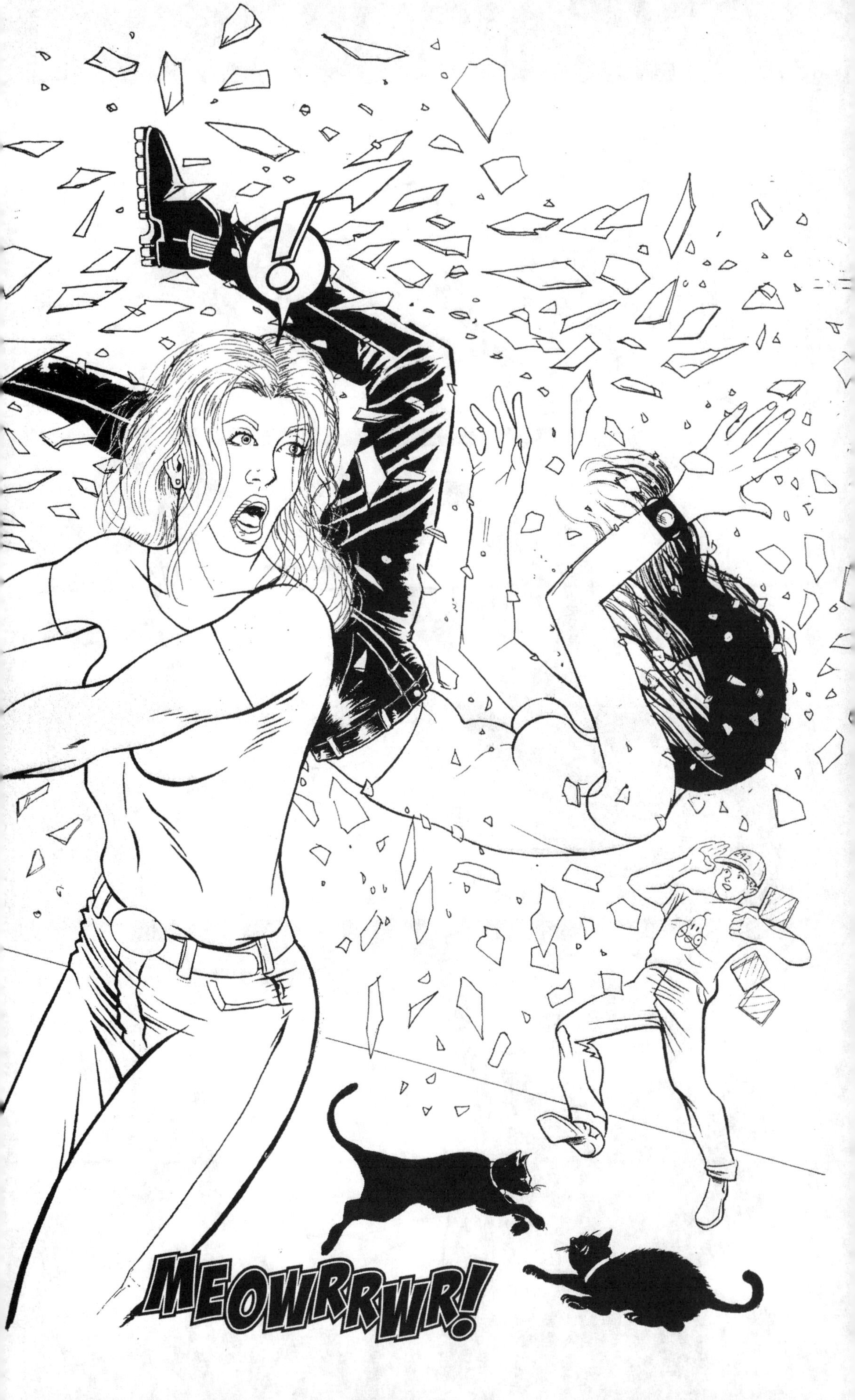
!
MEOWRRWR!

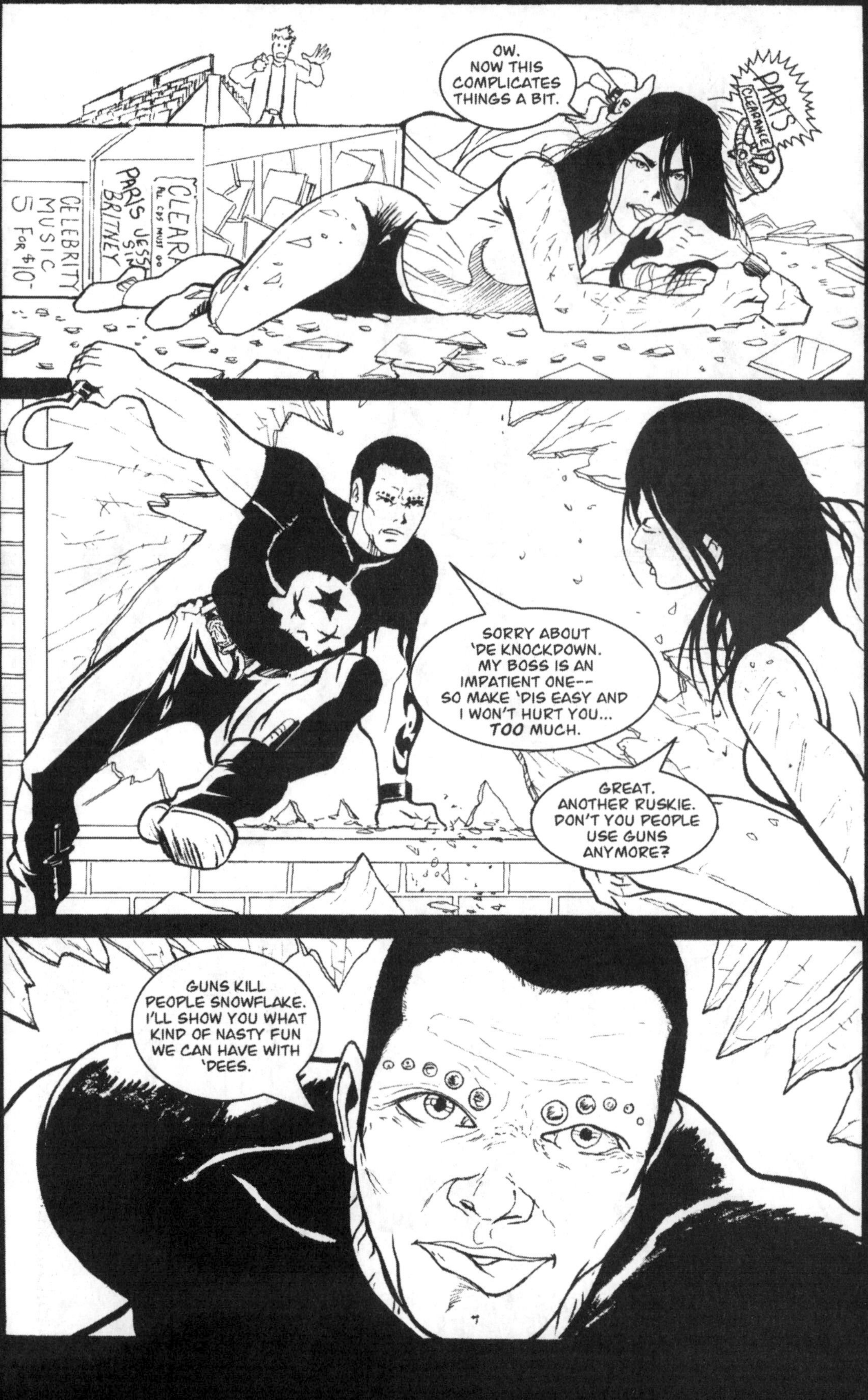
OW. NOW THIS COMPLICATES THINGS A BIT.
PARIS CLEARANCE
CLEARA ALL CDS MUST GO
PARIS JESS SIM BRITNEY
CELEBRITY MUSIC 5 FOR $10-
SORRY ABOUT 'DE KNOCKDOWN. MY BOSS IS AN IMPATIENT ONE-- SO MAKE 'DIS EASY AND I WON'T HURT YOU... TOO MUCH.
GREAT. ANOTHER RUSKIE. DON'T YOU PEOPLE USE GUNS ANYMORE?
GUNS KILL PEOPLE SNOWFLAKE. I'LL SHOW YOU WHAT KIND OF NASTY FUN WE CAN HAVE WITH 'DEES.

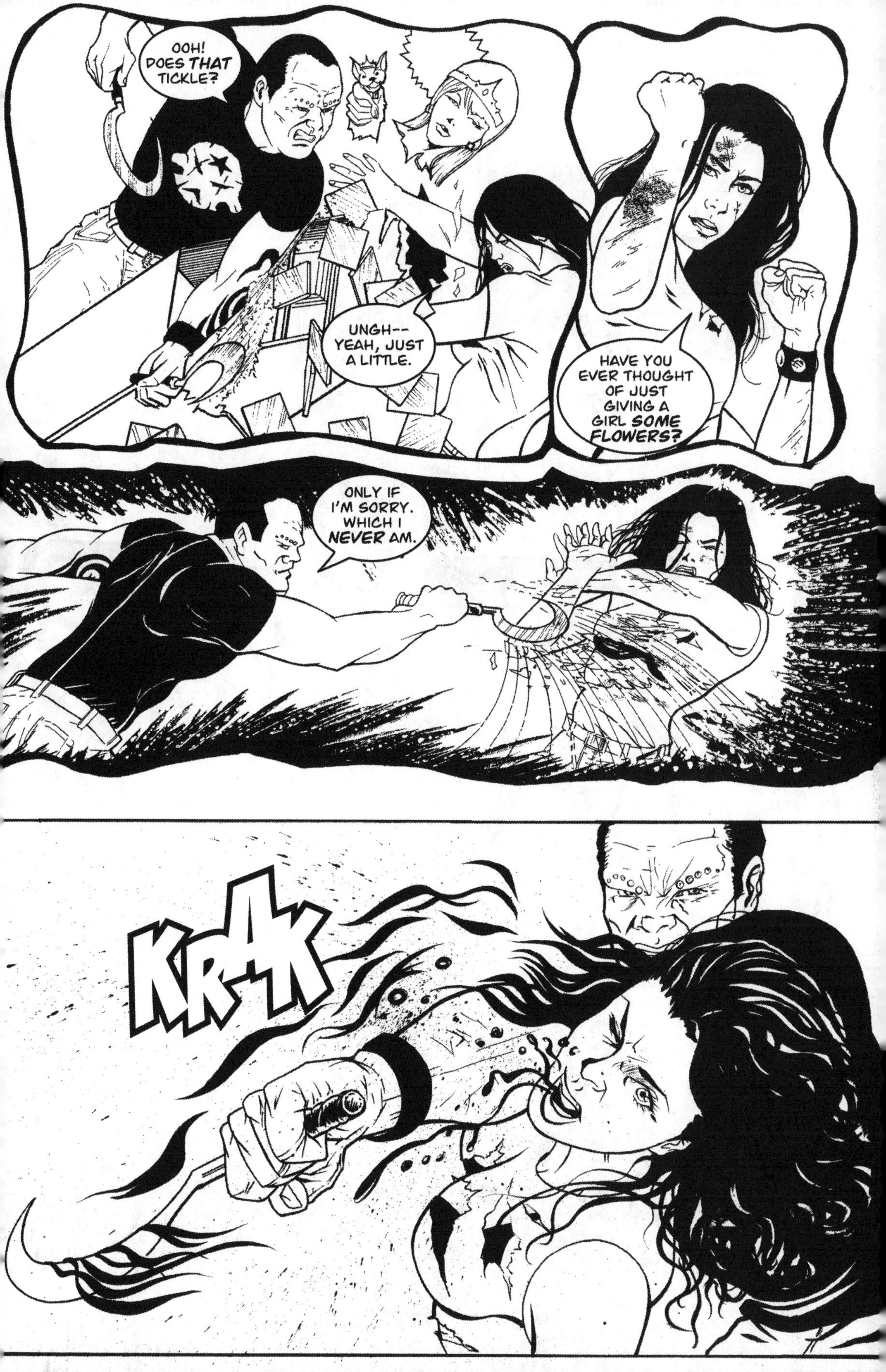
OOH! DOES THAT TICKLE?
UNGH-- YEAH, JUST A LITTLE.
HAVE YOU EVER THOUGHT OF JUST GIVING A GIRL SOME FLOWERS?
ONLY IF I'M SORRY. WHICH I NEVER AM.
KRAK

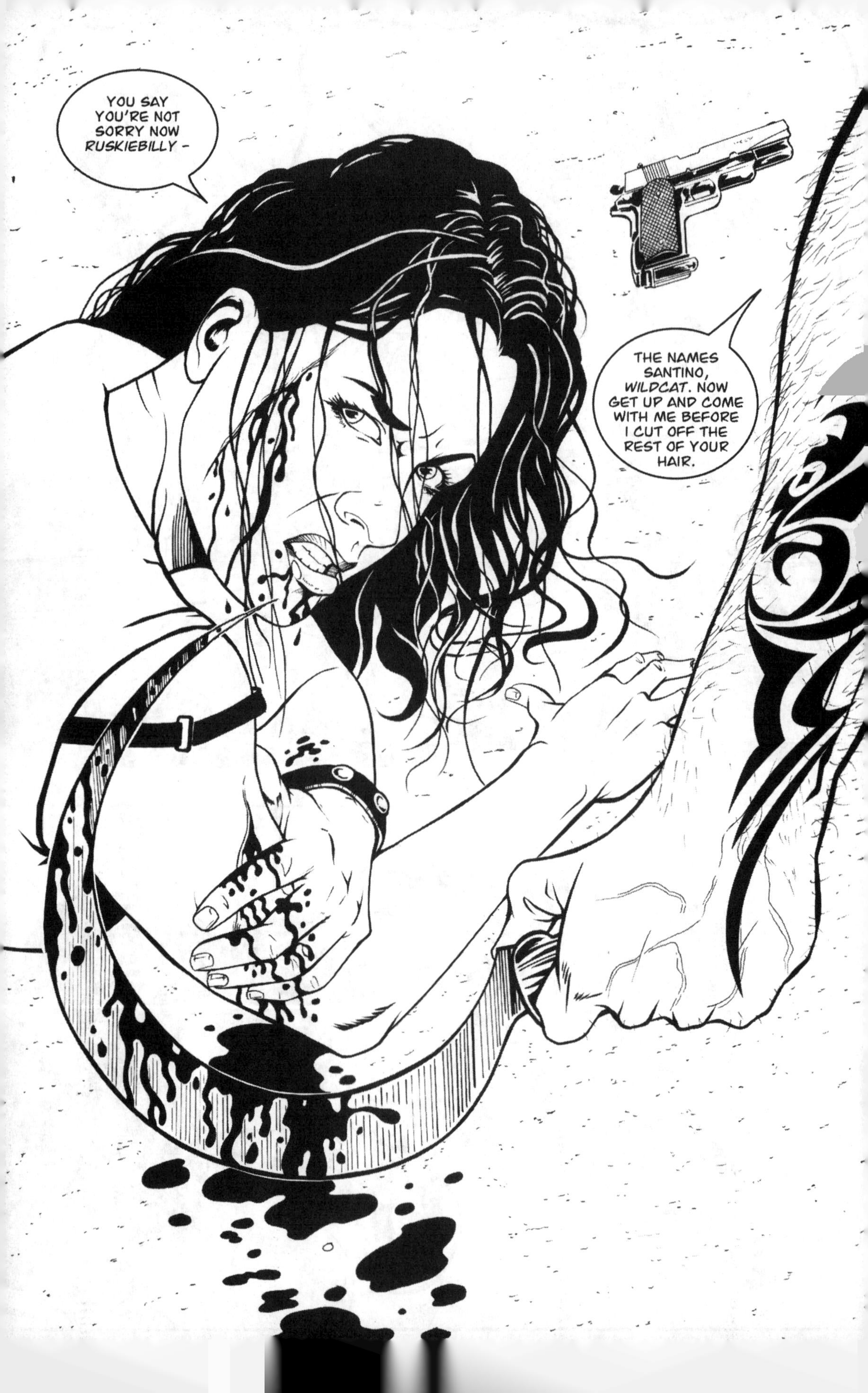
YOU SAY YOU'RE NOT SORRY NOW RUSKIEBILLY -
THE NAMES SANTINO, WILDCAT. NOW GET UP AND COME WITH ME BEFORE I CUT OFF THE REST OF YOUR HAIR.

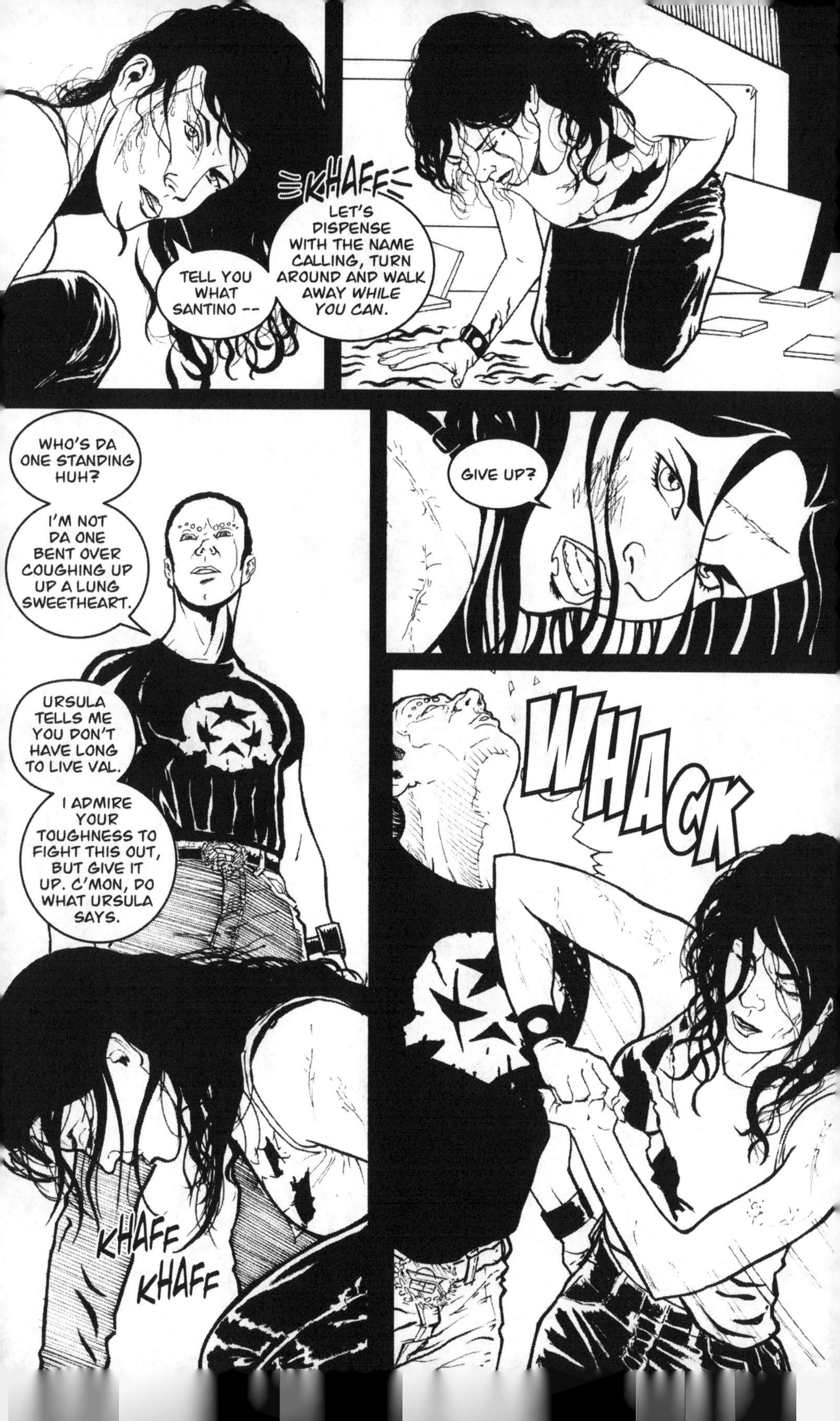
KHAFF
TELL YOU WHAT SANTINO --
LET'S DISPENSE WITH THE NAME CALLING, TURN AROUND AND WALK AWAY WHILE YOU CAN.
WHO'S DA ONE STANDING HUH?
I'M NOT DA ONE BENT OVER COUGHING UP A LUNG SWEETHEART.
URSULA TELLS ME YOU DON'T HAVE LONG TO LIVE VAL.
I ADMIRE YOUR TOUGHNESS TO FIGHT THIS OUT, BUT GIVE IT UP. C'MON, DO WHAT URSULA SAYS.
KHAFF KHAFF
GIVE UP?
WHACK

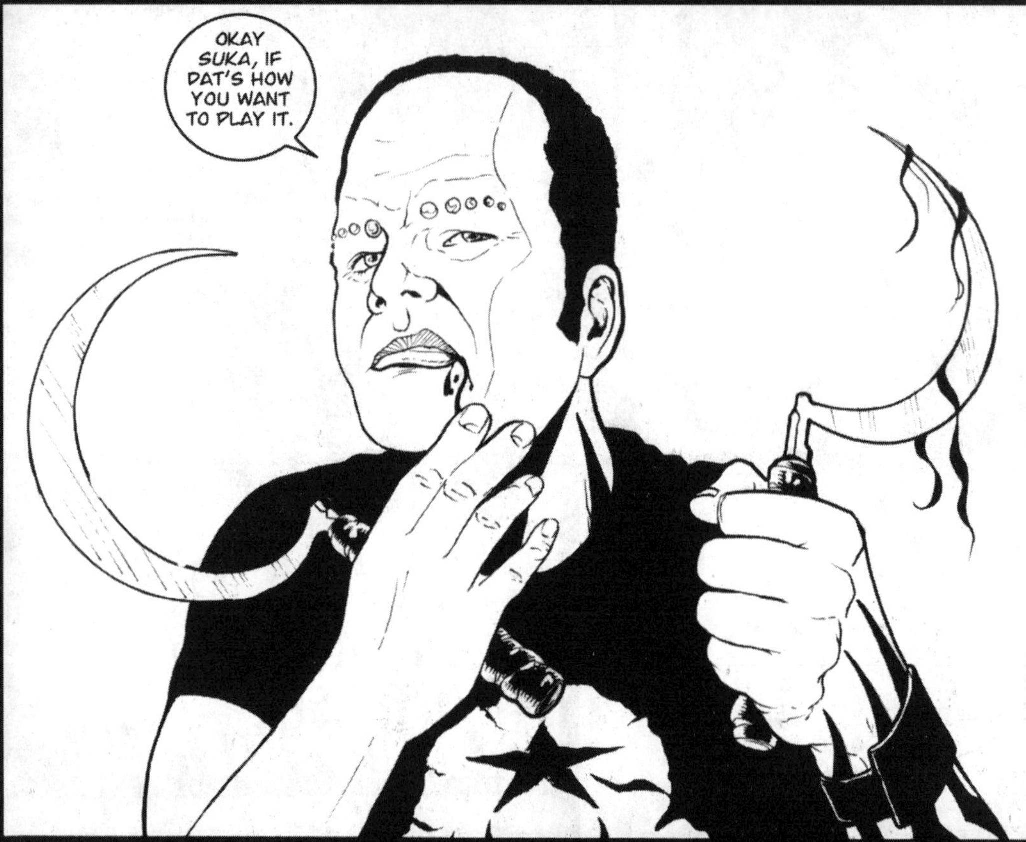
OKAY SUKA, IF DAT'S HOW YOU WANT TO PLAY IT.

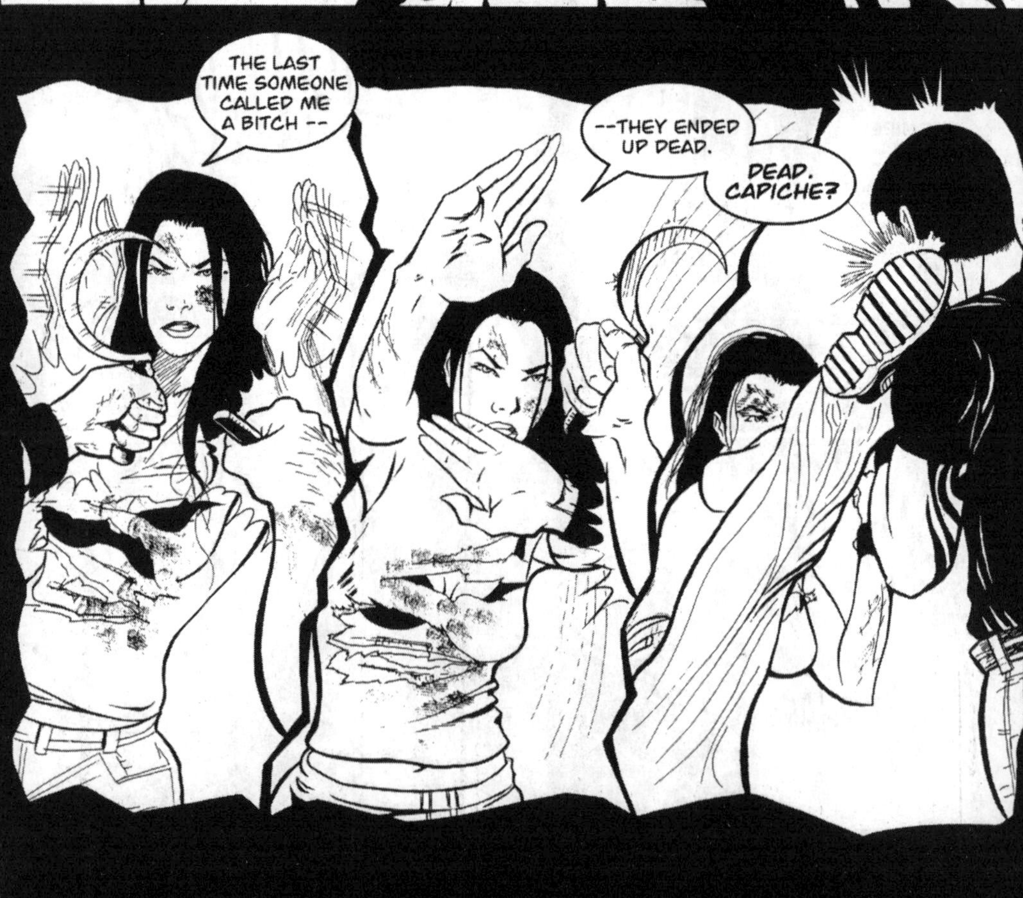
THE LAST TIME SOMEONE CALLED ME A BITCH --
--THEY ENDED UP DEAD.
DEAD. CAPICHE?

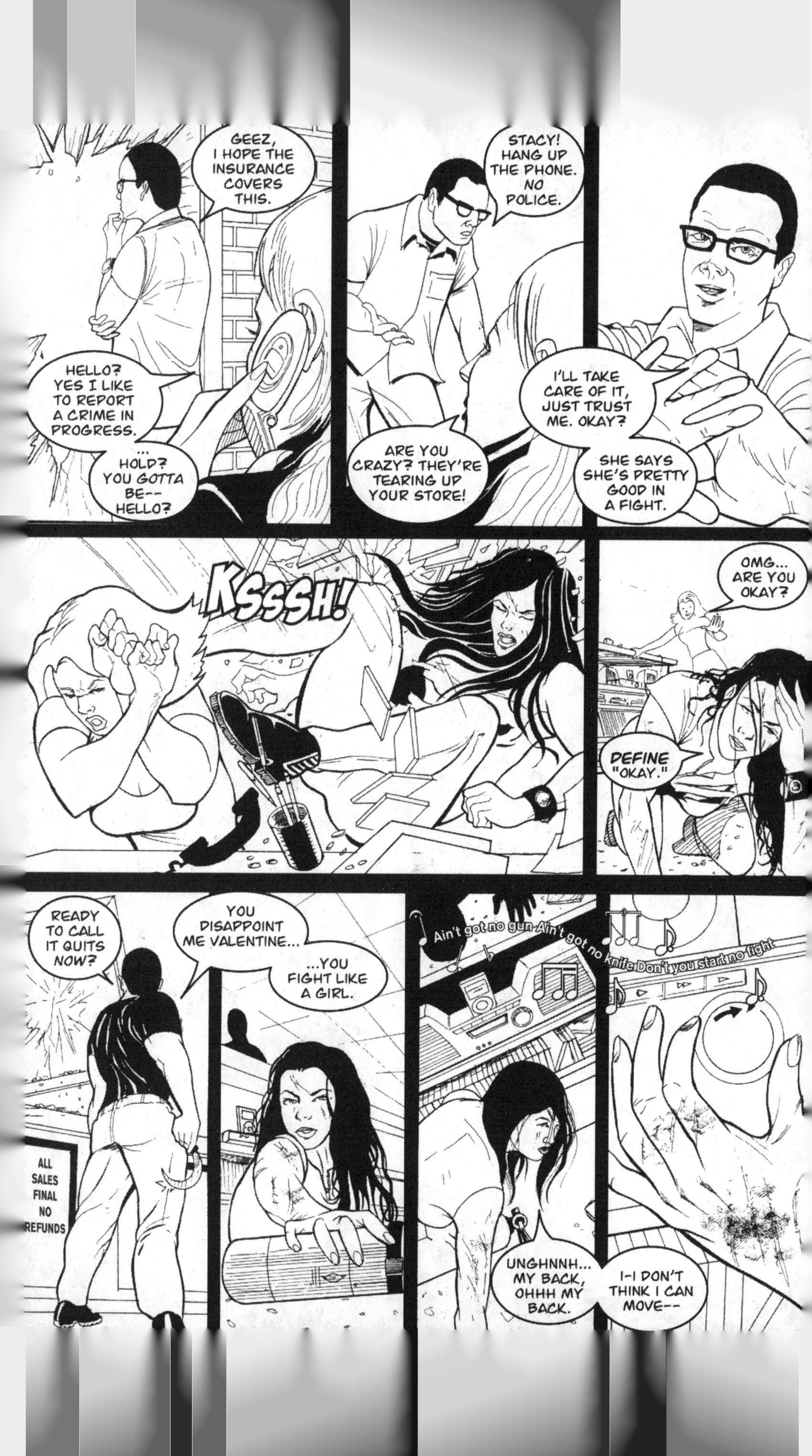
GEEZ, I HOPE THE INSURANCE COVERS THIS.
HELLO? YES I LIKE TO REPORT A CRIME IN PROGRESS.
... HOLD? YOU GOTTA BE-- HELLO?
STACY! HANG UP THE PHONE. NO POLICE.
ARE YOU CRAZY? THEY'RE TEARING UP YOUR STORE!
I'LL TAKE CARE OF IT, JUST TRUST ME. OKAY?
SHE SAYS SHE'S PRETTY GOOD IN A FIGHT.
KSSSH!
OMG... ARE YOU OKAY?
DEFINE "OKAY."
READY TO CALL IT QUITS NOW?
ALL SALES FINAL NO REFUNDS
YOU DISAPPOINT ME VALENTINE...
...YOU FIGHT LIKE A GIRL.
Ain't got no gun Ain't got no knife Don't you start no fight
UNGHNNH... MY BACK, OHHH MY BACK.
I-I DON'T THINK I CAN MOVE--

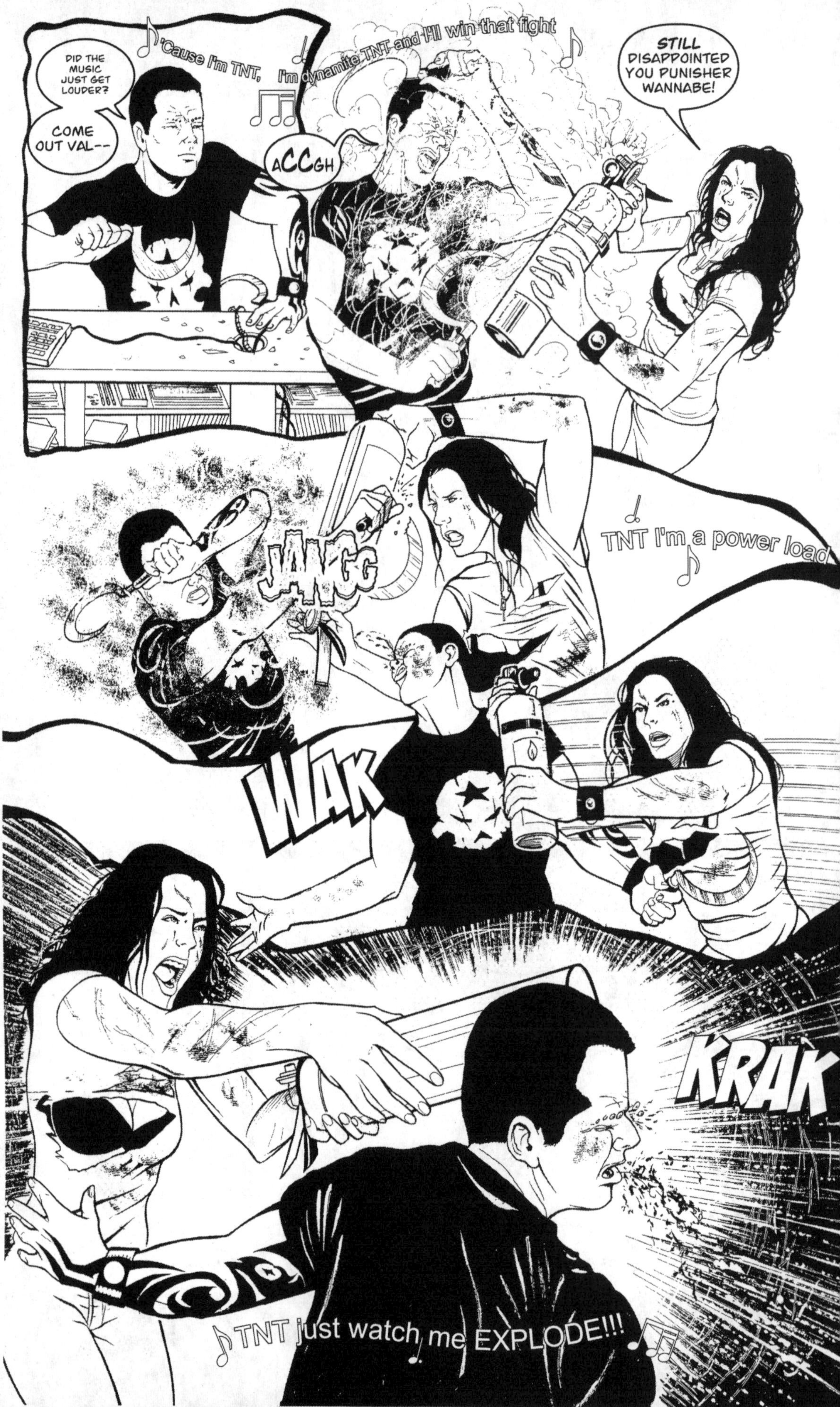
DID THE MUSIC JUST GET LOUDER?
COME OUT VAL--
'Cause I'm TNT, I'm dynamite TNT and I'll win that fight
ACCGH
STILL DISAPPOINTED YOU PUNISHER WANNABE!
JANGG
TNT I'm a power load
WAK
KRAK
TNT just watch me EXPLODE!!!

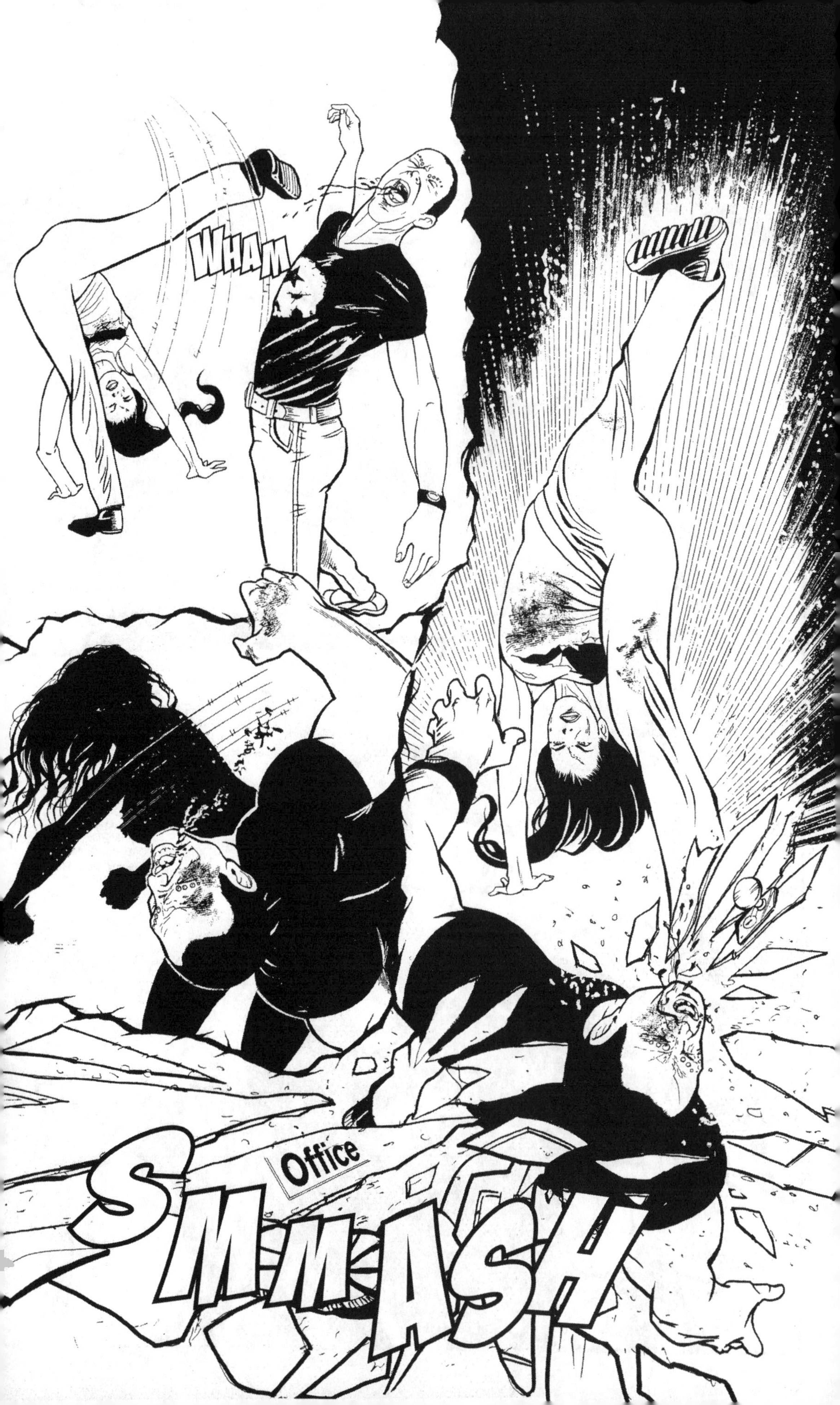
WHAM
Office
SMMASH

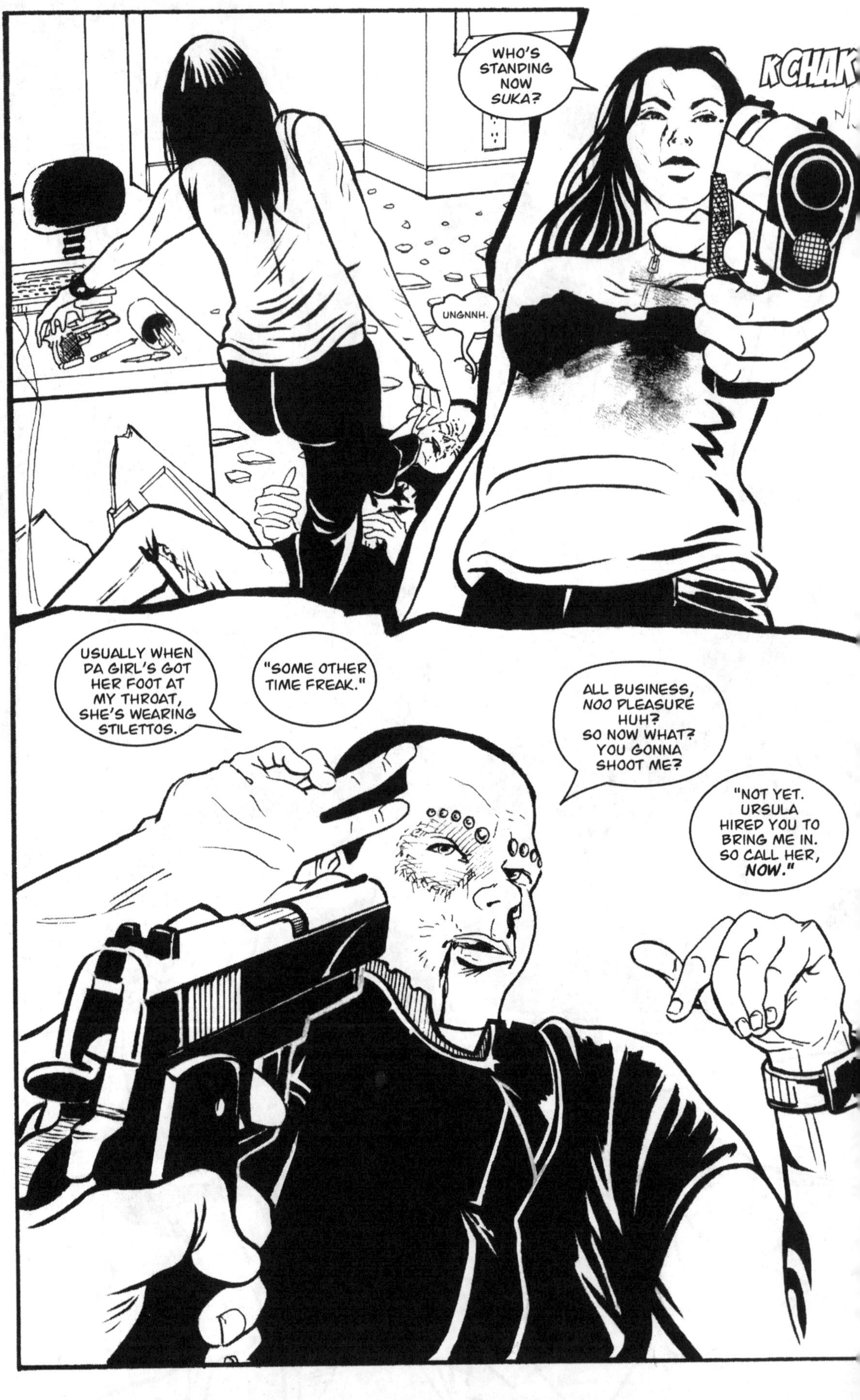
WHO'S STANDING NOW SUKA?
KCHAK
UNGNNH.
USUALLY WHEN DA GIRL'S GOT HER FOOT AT MY THROAT, SHE'S WEARING STILETTOS.
"SOME OTHER TIME FREAK."
ALL BUSINESS, NOO PLEASURE HUH? SO NOW WHAT? YOU GONNA SHOOT ME?
"NOT YET. URSULA HIRED YOU TO BRING ME IN. SO CALL HER, NOW."

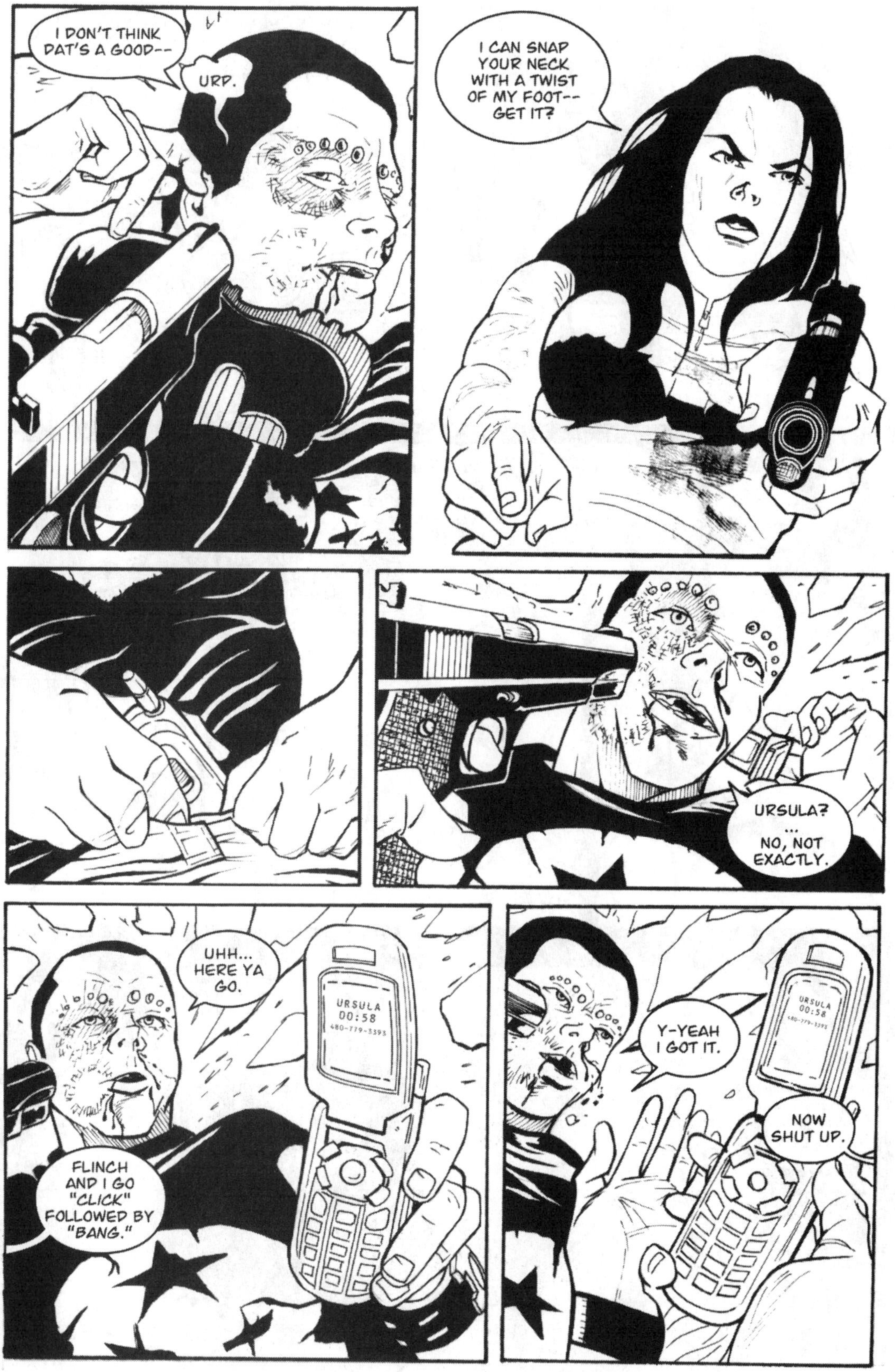
I DON'T THINK DAT'S A GOOD--
URP.
I CAN SNAP YOUR NECK WITH A TWIST OF MY FOOT-- GET IT?
URSULA? ... NO, NOT EXACTLY.
UHH... HERE YA GO.
URSULA
00:58
480-779-3393
FLINCH AND I GO "CLICK" FOLLOWED BY "BANG."
Y-YEAH I GOT IT.
NOW SHUT UP.

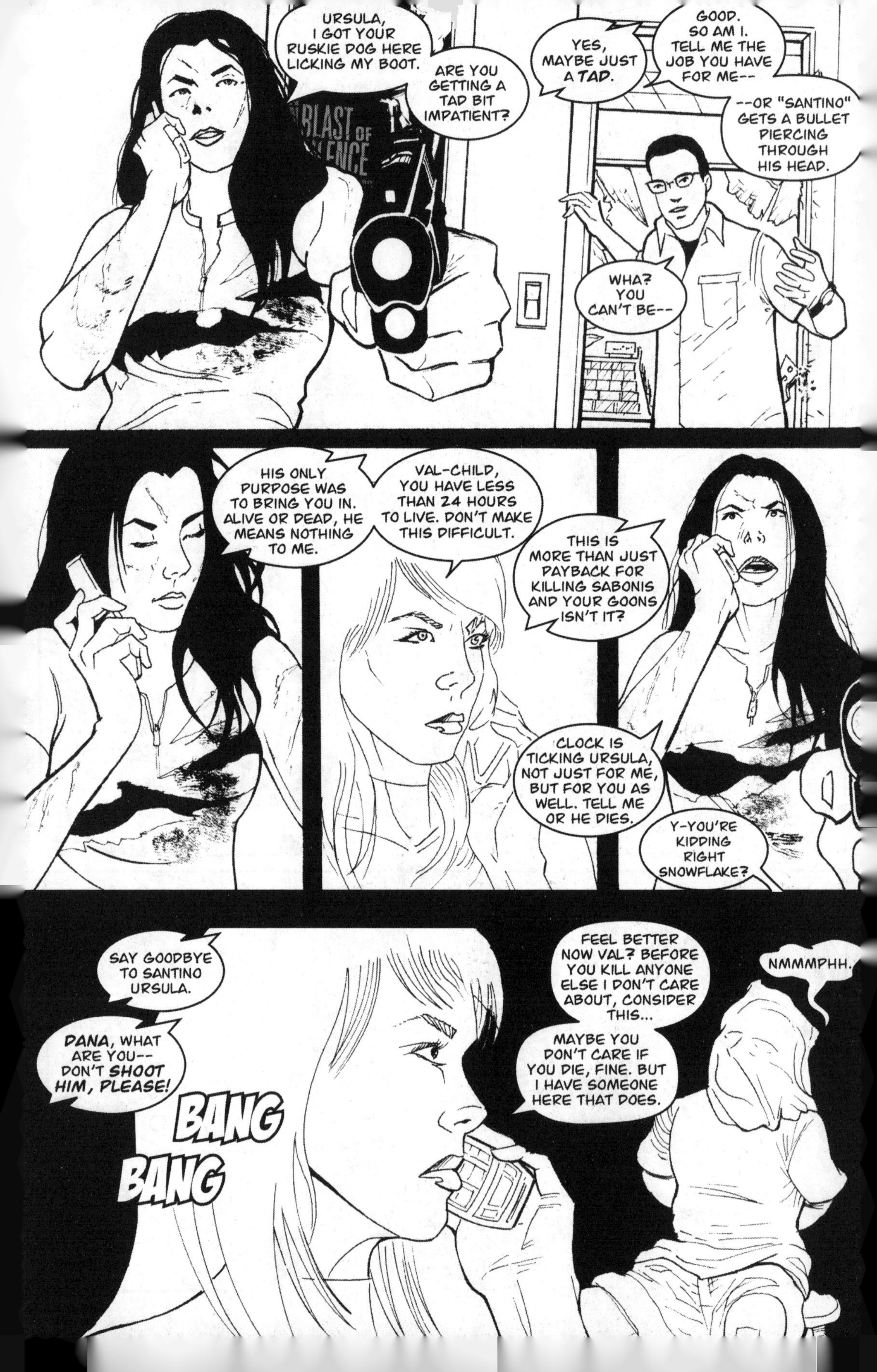
URSULA, I GOT YOUR RUSKIE DOG HERE LICKING MY BOOT.
ARE YOU GETTING A TAD BIT IMPATIENT?
BLAST OF
YES, MAYBE JUST A TAD.
GOOD. SO AM I. TELL ME THE JOB YOU HAVE FOR ME--
--OR "SANTINO" GETS A BULLET PIERCING THROUGH HIS HEAD.
WHA? YOU CAN'T BE--
HIS ONLY PURPOSE WAS TO BRING YOU IN. ALIVE OR DEAD, HE MEANS NOTHING TO ME.
VAL-CHILD, YOU HAVE LESS THAN 24 HOURS TO LIVE. DON'T MAKE THIS DIFFICULT.
THIS IS MORE THAN JUST PAYBACK FOR KILLING SABONIS AND YOUR GOONS ISN'T IT?
CLOCK IS TICKING URSULA, NOT JUST FOR ME, BUT FOR YOU AS WELL. TELL ME OR HE DIES.
Y-YOU'RE KIDDING RIGHT SNOWFLAKE?
SAY GOODBYE TO SANTINO URSULA.
DANA, WHAT ARE YOU-- DON'T SHOOT HIM, PLEASE!
BANG
BANG
FEEL BETTER NOW VAL? BEFORE YOU KILL ANYONE ELSE I DON'T CARE ABOUT, CONSIDER THIS...
MAYBE YOU DON'T CARE IF YOU DIE, FINE. BUT I HAVE SOMEONE HERE THAT DOES.
NMMMPHH.

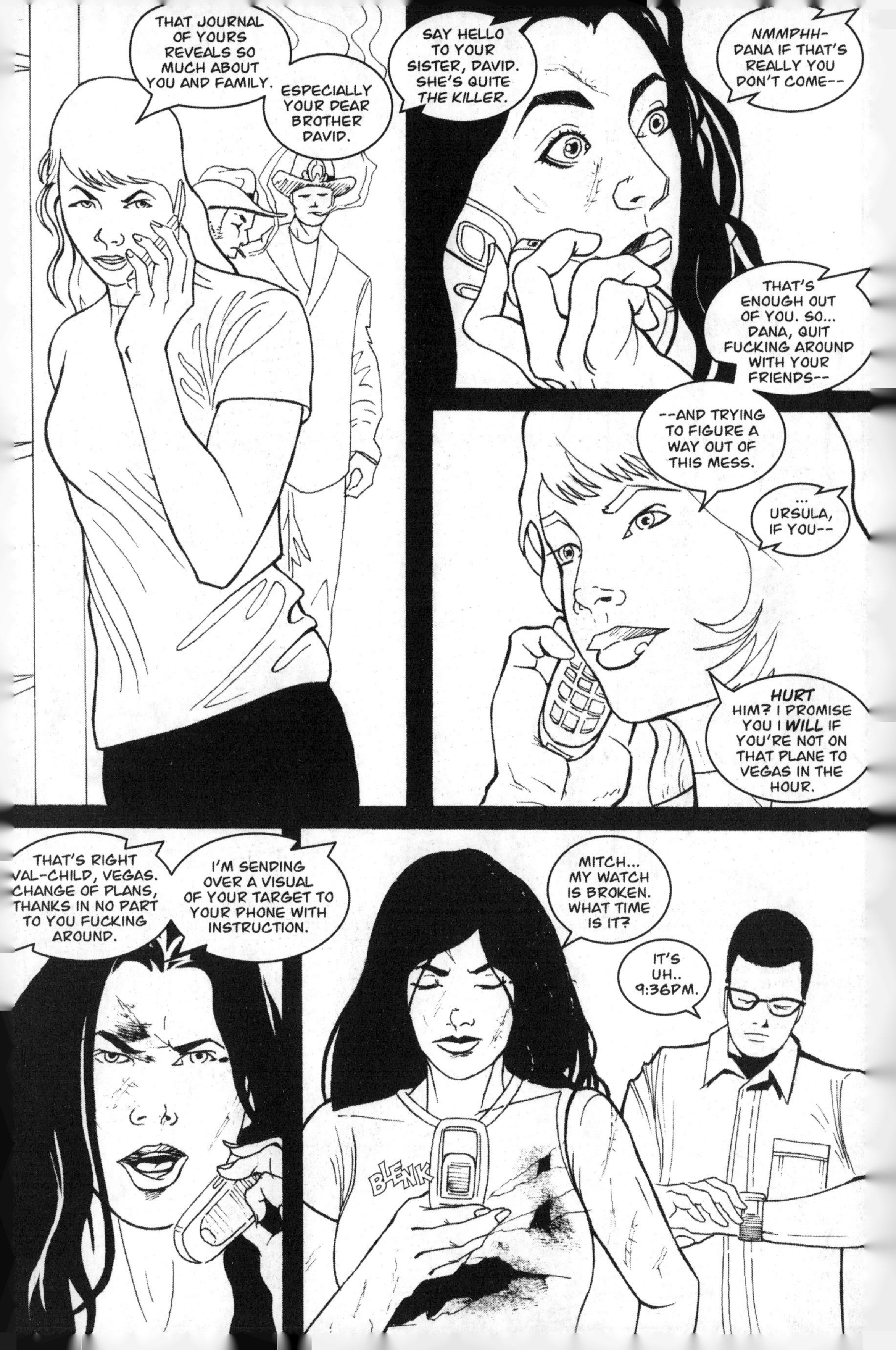

THAT JOURNAL OF YOURS REVEALS SO MUCH ABOUT YOU AND FAMILY.
ESPECIALLY YOUR DEAR BROTHER DAVID.
SAY HELLO TO YOUR SISTER, DAVID. SHE'S QUITE THE KILLER.
NMMPHH- DANA IF THAT'S REALLY YOU DON'T COME--
THAT'S ENOUGH OUT OF YOU. SO... DANA, QUIT FUCKING AROUND WITH YOUR FRIENDS--
--AND TRYING TO FIGURE A WAY OUT OF THIS MESS.
... URSULA, IF YOU--
HURT HIM? I PROMISE YOU I WILL IF YOU'RE NOT ON THAT PLANE TO VEGAS IN THE HOUR.
THAT'S RIGHT VAL-CHILD, VEGAS. CHANGE OF PLANS, THANKS IN NO PART TO YOU FUCKING AROUND.
I'M SENDING OVER A VISUAL OF YOUR TARGET TO YOUR PHONE WITH INSTRUCTION.
MITCH... MY WATCH IS BROKEN. WHAT TIME IS IT?
IT'S UH.. 9:36PM.
BLENK

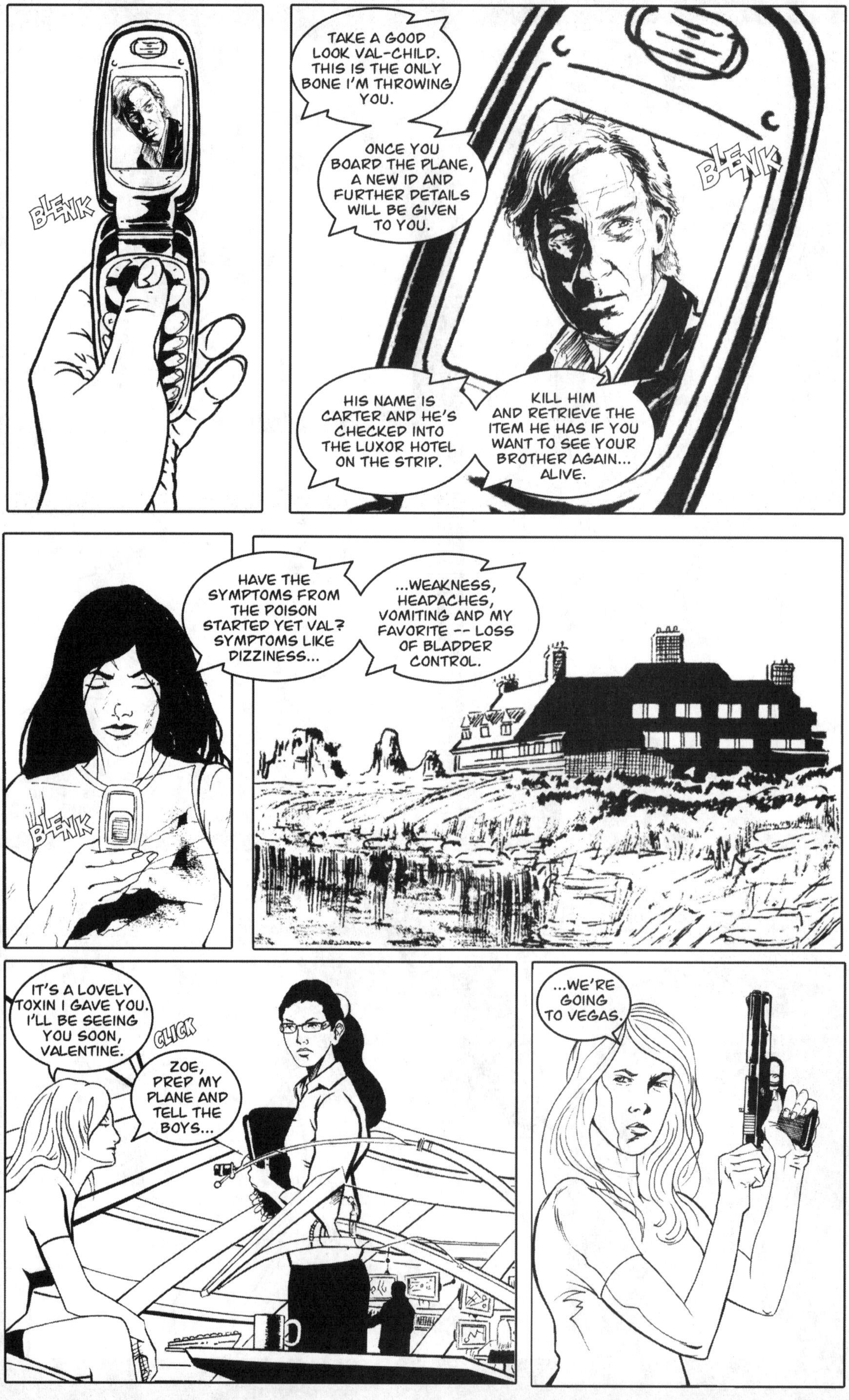
BLENK
TAKE A GOOD LOOK VAL-CHILD. THIS IS THE ONLY BONE I'M THROWING YOU.
ONCE YOU BOARD THE PLANE, A NEW ID AND FURTHER DETAILS WILL BE GIVEN TO YOU.
BLENK
HIS NAME IS CARTER AND HE'S CHECKED INTO THE LUXOR HOTEL ON THE STRIP.
KILL HIM AND RETRIEVE THE ITEM HE HAS IF YOU WANT TO SEE YOUR BROTHER AGAIN... ALIVE.
BLENK
HAVE THE SYMPTOMS FROM THE POISON STARTED YET VAL? SYMPTOMS LIKE DIZZINESS...
...WEAKNESS, HEADACHES, VOMITING AND MY FAVORITE -- LOSS OF BLADDER CONTROL.
IT'S A LOVELY TOXIN I GAVE YOU. I'LL BE SEEING YOU SOON, VALENTINE.
CLICK
ZOE, PREP MY PLANE AND TELL THE BOYS...
...WE'RE GOING TO VEGAS.

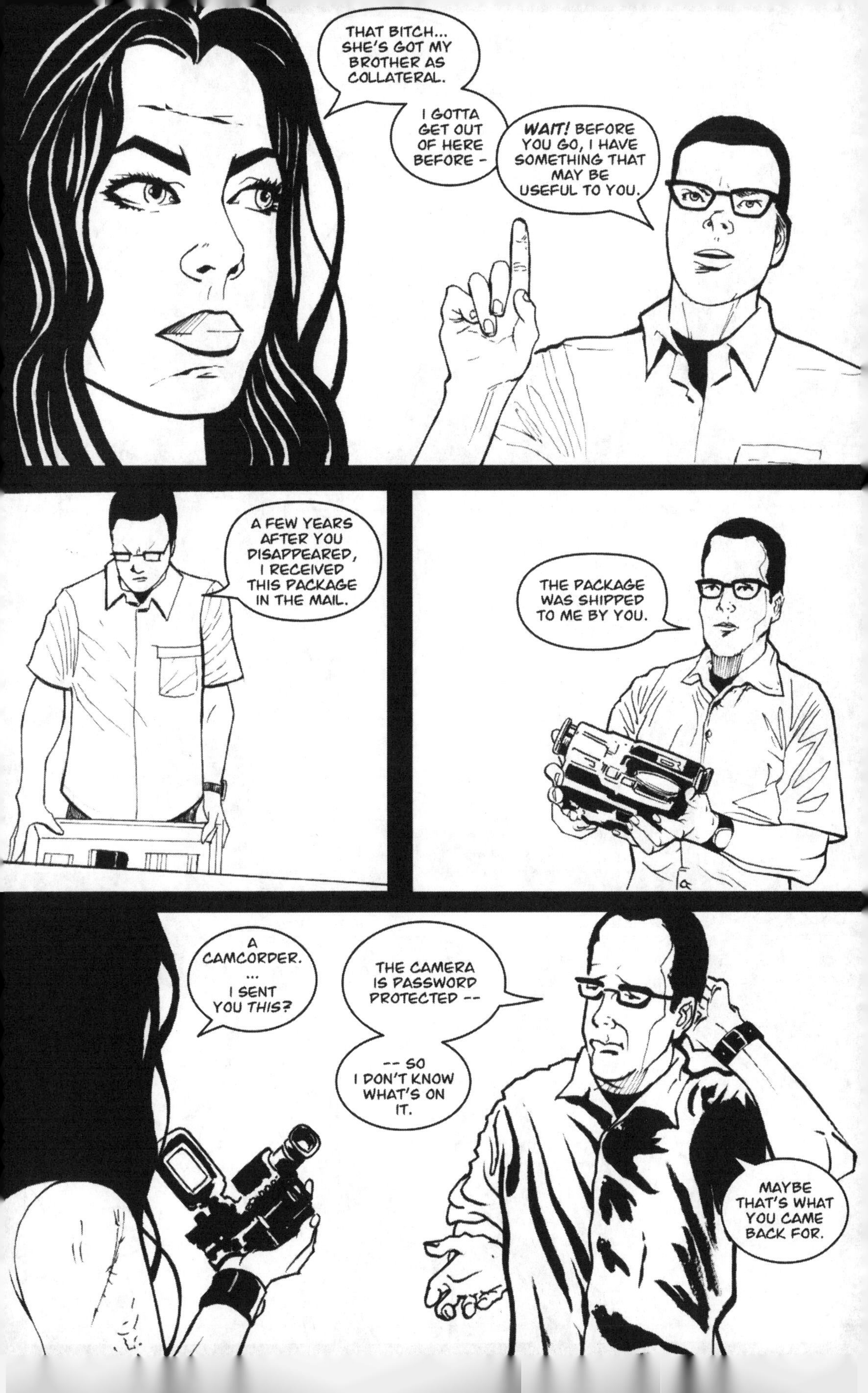
THAT BITCH... SHE'S GOT MY BROTHER AS COLLATERAL.
I GOTTA GET OUT OF HERE BEFORE -
WAIT! BEFORE YOU GO, I HAVE SOMETHING THAT MAY BE USEFUL TO YOU.
A FEW YEARS AFTER YOU DISAPPEARED, I RECEIVED THIS PACKAGE IN THE MAIL.
THE PACKAGE WAS SHIPPED TO ME BY YOU.
A CAMCORDER. ... I SENT YOU *THIS?*
THE CAMERA IS PASSWORD PROTECTED --
-- SO I DON'T KNOW WHAT'S ON IT.
MAYBE THAT'S WHAT YOU CAME BACK FOR.

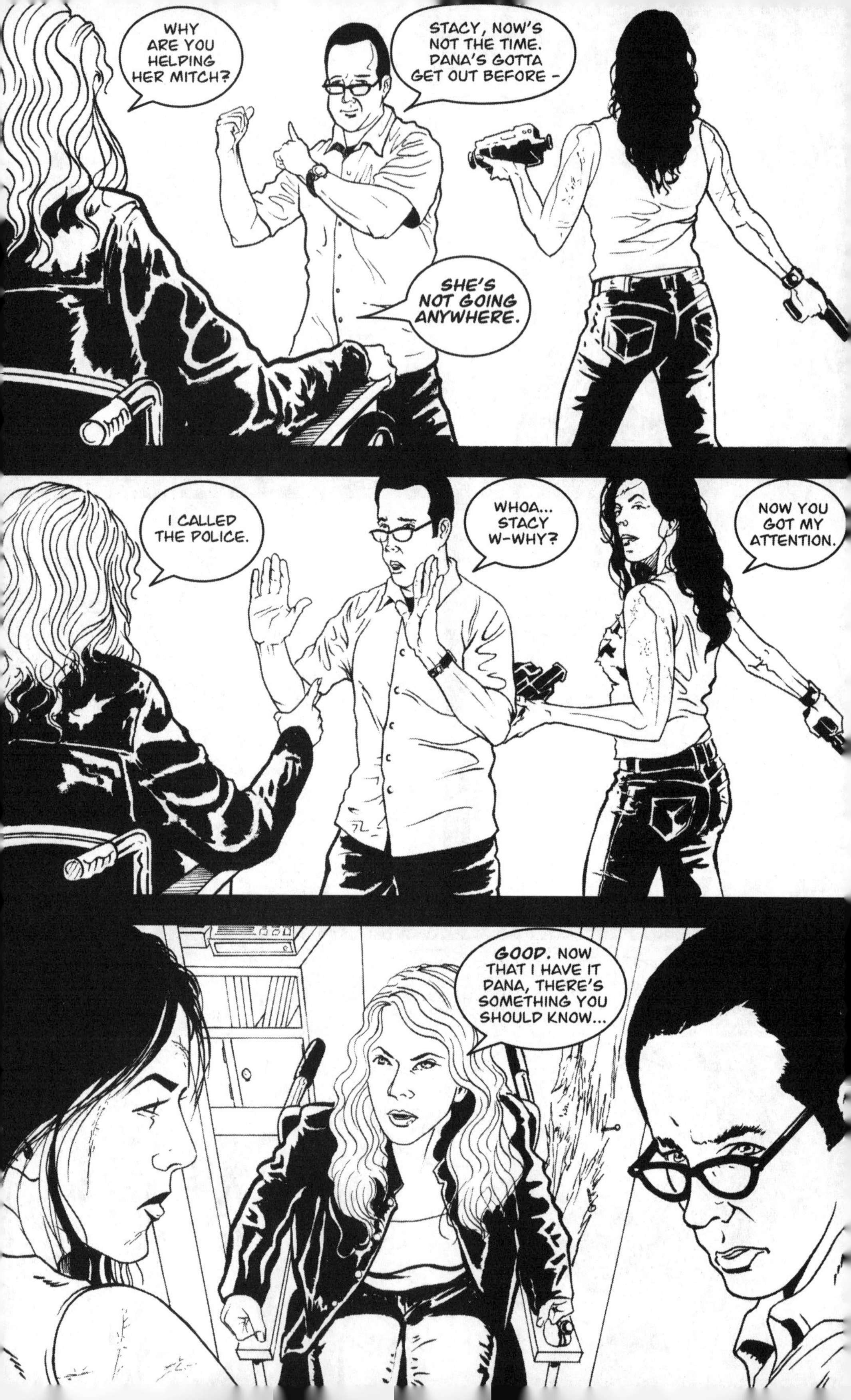
WHY ARE YOU HELPING HER MITCH?
STACY, NOW'S NOT THE TIME. DANA'S GOTTA GET OUT BEFORE -
SHE'S NOT GOING ANYWHERE.
I CALLED THE POLICE.
WHOA... STACY W-WHY?
NOW YOU GOT MY ATTENTION.
GOOD. NOW THAT I HAVE IT DANA, THERE'S SOMETHING YOU SHOULD KNOW...

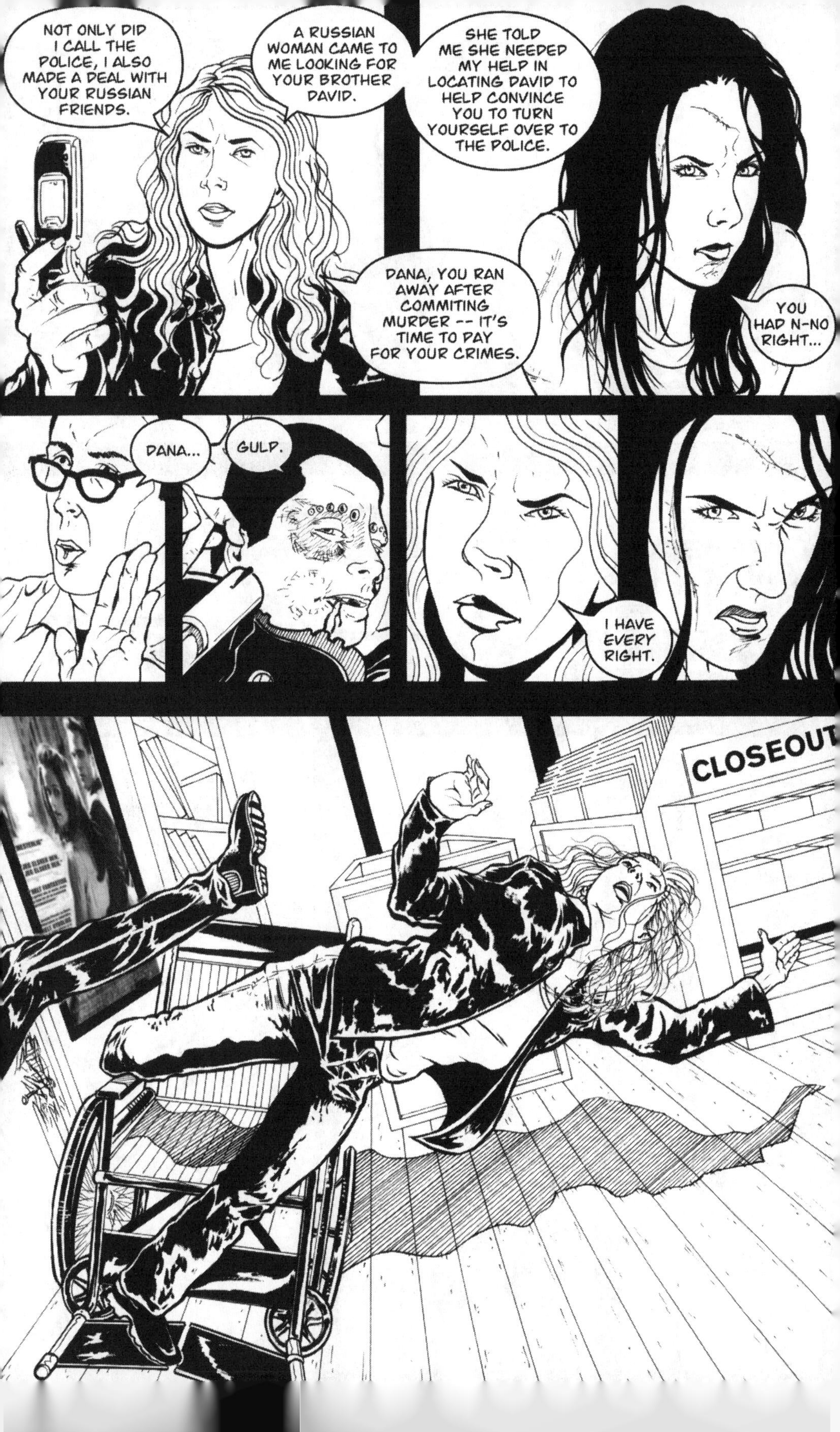
NOT ONLY DID I CALL THE POLICE, I ALSO MADE A DEAL WITH YOUR RUSSIAN FRIENDS.
A RUSSIAN WOMAN CAME TO ME LOOKING FOR YOUR BROTHER DAVID.
SHE TOLD ME SHE NEEDED MY HELP IN LOCATING DAVID TO HELP CONVINCE YOU TO TURN YOURSELF OVER TO THE POLICE.
DANA, YOU RAN AWAY AFTER COMMITING MURDER -- IT'S TIME TO PAY FOR YOUR CRIMES.
YOU HAD N-NO RIGHT...
DANA...
GULP.
I HAVE EVERY RIGHT.
CLOSEOUT

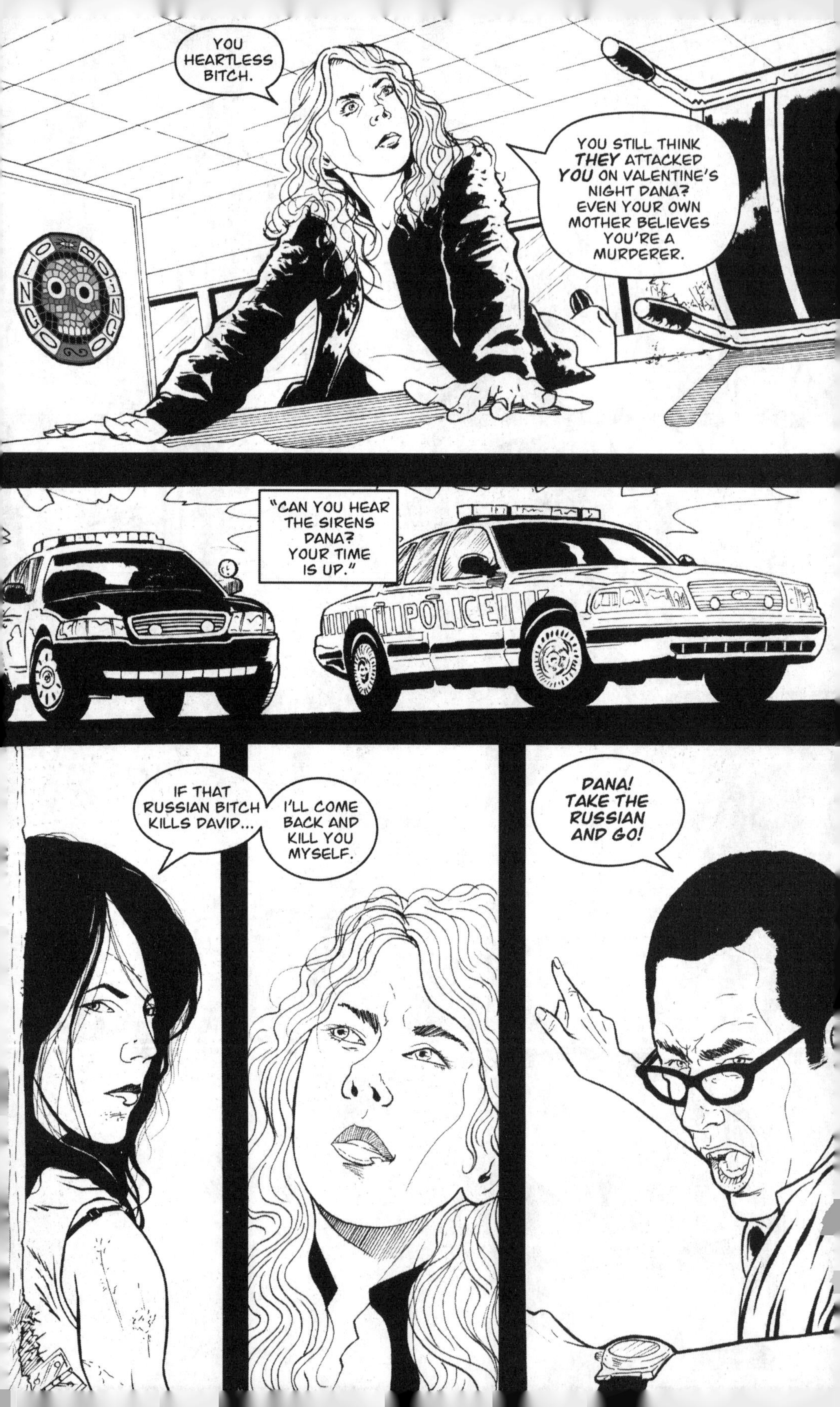
YOU HEARTLESS BITCH.
YOU STILL THINK THEY ATTACKED YOU ON VALENTINE'S NIGHT DANA? EVEN YOUR OWN MOTHER BELIEVES YOU'RE A MURDERER.
BOINGO BOINGO
"CAN YOU HEAR THE SIRENS DANA? YOUR TIME IS UP."
POLICE
IF THAT RUSSIAN BITCH KILLS DAVID...
I'LL COME BACK AND KILL YOU MYSELF.
DANA! TAKE THE RUSSIAN AND GO!

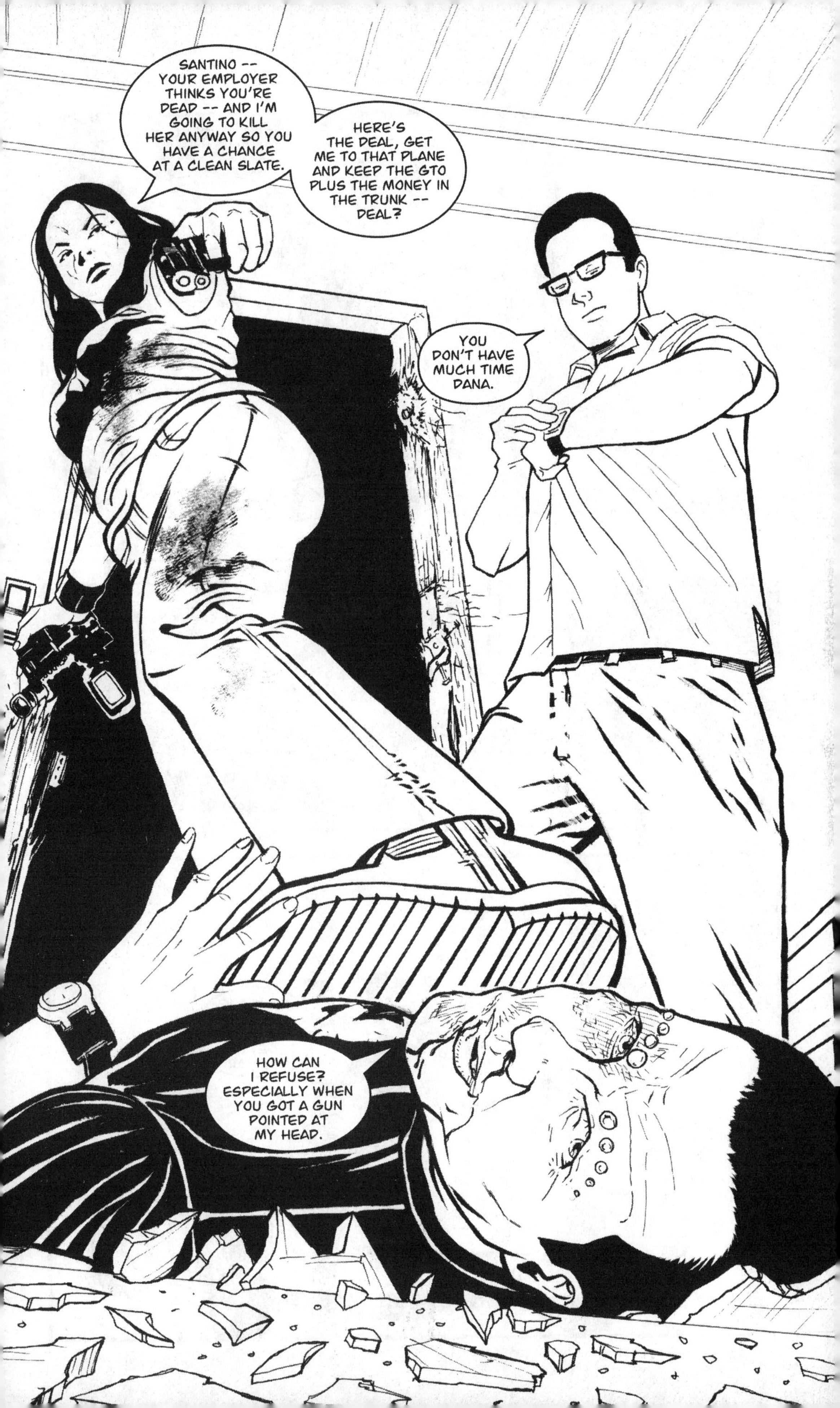
SANTINO -- YOUR EMPLOYER THINKS YOU'RE DEAD -- AND I'M GOING TO KILL HER ANYWAY SO YOU HAVE A CHANCE AT A CLEAN SLATE.
HERE'S THE DEAL, GET ME TO THAT PLANE AND KEEP THE GTO PLUS THE MONEY IN THE TRUNK -- DEAL?
YOU DON'T HAVE MUCH TIME DANA.
HOW CAN I REFUSE? ESPECIALLY WHEN YOU GOT A GUN POINTED AT MY HEAD.

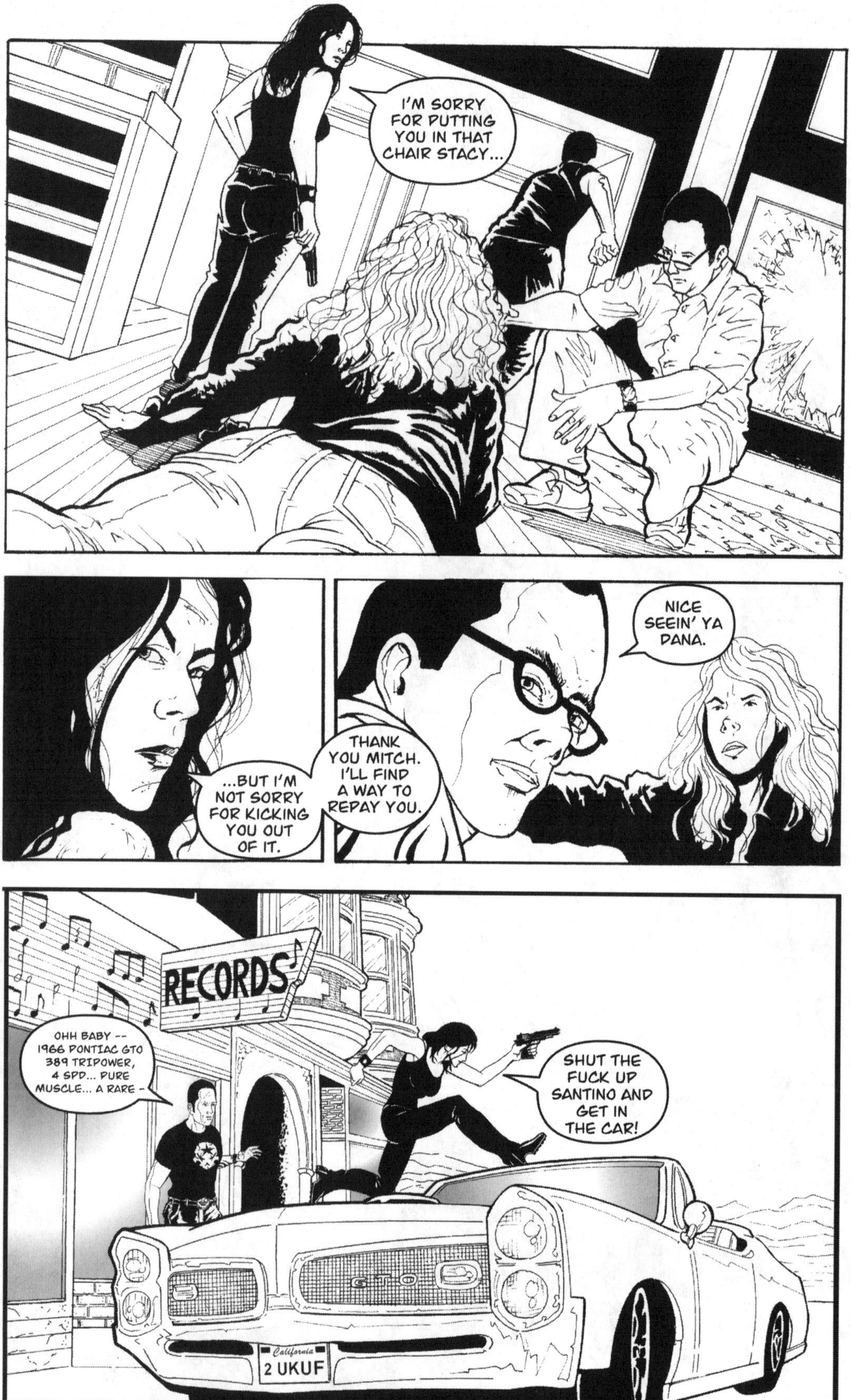
I'M SORRY FOR PUTTING YOU IN THAT CHAIR STACY...
...BUT I'M NOT SORRY FOR KICKING YOU OUT OF IT.
NICE SEEIN' YA DANA.
THANK YOU MITCH. I'LL FIND A WAY TO REPAY YOU.
RECORDS
OHH BABY -- 1966 PONTIAC GTO 389 TRIPOWER, 4 SPD... PURE MUSCLE... A RARE -
SHUT THE FUCK UP SANTINO AND GET IN THE CAR!
GTO
California
2 UKUF

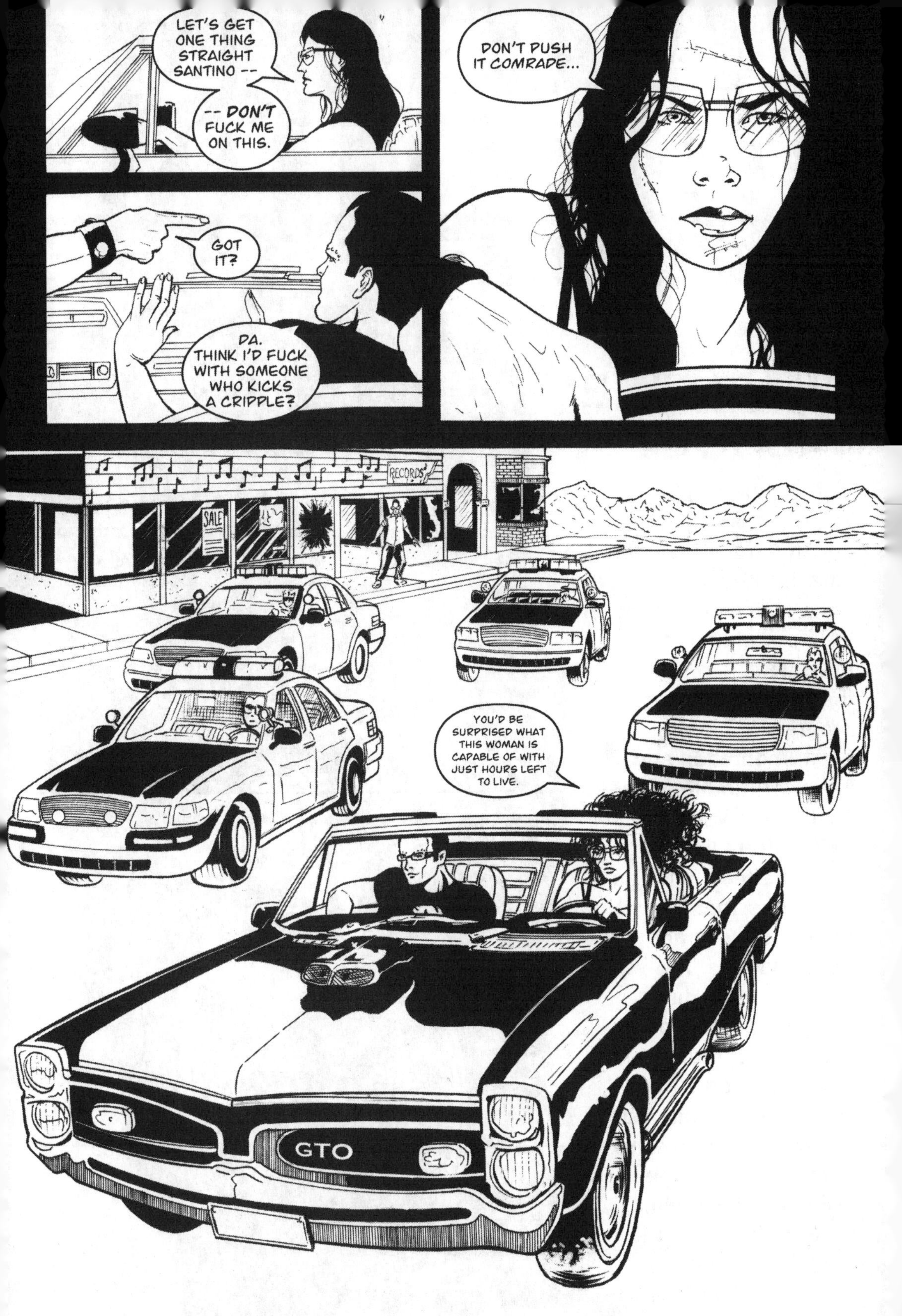
LET'S GET ONE THING STRAIGHT SANTINO --
-- DON'T FUCK ME ON THIS.
GOT IT?
DA. THINK I'D FUCK WITH SOMEONE WHO KICKS A CRIPPLE?
DON'T PUSH IT COMRADE...
RECORDS
SALE
YOU'D BE SURPRISED WHAT THIS WOMAN IS CAPABLE OF WITH JUST HOURS LEFT TO LIVE.
GTO

VALENTINE
DOSSIER

DANA "VALENTINE" VASQUEZ

Little is known about Valentine prior to her becoming a professional killer for hire. It is believed Dana was a participant of the now infamous MKULTRA: the CIA's top secret program in human experimentation and behavior modification. To this day, Valentine suffers from lingering mental effects such as migraines, memory breaks, nausea and hallucinations. The most disconcerting feeling Valentine deals with are her memories: real, imagined, suggested--or altered to serve the program's purpose? Only time will tell. For Valentine, it's life that's become a death sentence.

-COONEY.

VALENTINE
DOSSIER

CIA AGENT
KEVIN HARPER

A CIA Internal Affairs agent, Harper is often called upon to go undercover in order to expose government contracts to companies domestically and abroad. Divorced and often disheartened with the bureaucracy of the CIA, Agent Harper continues to fight the good fight. Agent Harper recently thwarted an assassination attempt by a rogue CIA operative, Damon Killian. Rumors have been circulating inside the walls of CIA Headquarters regarding Agent Harper's suspected involvement with a female assassin.

VALENTINE DOSSIER

URSULA STANIMIR

Described as having ice in her veins and calculated fire in her eyes, Ursula Oksana Stanimir is a Southern Russian immigrant from the Chechnya region. She has been involved for several years with the Russian mob outfit The Red Faction trafficking weapons and coordinating assassinations along with the buying and selling of goverment secrets to terrorist organizations. It is unknown where her loyalty truly lies; with The Red Faction or to the rebel fighters for an independent Chechnya.

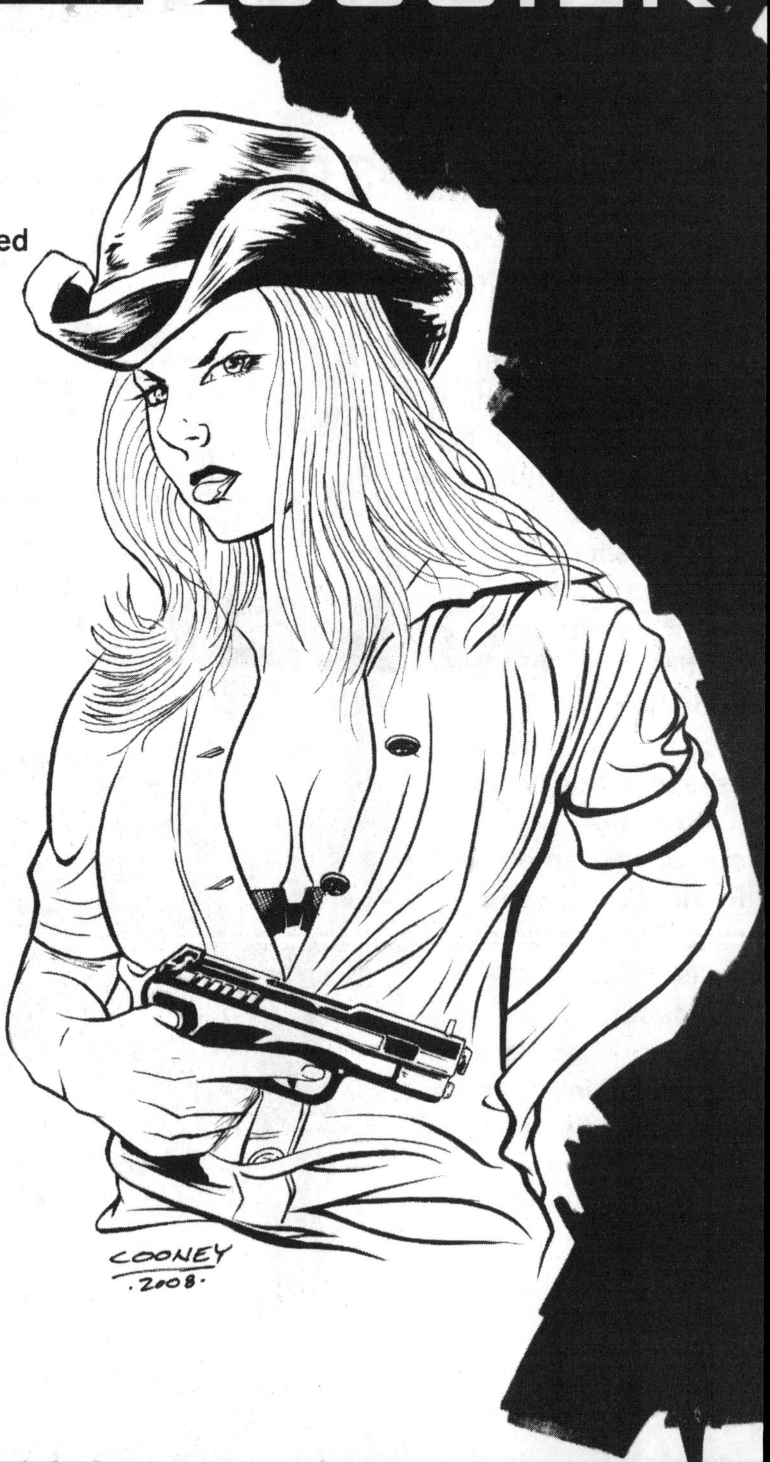
COONEY
·2008·

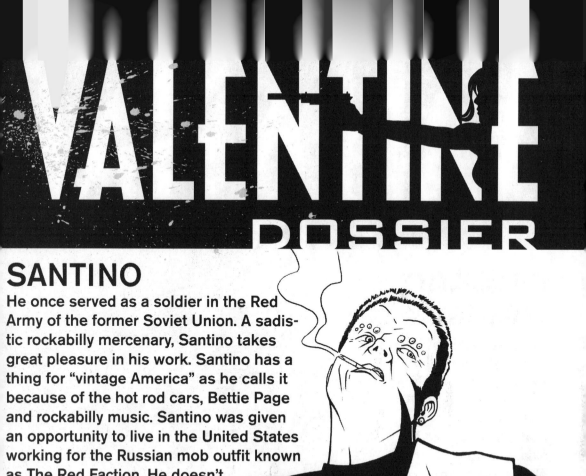

VALENTINE
DOSSIER

SANTINO

He once served as a soldier in the Red Army of the former Soviet Union. A sadistic rockabilly mercenary, Santino takes great pleasure in his work. Santino has a thing for "vintage America" as he calls it because of the hot rod cars, Bettie Page and rockabilly music. Santino was given an opportunity to live in the United States working for the Russian mob outfit known as The Red Faction. He doesn't care for their politics or agenda -- just as long as they pay well enough to live his lifestyle.

VALENTINE DOSSIER

DELGADO

Little is known about Delgado's background. Although an intelligence voice analysis reveals he has spent a lot of time in Valencia, Spain, he routinely changes his alliances, and his true allegiance seems to be only to himself. He is notorious for his violent temper and his ability to evade capture.

Delgado has been tied to several criminal organizations and has been instrumental arming Chechen rebels for their fight to become a nation independent of Russia. The CIA has made several attempts to bring Delgado into custody, not only for his criminal record but for his connection to wanted terrorists worldwide.

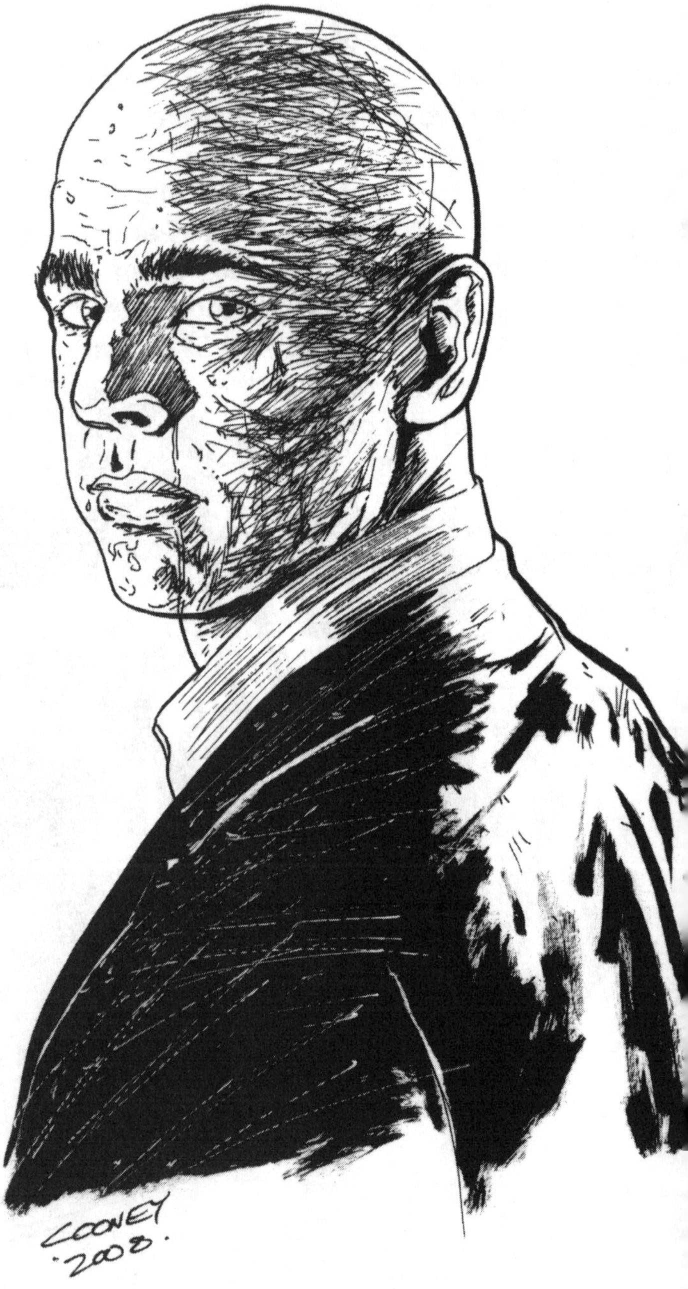
COONEY
2008.

VALENTINE DOSSIER

CARTER

This man has led a relatively quiet life in terms of criminal activity on the books. A relic of the Cold War between the United States and the Soviet Union, Carter was the liaison for the criminal underworld, facilitating arms deals and intelligence espionage. He is rumored to have been involved in the MKULTRA project for the CIA. Intelligence has reported that Carter has recently resurfaced publicly in the United States. He is a wanted man by both the CIA and former members of the KGB.

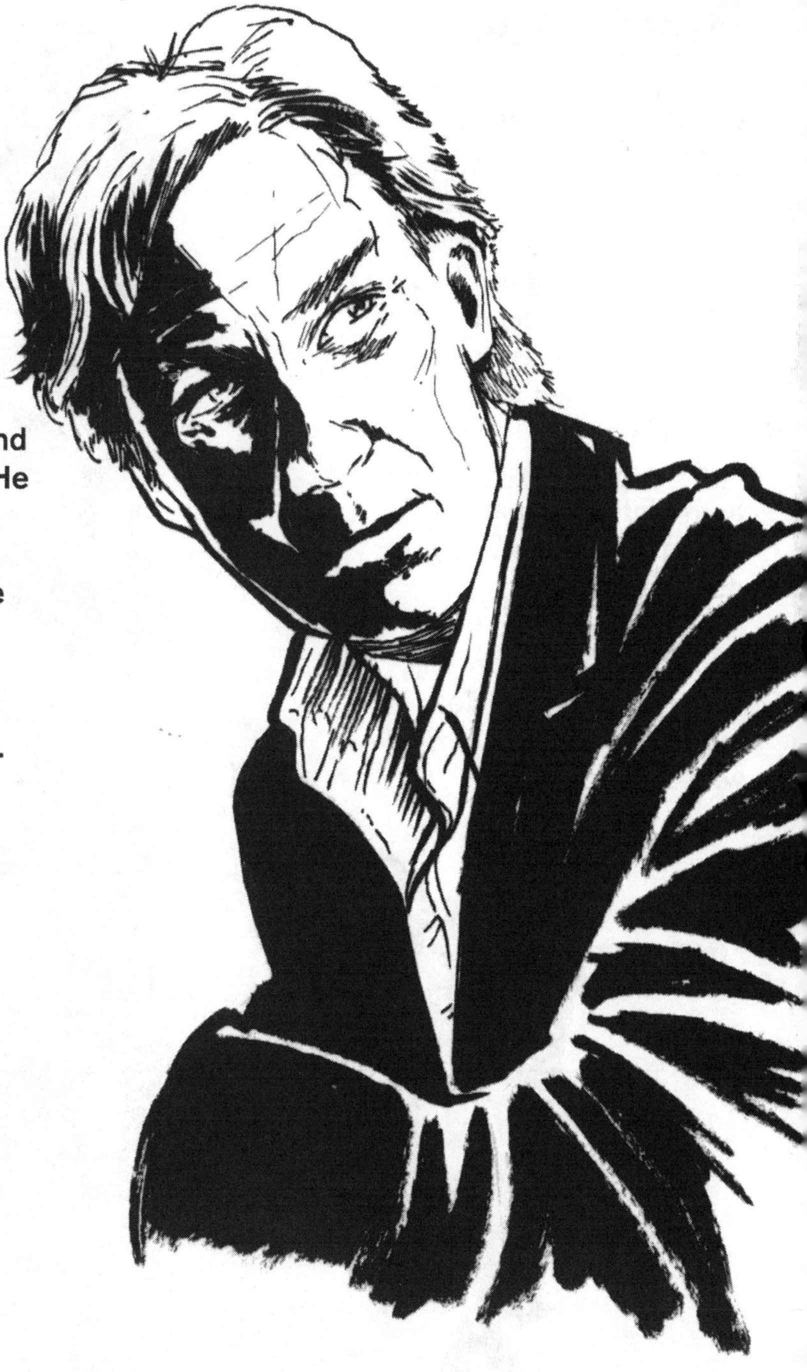

VALENTINE DOSSIER

Black Dog

This mysterious man is known only as "Black Dog." Black Dog is an enigma of sorts to the criminal world and no government agency has a valid record of his true identity. The question could be raised that he even exists at all. His name has been connected to the international criminal Delgado but only during recorded conversations and never spoken to in person. His motivations are unclear regarding his involvement with Delgado.

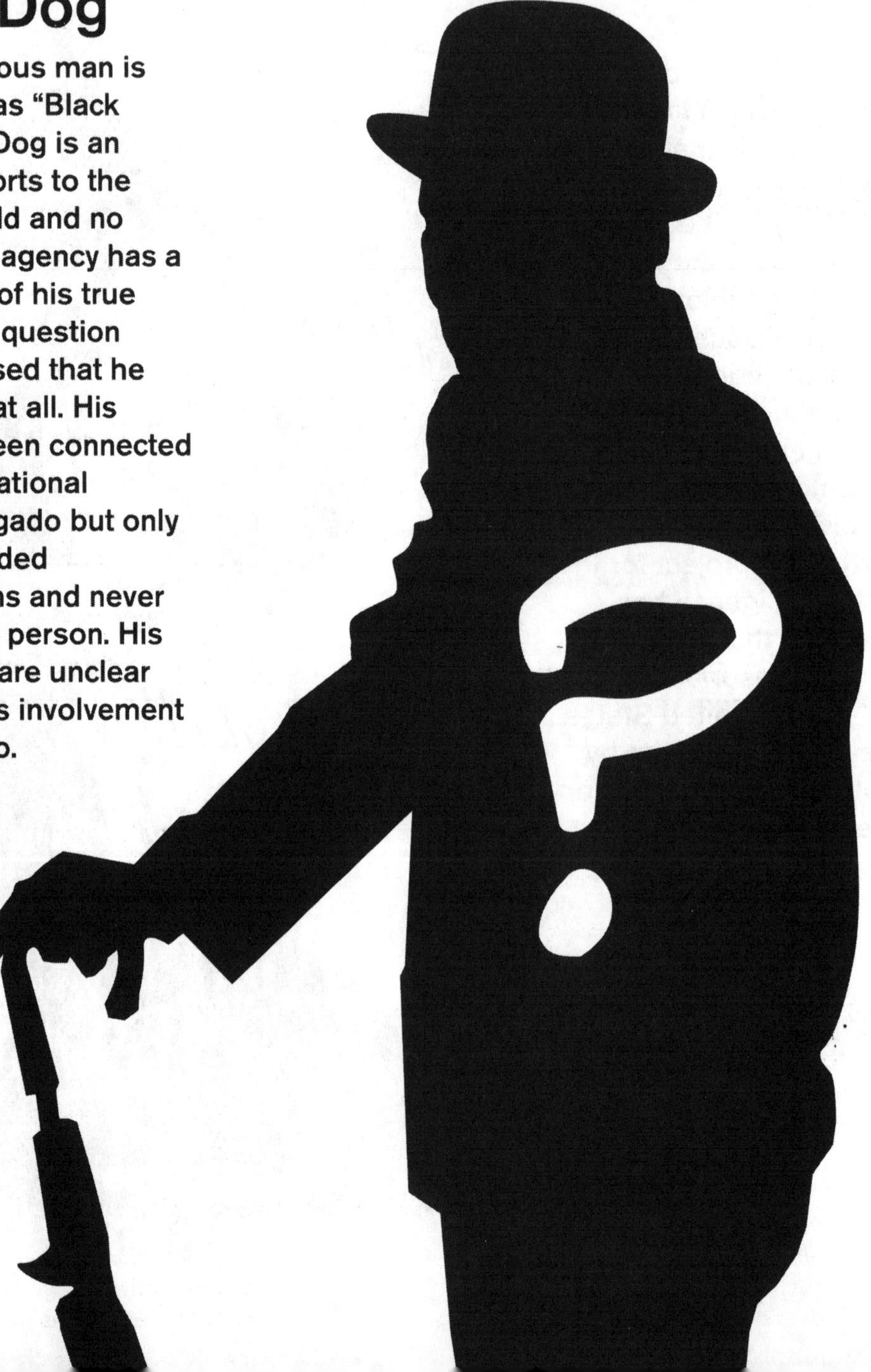

VALENTINE BOOKS

Other books by DAN COONEY...

VALENTINE: FULLY LOADED
VOL. 1 TPB

$14.95 US 160 pgs. B/W
ISBN 0-9724673-5-1

Retouched, re-edited, and reloaded: This first Valentine trade paperback collects hard-to-find issues 1 - 6, for old and new fans alike. Comes complete with cover work by Daniel Cooney, Bill & Linda Reinhold (Earth X, Punisher), inks by Peter Palmiotti (Aquaman), a psyche profile of Ms. Valentine, a production gallery, sketchbook and more!

VALENTINE: RED RAIN
VOL. 2 TPB

$12.95 US 120 pgs. B/W
ISBN 0-9724673-6-X

Can an assassin ever quit the business? Meet Dana Valentine, a gun for hire – who abandoned her profession for a clean slate at life. She has taken shelter with an Italian restaurant owner, who saved her life at one time. Now, burdened with debt and the Russian mob on his back, he's on the brink of losing it all. Can a former assassin, risk all to save another? New problems abound for Valentine, bringing her past full circle and a decision that will change the outcome of her future... if she survives to have one first.

AVAILABLE AT FINER BOOKSTORES EVERYWHERE.

For a comics store near you,
call **1-888-COMIC-BOOK**
or visit **www.the-master-list.com**

For more information, go to:
www.valentinecomic.com
www.redeyepress.net

DANIEL COONEY

Daniel Cooney has worked in comic art and illustration since 1997. Cooney has done all aspects of producing comic books and graphic novels -- writing, penciling, inking, coloring, lettering, and book design, all the way through pre-press for publication. A lifelong fan of comics, Cooney graduated with a BFA from New York's School of Visual Arts in 1998. His client list includes illustration/graphic design work for Rolling Stone, Sony, Tower Records, Marvel Trading Cards, Aliens vs. Predator 2, Heroes, LFL Indiana Jones, Iron Man, and Star Wars: The Clone Wars, along with writing and illustrating his own stylish action comic thriller, Valentine, under the Red Eye Press imprint. Cooney currently lives in the San Francisco Bay area, where he teaches numerous classes at the Academy of Art University, writes online classes for the University, and stays busy with a variety of freelance and comic work. He lives with his ravishing and industrious wife, Carolina, and their two quirky black cats, Shorty Doo Wop and Greenly Beans. To learn more about Dan and his work go to www.dancooneyart.com.